CW00621980

Training
Problem
Dogs

TS-283

© **1997 by T.F.H. Publications, Inc.**

Distributed in the UNITED STATES to the Pet Trade by T.F.H. Publications, Inc., One T.F.H. Plaza, Neptune City, NJ 07753; distributed in the UNITED STATES to the Bookstore and Library Trade by National Book Network, Inc. 4720 Boston Way, Lanham MD 20706; in CANADA to the Pet Trade by H & L Pet Supplies Inc., 27 Kingston Crescent, Kitchener, Ontario N2B 2T6; Rolf C. Hagen Inc., 3225 Sartelon St. Laurent-Montreal Quebec H4R 1E8; in CANADA to the Book Trade by Vanwell Publishing Ltd., 1 Northrup Crescent, St. Catharines, Ontario L2M 6P5 ; in ENGLAND by T.F.H. Publications, PO Box 15, Waterlooville PO7 6BQ; in AUSTRALIA AND THE SOUTH PACIFIC by T.F.H. (Australia), Pty. Ltd., Box 149, Brookvale 2100 N.S.W., Australia; in NEW ZEALAND by Brooklands Aquarium Ltd. 5 McGiven Drive, New Plymouth, RD1 New Zealand; in Japan by T.F.H. Publications, Japan— Jiro Tsuda, 10-12-3 Ohjidai, Sakura, Chiba 285, Japan; in SOUTH AFRICA by Lopis (Pty) Ltd., P.O. Box 39127, Booysens, 2016, Johannesburg, South Africa. Published by T.F.H. Publications, Inc.

Manufactured in the
United States of America
by T.F.H. Publications, Inc.

Training Problem Dogs

ADVICE FROM A LEADING VETERINARIAN ON HOW TO REMEDY CANINE BEHAVIOR PROBLEMS

Dr. Louis Vine

Illustrations by Kate Salley Palmer

Contents

Normal Behavior and Normal Instincts
• Personality and Intelligence

Physical Causes of Abnormal
Behavior • Inherited
Emotional and Instinctual
Causes of Neurotic Behavior
• People and Other
Environmental Causes of
Neurotic Behavior

Common Neuroticisms
• Sexual Disorders
• Psychosomatic Neuroticisms
• Overaggression

Bad Habits

About the Author

Dr. Louis Vine attended Cornell University and Middlesex University. He has been practicing veterinary medicine in Chapel Hill, North Carolina for 40 years and is a frequent lecturer and demonstrator at veterinary symposiums on the subject of corrective (plastic) surgery on the ears of dogs. Professional journals carry his articles on varied subjects in veterinary medicine. Dr. Vine is a member of the American Veterinary Society of Animal Behavior and a member of the International Animal Behavior Society.

Dr. Vine's first book *Dogs in My Life*, published in 1961, was widely acclaimed in the United States and Great Britain and has been translated into several European languages, as have many of his subsequent books. Dr. Vine is also the author of *The Total Dog Book*, which was acclaimed "Best Technical Book of the Year" by the Dog Writers Association of America, Inc. His book *Common Sense Book of Complete Cat Care* was selected as an alternate selection for the Literary Guild Book Club.

Other books by Dr. Vine in the United States include: *Dogs Are My Patients*; *Your Dog, His Health and Happiness*; *Breeding, Whelping and Natal Care*; *Behavior and Training of Dogs and Puppies*; *Your Neurotic Dog*; *Dogs, Devils and Demons* and *Dogs Are People, Too!*

In Europe, Dr. Vine is the author of: *Mon Chien a des Problems* (France); *Hunde Liebsten Freunde* (Germany); *Dogs Are My Patients*-(Great Britain); *Leilkibeteg Kutya* (Hungary) and *Vas Neuroticky Pes* (Czechoslovakia).

Dedication

To all the dog lovers who enjoy spoiling their dogs:
Spoil anyone you love, be it a dog or a human.

Introduction

"Like master, like dog" is one of those old sayings that has a core of truth. That is not to say that all neurotic dogs have neurotic owners. Neuroses in dogs can be caused by heredity, brain injury, and some physiological conditions. Most problem dogs are neurotic or otherwise abnormal (that is, they do not behave as we expect them to) because of human mismanagement. As we shall see, neurotic dogs often mirror neurotic members of their human families. Sometimes they are the product of human ignorance, neglect, or cruelty—and sometimes misguided love, overindulgence, and overprotectiveness. Whatever the reason, the fact remains that most dogs are not born problem dogs but become that way as a result of human shortcomings.

In that fact lies the chief hope for improvement. If you, as a dog owner, become better informed about the causes of neurotic and other problem behavior in your pets and about ways of dealing effectively with it, then there will be fewer problem dogs. The result will be happier owners and happier pets.

When behavior problems develop, the obvious first step is a trip to a veterinarian for a physical checkup. If the dog's health is fine, an environmental factor might be at the root of the problem. You must recognize that you, as the owner, are the only one with the power to change the environmental factors that cause neuroses and bad habits in your dog. You must recognize your contribution to behavior problems and your responsibility to try to correct them.

Anyone who cares for dogs should realize that the growing number of neurotic pets—and those who, for other reasons, develop undesirable behavior—has helped create a crisis for dogs. Every year several million dogs are put to death in this country. Most of them have been abandoned by their owners. Often these owners see the cute puppies they have purchased grow into adult dogs they don't like, don't want, or can't handle. In most cases these abandoned dogs are problem dogs whose behavior is neurotic or, for some other reason, intolerable to their owners.

How different the fate of such dogs might be if all owners appreciated their responsibility to train their dogs in desirable behavior, and to give them the attention and affection they need.

"A dog is like an eternal Peter Pan, a child who never grows old and who therefore is always available to love and be loved." That is how Dr. Aaron Katcher, associate professor of psychiatry at the University of Pennsylvania, described the role of dogs in our lives at the International Conference on the Human/Companion Animal Bond in Philadelphia. Dog lovers will recognize the truth in Dr. Katcher's statement, but as that conference indicated, it is not the whole truth. These "Peter Pans" have for a long time made valuable contributions to human beings—as guard dogs, Seeing Eye Dogs, shepherds, and faithful companions. It is now being realized that dogs have an important contribution to make in therapy for heart patients, disturbed children, the mentally ill, older people, prisoners, and others who can benefit from the faithful attention and affection of an uncritical friend. In short, dogs are far too valuable to be treated as many of us have been treating them.

My chief hope is that this book will help dog owners to avoid most behavior problems in their pets and to deal effectively with those that do occur.

The Normal Dog

NORMAL BEHAVIOR AND NORMAL INSTINCTS

When I was an intern at a veterinary hospital in Massachusetts, a well-dressed young couple came into the clinic late one afternoon. The man was carrying a young Dachshund in his arms. Before I could ask any questions, he put the dog on the examining table and said, without a trace of emotion, "We want you to put him to sleep."

"Why?" I asked.

"Never you mind why," the man said. "Just do it."

I examined the dog briefly. He was about six months old. He was healthy, and he was beautiful.

"You must be crazy," I said. "There's nothing wrong with this dog."

The woman had said nothing. I turned to her now. "Look," I said, "you can't ask me to do that. This dog isn't sick."

"We want you to put that dog to sleep," the man repeated. "And we're going to stay right here until you do it. Now go on and get it over with."

"Good God!" I exploded. "What kind of people are you?"

Their expressionless faces stared straight ahead. The Dachshund looked first at one, then the other. As I took the hypodermic needle out of the cabinet, I stalled for time, hoping that something would happen to change their minds. Today, with all my years of experience and living behind me, I would now know how to handle such a situation. Then, young and inexperienced, I was baffled. Suddenly, I had what I thought was an inspiration.

"If you don't want the dog, why not let me have him?" I said.

"Will you do as I say, or shall I take him somewhere else?" The man's voice was steady. Not once had he looked at the woman, nor had she looked at him.

So I did what they wanted—as quickly, as painlessly, as I knew how.

The instant the little dog lay still, the woman rushed forward. She grabbed the limp body. She hugged it to her breast, covering it with kisses and murmuring words into the ears that could not longer hear. I looked, disbelieving, from her to the man. His eyes were blinded with tears. He reached forward and tried to get the dead dog away from the woman. For a moment I had the insane notion that they would tear the dog in two, so violently did they struggle for possession of the body. Then I began to feel an anger as I had never experienced before.

"Damn you both!" I said. "If you loved that dog so much, why did you make me kill him? Stop it, both of you! Stop it!"

I think I pounded the man on the arm. Anyway, they calmed down a bit. The woman still held the dog in her arms. The man covered his face with both hands and sobbed like a child.

"I think you owe me an explanation," I said. "My job is to save dogs, not destroy them."

"We're getting a divorce," the man muttered, "and neither one of us could give up the dog."

"We loved him, you see," the wife said, and began to cry again.

"Queer sort of love," I said bitterly. "I asked you to give the dog to me."

"Oh, no," the husband replied. "We made up our minds that if we couldn't have him then no one could."

When they regained control of themselves, they left the hospital, taking the body. The last I saw of them they were driving off in a big car. The husband was behind the wheel. The wife sat as far as possible from him on the front seat. The sacrifice to a selfish love lay motionless between the two of them.

What happened on that long-ago afternoon in Massachusetts has haunted me over the years. I knew almost as soon as the episode ended that I would never again accede to such a request. That did not assuage the guilt I felt for allowing myself to be used to destroy the dog.

As I have thought about it again and again, I have realized certain simple, and obvious, truths: Our dogs are at our mercy. They depend on us for health, for happiness, for the preservation of life. We are their all-powerful beings, who can guide, nourish, and protect them, who can return the love they give so unstintingly—or who can sicken and destroy them.

The Normal Dog

As I began to prepare this book, I thought again of that unhappy husband and wife. I do not know if they were emotionally unbalanced or if what happened that afternoon was an aberration. What I do know is that the Dachshund was the victim of their unstable behavior and that many thousands of other dogs every year are also victims of their owners. I do not mean to say or imply that all neurotic dogs are the victims of unstable people, for that is not true. There are, as we shall see, many causes of problem behavior in dogs, other than the people they rely on. In order to better understand what neurotic dogs are like and how they differ from normal dogs, let us first look briefly at the behavior, the instincts, and the personalities of normal dogs.

Although I suspect that many dogs, like many people, might resent being labeled normal, I use the term as a convenient catch-all for the characteristics of well-adjusted dogs with generally desirable behavior. For similar convenience I use the term abnormal for those dogs who are not well adjusted and who are chronic misbehavers. When the misbehavior is caused—wholly or partially—by mental or emotional disorders, I use the term neurotic to describe such behavior.

Remember, what is desirable behavior in one situation may be undesirable in another. The term normal encompasses a variety of temperaments, habits, and idiosyncrasies even among dogs of the same breed.

The normal dog—that model companion we all hope to see in the pets we love—is a self-assured dog who is outgoing and friendly with people and other dogs, with a fine pride in his own intelligence. He will greet guests with a wagging tail rather than jump all over them. He will not bite or fight except to protect himself or his family. He is neither overfriendly nor shy. He is "well adjusted" because he has no bad personality traits that have to be corrected before training. The normal dog is usually a happy dog. A happy dog is the product of mutual cooperation between owner and pet.

At times it is difficult to distinguish between normal and neurotic behavior in dogs (or humans). A docile little pet might turn into a ferocious tiger when being groomed or during nail clipping. It would not be considered abnormal behavior if he were to bite his owner. This is a normal reaction to grooming in an untrained dog. It is obvious that such a dog needs some training, and most dogs actually want to be obedient—they respect you more if you demand obedience, and they like to learn. Dogs are pleased when they master commands and are praised for doing so.

Distinctive Breed Behaviors

Certain breeds have distinct inherited physical and behavioral characteristics that are passed from generation to generation. The guard dogs (Doberman Pinschers and German Shepherds) have strong bodies and a great desire for territorial defense, so they make excellent sentries. It is interesting to watch puppies of these breeds as they begin to assume protective custody of both the house they live in and their human family. Although this behavior is normal and cannot be taught, it can be developed as the dogs mature.

Hunting dogs, because of their keen eyesight and sense of smell, have been bred for centuries to pursue various game.

The Normal Dog

Saluki and Whippets, because of their great speed, can actually catch their game. Larger breeds, such as Irish Wolfhounds and Scottish Deerhounds, spot their prey. Bird dogs—spaniels, setters, pointers, and retrievers—also hunt by eyesight but primarily employ the sense of smell. Hound breeds, which include Bloodhounds, Foxhounds, and Beagles, hunt mainly by scent, with their noses close to the ground. Small breeds, such as terriers, were originally trained to hunt rodents. They are aggressive and quick and go after their prey assertively. Dachshunds were bred for hunting badgers, and their body and leg formation makes them ideally suited for catching their particular quarry.

Through the years, these and other breeds of dogs have come to be used more and more for companionship, often to the neglect of their inbred skills. While this kind of domestication has brought great pleasure to humans and, no doubt, to many dogs, it has not been without its price...as we shall see.

Normal Instincts

A dog has many curiosities and instincts. When you own a dog, you have a breath of the wild in your home, an animal that still retains traces of the days when his ancestors roamed the wilderness, matching wits and courage with wild boars and tigers. One of the curiosities is the nose; it is split into a backward curve and trembles with sensitivity. Keenness of scent was especially valuable to primitive dogs. They slept with their noses pointed upward to catch the scent of approaching enemies; bedding down involved walking in circles to catch the proper direction of the wind, which is why dogs still walk in circles before lying down.

Maternal Instincts

One of the basic instincts involves the mother-pup relationship. In the wild, the father helped rear the puppies, but domestication has generally eliminated him from this role.

The maternal instinct is a prominent factor in raising puppies. One of the earliest signs of this instinct is nest making before the onset of whelping. The bitch's licking and eating of the placenta seems to be a necessary preliminary to the cleaning of the young. It also seems to be the basis of the maternal attachment to the offspring;

14

experience has shown that if the bitch is prevented from cleaning and eating the placenta, the usual close links between mother and puppies are not formed.

Quite normally a bitch will push aside sick and dying puppies and will sometimes even bury them.

Normally the bitch tends the litter and stays close for about three weeks. Then gradually she leaves the pups more and more. She will clean the puppies by licking them and by eating the urine and feces until they are about four weeks old; by then they will have been taught to leave the box to eliminate. At about three weeks she starts training them, she punishes them, growls at them, and knocks them over. At the onset of the weaning period, in order to introduce the puppies to solid food, she regurgitates their food for them. She begins to lose her maternal affection when the puppies start taking solid food, at around four to five weeks.

Caring for the needs of her puppies is instinctive with the mother dog. She sometimes engages in an advanced type of social behavior—a grooming process, which is a toothful combing for fleas or foxtails—either on her young, on another dog, or on her owner. It is normal for the male as well as female dogs to "groom" someone in their human family. They will lick the ear and neck in an affectionate way, the expression of extreme love.

Suckling, of course, is also a strong instinct. If puppies are not suckled by the mother, there must be some substitute. Even a pacifier will do. However, it is best to use a bottle with a tiny opening so the puppy will have to work to get the milk out. If the puppy is not allowed to suckle, a non-nutritional sucking habit is apt to develop and persist into adulthood.

Sex

Puppies, like children, have early sexual sensations, and can be sexually stimulated. The mother licks her puppies, stimulating the genitals and other sensitive areas. Litter mates rub against one another and their mother for pleasurable sensations. During early growth, long before sexual maturity, puppies exhibit sexual excitement during oral and bodily contact. There is no differentiation between the sexes—males ride males and females are stimulated by females. This is normal behavior for puppies.

The Normal Dog

Domestication has so altered dogs' sexual behavior that today a male dog is likely to breed with any female, and vice versa. Primitive dogs tended to pair up for long periods of time.

Sex play is normal in dogs and important in breeding. The mating pair should be put in a room by themselves and allowed their pleasures. It is stimulating to both sexes, and often an aggressive romantic male can win over a blatantly frigid female.

I knew one beautiful Miniature Poodle who would have nothing at all to do with a champion stud picked out for her. However, at her first opportunity, she slipped out of the house and bred with the mongrel dog next door.

Frequently, when a female in heat is kept from male dogs, she will become so aroused sexually during the middle of her estrous cycle that she will ride other females to try to satisfy her sexual needs. Likewise, males cooped up for long periods without female companionship will ride one another.

In the male dog, the raising of the hind leg when urinating is usually controlled by male hormones and is not learned from other male dogs. This usually occurs at the beginning of puberty when the dog is six to nine months old, depending on the breed. There is also a strong link between the sexual urge of the male and the hormonal smell of female urine. Male dogs are attracted to female dogs in heat by the odor of their urine and instinctively know when the female is ready for breeding.

Dogs have a habit of smelling one another under the tail; this is a normal instinct. It has to do with the odor produced by the anal glands. Under severe emotional stress, evacuation of these glands can occur, and the odor is quite putrid. These are similar to the glands used as a defense mechanism in the skunk. Some authorities believe these secretions may be a sexual attraction as well, containing hormonal odors that identify at which stage in the heat cycle the female dog is in.

Herding-Roaming Instinct

Dogs are born with the instinct to herd and roam. They should be prevented from traveling in packs because such behavior is a reversion to the wild. When they travel in packs, they frequently get into trouble by attacking other dogs, animals, and even people.

During the mating season, it is normal for a male to join with a group of dogs and follow the trails of females in heat. Laddie, a male Collie I know, completely changes in behavior during the mating season. Usually a very easygoing dog, but at these times Laddie changes into an aggressive roaming "Casanova." He joins a pack of dogs and stays with them for several days at a time, eventually coming home with many tell tale wounds from all his battles.

Territorial Instinct

Both male and female dogs mark off their territory by urinating around the edges of their property, and they do this repeatedly to keep the scent fresh. Male dogs sometimes do this in their homes when they feel threatened by another animal or when a human causes them to become especially nervous.

Homing Instinct

The homing instinct seems stronger in some dogs than in others. It is linked to the territorial instinct and requires a sense of direction, and a certain amount of sight and sound memory.

One of the more unusual examples of the homing instinct that I ever saw involved a four-year old Miniature Poodle named Doodlebug who, although well adjusted and happy, was completely blind. He was stolen from his front yard apparently by a passing motorist. His frantic owner tried in vain to find him. Three weeks passed. Then the owner received a phone call from a neighbor who lived only a few blocks away. Doodlebug had been found in the neighbor's yard, too weak to travel farther. His coat was a mass of burrs, his ribs stuck out from his undernourished body, the pads of his feet were worn and bleeding, and he was suffering from hunger and exhaustion.

No one knows whether Doodlebug had escaped from his dognapper or had been discarded when his blindness was discovered. It was apparent that he had walked a long time and distance. Somehow, he knew the way home.

The Normal Dog ───────────────

Play Instinct

The play instinct is ever-fascinating and never more so than when it involves mock fighting, because most dogs seem to know how far they can go and when to stop. Ears are pulled, mouths are locked together, tails are furled, and then one real yip and they stop. Afterward, oftentimes, they curl up and rest together.

Communication

There are many communication patterns between dogs. When danger threatens, a dog adopts a certain posture. He has a distinctive way of slinking when submitting. Putting his tail between his legs and raising a paw are also signs of submission, as is lying on his back with the flanks exposed.

Vocalization varies from breed to breed. Some breeds, like the hounds, howl, while smaller breeds yap. Guard dogs bark to let both people and animals know they are protecting their territory. Hunting dogs bay to express themselves.

Only tame or domesticated dogs bark. Wild dogs and wolves howl. Barking is an imitation. As the early masters urged their dogs to go after game, the dogs, in their excitement, imitated their humans' sounds and in time developed the barking habit.

Howling in the domestic dog is the nostalgic expression of instincts developed when wild dogs hunted in packs; the howl is their rallying call.

It is important for owners to study the postures and vocal patterns of their dogs in order to understand them and to be better prepared to communicate feelings and commands.

PERSONALITY AND INTELLIGENCE

Personality

Just as with the human species, no two dogs are exactly alike in their features, behavior, temperament, personality, or intelligence. In a group of dogs you will find almost every personality type and temperament: the leader, the follower; the brave dog, the coward; the sly one, the dumb one; a friendly dog, a timid one; and, of course, the bully. And even though you may often hear alleged "authorities" declare flatly that mutts are smarter than pedigreed dogs, that all

Kate Solley Palmer

poodles are exceptionally smart, all retrievers friendly, and all German Shepherds suspicious of people and not to be trusted, none of these statements are true. There are general breed characteristics, but every personality type and degree of intelligence can be found in every breed and mixture.

An owner's close association with his dog produces an animal that often times develops a similar personality. The dog will usually attempt to imitate his owner's behavior. Not only does the person and his dog act alike, they sometimes even look alike.

Dogs are born with certain instincts. The training of these instincts and the surrounding environment mold their personalities. Proper training and a favorable environment produce a dog of even temperament with a pleasant personality.

The Normal Dog ————————————

Intelligence

Most dogs know us better than we know them. Their lives are centered on us and they are observant. I firmly believe that many dogs understand much more than people realize and that often they understand what we're saying—not every word and detail, of course, but the essential feeling and sometimes the meaning.

A number of my patients definitely understand words, and their owners have to spell out words they don't want their dogs to overhear. Just the other day a woman brought her Miniature Poodle, Dolly, to be spayed. She spelled out the word operation because Dolly's master is a surgeon and it's a word she well knows.

Reasoning Power

There is a growing controversy between some psychologists and dog owners as to whether remarkable performances of dogs are the result of training or indicate reasoning power and judgment.

I am not a psychologist and besides, I'm prejudiced. I am convinced that many dogs are highly intelligent. However, psychologists contend that as dog training mostly involves repetition, dogs learn only by conditioned reflexes. Anyone who has ever trained a dog has surely found that the time comes when one really has to mentally exert oneself to stay one step ahead of the canine pupil; the dog shows reasoning power either in cleverly avoiding the work at hand or in becoming an obedience champion. I have seen many dogs appraise certain situations and then carefully take the right action. Certainly the judgment exercised by some Seeing Eye Dogs shows intelligence far beyond conditioned reflexes acquired by training. During their daily work they make many on-the-spot decisions that are quite remarkable and sophisticated, to safeguard their masters.

An amusing example of reasoning power was told to me by the mother of a new baby. She had trained her dog to fetch a clean diaper from a closet shelf every time the baby needed to be changed. One day her infant had an upset stomach and needed changing every half hour or so. The dog made the trip to the closet nine times and returned with the needed diaper as requested. On the tenth trip, obviously fed up, he pulled all the diapers off the closet shelf and deposited them in a neat pile beside the baby's crib, then stalked out of the room with his head high in the air.

Another good example involves a very intelligent Kerry Blue Terrier who is always brought to my kennel for boarding when his family goes out of town. He loves the kennel and especially enjoys being with the other dogs. One time his family decided to let him stay at home with a baby-sitter friend while they were away for the weekend. The dog wasn't apprised of the arrangement and disappeared from the house when he saw his family drive off. While the baby-sitter was frantically looking for her charge, the dog was walking the three miles through town to my kennel to present himself to be boarded.

Another time, this dog appeared at my hospital door and barked to be let in. He limped in holding up his front paw. The paw was cut. I sutured and bandaged it and then phoned his, mistress to tell her he was on his way home and that his medication was taped inside his collar. He arrived while she was still on the phone.

Dogs have their own way of figuring things out. Their reasoning power may vary, depending on their intelligence.

Mort, a Wire-Haired Terrier, was the bully of the neighborhood. Every dog and cat was afraid of him. He killed cats and picked on male and female dogs alike. Size or sex made no difference. Finally, lawsuits against his owner confined Mort to the house. They only took him out on a leash.

When the other dogs realized this, they came by the house every day, barking at Mort through the glass doors. This drove Mort crazy. He could not get at those teasing dogs. He would charge the glass, which fortunately was heavily reinforced, and hit it so hard that several times he knocked himself out.

Acute Perception

Telling the time of day and day of week is an accepted ability in dogs. Just about every dog owner has at least one story to corroborate his or her dog's time sense.

There is a little mixed spaniel I know named Nellie who knows exactly what time her mistress comes home from work everyday, and at 5:00 p.m. every afternoon she sits at the door waiting for

Kate Salley Palmer

her. However, Nellie knows that on Thursdays her mistress is late, returning home at about 6:30. On Thursdays, therefore, Nellie takes up her position at the door an hour and a half later than on other work days.

Porky, a mixed terrier, is another one of my patients, who knows exactly which day of the week is Tuesday and which is Thursday. On those days his mistress stops on her way home from work and buys Porky a hamburger, his favorite food. And each Tuesday and Thursday evening—but on no other days of the week—Porky meets her at the front door carrying his food bowl.

Predicting storms is also a faculty that dogs are acknowledged to have. Sometimes hours before an impending storm they become restless and start to whine and act in a peculiar fashion. Dogs feel barometric pressures beyond the threshold of human perception and so they often "know" when a thunderstorm is coming.

Kate Salley Palmer

There is also a ten-part dog intelligence test developed by a psychologist. On a scale of 0 to 10—very dumb to brilliant—the mean test score among the 10 dogs studied was 5.75. Purebred hounds scored the highest, with a 7.63 average. Obedience school dogs did no better than unschooled dogs. Mixed breeds were about as smart as purebreds. Neither male nor female dogs were significantly smarter.

Owners whose dogs do not score high on intelligence tests should not be discouraged. The important thing to remember is that any normal dog—and owner—can develop a loving relationship no matter whether the dog has a high IQ or not.

Extrasensory Perception (ESP)

Many scientists even believe that dogs are blessed with a sixth sense. There are many reports on the homing instinct in dogs that cite cases of dogs returning to their old homes after traveling hundreds and even thousands of miles.

The Normal Dog

Kate Salley Palmer

Some of this ability can be attributed to the marking of territory. Also, a dog has a built-in compass of sorts. However, behavioral scientists investigating animal navigation cannot at the present time account for all their extrasensory capabilities, such as reports of dogs who have found owners newly relocated in places where the animal had never been. Such behavior rules out the possible exercise of basic senses as well as memory. The ability is called psi-trailing, and hundreds of cases have been reported.

One of the earliest and most famous cases was a dog named Prince who crossed the English Channel during World War I and, somehow found his master in the trenches in France. Another dog was left behind in New York when his family moved to California. Eleven months later he appeared at their new home in California.

It is clear that dogs have extraordinary sensory abilities that we do not understand.

Causes of Abnormal and Neurotic Behavior

PHYSICAL CAUSES OF ABNORMAL BEHAVIOR

The underlying causes of abnormal behavior in dogs cannot be discovered by simply observing particular actions. Obsessive barking at strangers, biting children, cringing during a thunderstorm, house soiling—none of these acts, or any combination of various other acts, can tell you what causes the problem. The dog who goes berserk at loud noises, for example, may or may not be reliving the fear of an earlier event. Even though he acts fearful, he may not feel any fear whatsoever. Instead he may have learned to act fearfully to get attention. Perhaps somewhat along the way he was indeed startled by a loud sound; when that happened, his human family lavished him with hugs, kisses, cooing, and the like. So he learned to repeat his erratic behavior to get more of this enjoyable attention.

Or his behavior may have nothing at all to do with his human family and their treatment of him. Perhaps he has an ear disease or disorder that causes pain when certain sounds occur; or perhaps something else is the problem.

Physical condition, diet, inherited instincts, abnormalities in the environment in which the dog is raised, and the owner-family environment, the outside environment, all must be considered in determining the cause of undesirable behavior. The specific cause can be elusive, and treatment must be carried out on a trial-and-error basis. For the most part, though, careful observation, along with an understanding of how canine and human expectations differ, will bring the concerned owner a long way toward identifying the cause of abnormal behavior.

General Physiological Causes

When I examine a dog brought to my hospital because of abnormal behavior, I consider many factors, the first of which

Abnormal and Neurotic Behavior

Kate Salley Palmer

are physical disorders. Many times an animal doesn't feel well and acts in a peculiar manner because of an organic problem. During the examination, I look for worms, a thyroid condition, a spinal disc problem, poisoning, constipation, diarrhea, anal gland infection, colitis, pancreatitis, urinary ailments, allergic reactions, milk fever in a nursing bitch, false pregnancy, and sex organ malfunction, among others. Any one of these could cause a behavior problem. Poor eyesight caused by excessive facial hair, cataracts, glaucoma, or pannus (a thickening of the cornea) will naturally cause abnormal behavior, as will ear mites and ear infection. The pain of arthritis can cause the mildest dog to be snappish. Even a sore paw or broken nail can affect behavior.

Many diseases, such as rabies, spinal meningitis, distemper, and epilepsy cause disruptive behavior. Brain tumors, abscesses, and such traumatic things as a blow to the head can also alter behavior and even affect a dog's temperament. I have seen dogs with head injuries undergo changes such as: loss of social and sexual drives, loss of hunting tendencies, complete lethargy, regress to puppy habits and further—back to the point of becoming wild and primitive. Sometimes a good-natured animal will turn vicious and unreliable. After the organic cause is eliminated, however, the abnormal behavior will usually clear up.

Tranquilizers or sedatives can also change behavior. Some drugs accumulate in the bloodstream and gradually, over a period of time, cause a derangement. If a dog becomes dopey or sleepy, or acts stupidly under a certain medication, the owner should have the veterinarian check to make sure the dog is not allergic and that the drug does not contain substances that are debilitating.

Even alcohol can be a problem with some dogs. Drinking generally starts as a gag at a party when someone gets the dog to lap up some booze. The dog takes liking to the stuff and becomes a sneaky party drinker.

Diet

Diets that are over 50 percent carbohydrates produce hyperactivity and make dogs overactive. So it just stands to reason that a hyperactive or excitable dog will benefit from more protein added to the diet. Sugar and starches also seem to stimulate dogs. Overfeeding, feeding too frequently, or feeding with an inadequate supply of fresh water can also contribute to abnormal behavior.

Diet is particularly important for older dogs. Obesity is especially dangerous if there is a reduction of vitality or any heart or kidney ailment. Often a loving owner is the unintentional cause of the pet's problem. Consider the case of Frieda, one of my Dalmatian patients.

The first time she was brought to my hospital she was so fat she had to be carried in. (Let me tell you, it is not easy to carry an obese Dalmatian).

"I don't know why she's so fat, Dr. Vine," her owner told me. "All she eats is half a can of food a day. "What about tidbits?" I asked. "Do you feed her at the dinner table or give her sweets?"

"Well, yes," her owner replied. "But that doesn't amount to much."

How many times through the years have I heard that story! Every time her owners ate, Frieda had just a little something.

Abnormal and Neurotic Behavior ———

Frieda loved candies, so they were given whenever she asked for them. The trouble was that the half a can of food a day wasn't sufficient nourishment for the dog. Fortunately for Frieda, her human family really did love her enough to cooperate wholeheartedly with me in helping their dog.

A good diet canned food or dry food, thyroid tablets to stimulate her metabolism, injections of hormone preparations, and eventually, long walks with her family helped Frieda to become a healthy, active dog again.

Aging

Senility affects the various organs of the body, so as a dog gets older there will be a gradual change in his or her behavior. Incontinence is one of the earliest problems. For example, when he was once housebroken he now begins to lose control, much to his embarrassment. Certain kidney diseases, such as nephritis and diabetes, can also cause the dog to wet. Then as the male dog gets older, his prostate gland often enlarges and produces an inflammation that causes him to urinate often. This condition is painful and needs medical attention.

An older dog usually suffers a loss of hearing. At first it is gradual, and people may not realize he is having trouble hearing them. As your animal deafens, you might find it useful to use high-pitched sounds, such as whistles, rather than voice commands.

Dogs are also prone to eye problems as they grow older, just like people. Cataracts form, and the dog may have trouble recognizing his human family. So there is a gradual loss of vision accompanied by changing behavior.

The older dog wants comfort and solitude more often, and may sometimes get a little irritable and not want to be handled. His wishes should be honored. It is also helpful if you can convince the senior citizen that you still love him by paying more attention to him.

Some dogs become jealous as they age. The cause could be a new pet, a new baby, or something else that challenges their dominant position. House soiling or destructiveness become methods of retaliation. In these cases, little generally can be done except to confine the displeased pet to a small area where damage can be controlled.

Abnormal and Neurotic Behavior

Inherited Physiological Causes

Some breeds, such as Wire-Haired Terriers and Dalmatians, and most white dogs, are prone to skin allergies (although all breeds and colors are susceptible). These dogs are generally nervous and jittery and tend to mutilate themselves by biting and scratching.

Several degenerative eye diseases can cause difficulty in seeing. Other vision problems arise in breeds with hair covering their eyes—they sometimes have a tendency, because of their impaired vision, to be hand-shy. They are apt to bite when surprised by sudden handling. Trouble in hearing, likewise, may be due to inherited difficulties.

Hip and elbow dysplasia are painful conditions in breeds such as German Shepherds, Saint Bernards, Golden Retrievers and others, and cause nervousness and a tendency to snap and bite.

Basset Hounds and Bulldogs are among the breeds prone to excessive salivation, which usually leads to eviction or scolding. This in turn can lead to undesirable behavior.

Some smaller breeds, like Dachshunds and Poodles, have intestinal problems. These dogs are especially apt to be house soilers.

In hydrocephalus (literally water head), a common inherited condition in the Chihuahua, an increase of fluid within the skull can cause pressure on the brain and, thus, nervous behavior.

Researchers are gaining insight into the causes of many inherited disorders. Scientists have located the genes that cause muscular dystrophy in Golden Retrievers and "shaking pup" syndrome in Welsh Springer Spaniels. They're working on identifying the genes responsible for failure-to-thrive problems in Giant Schnauzers, bleeding disorders in Scottish Terriers and Doberman Pinschers, and the hereditary deafness that affects about 30 percent of Dalmatians. And they believe that hip dysplasia may be the result of several defective genes working in concert.

Owners of English Springer Spaniels are encouraging one another not to breed dogs with "rage syndrome," a type of brain seizure that makes some dogs lose control of themselves. Researchers have developed a blood screening test in Portuguese Water Spaniels for two separate diseases. One

Abnormal and Neurotic Behavior ───────

disease causes blindness, and the other is a neurological disorder that can lead to death.

It is estimated that 15 to 25 percent of the 20 million purebred dogs in America have or carry a genetic disease, while many others suffer from lesser genetically related problems. Labrador Retrievers can have an allergic skin disease, and some are prone to dwarfing. An estimated 70 percent of Collies have genetic eye trouble; up to ten percent of those affected go blind. Cocker Spaniels, particularly those bred by puppy mills, have tended to be bad-tempered. Some Great Danes have weak hearts. English Bulldogs can suffer from congenital heart disease, and their large heads are the reason pups must often be delivered by cesarean section. Newfoundlands can die from cardiac arrest.

The object of all serious breeders is to be more aware of genetic defects and attempt to eliminate them by more careful planning.

INHERITED EMOTIONAL AND INSTINCTUAL CAUSES OF NEUROTIC BEHAVIOR

Inherited Emotional Causes

Although most neuroses are due to environmental factors, some are inherited, especially the tendency for certain personality traits. It is often difficult to decide which traits are inherited and which are acquired. The relative effects of environment and heredity on canine—and human—behavior have long been disputed by psychologists and geneticists. But as any good breeder knows, heredity does play a major role in determining canine behavior, so it must be investigated.

Certain generalizations can be made. Some breeds show more excitability or aggressiveness than others. And there are some inbred differences in their learning ability. Guard dogs, such as Doberman Pinschers and German Shepherds, have strong bodies and a great desire to defend their territory, while hunting dogs are bred for their aggressive quickness in retrieving game. Still, within each breed itself, there are individual genetic variability. Each dog has his own personality, and it is unwise to generalize too much about breed characteristics.

Abnormal and Neurotic Behavior

To discover the inherited cause of a neurosis, it is most important to know the temperament of a specific puppy's parents. Ancestry can tell us a lot about a puppy's potential personality. A shy, nervous bitch is likely to produce shy, nervous puppies, even if the sire isn't. Such pups are not easily trained.

A typical example is the case of Charlie and Gorgeous, two Cocker Spaniel puppies born of a shy, fearful, snappish mother. Suspecting that the temperamental mother might harm or even kill her puppies, the owner conscientiously gave the pups to two families, neither knowing the other family, but both eager to raise a puppy. The dogs were hard to train, but with a lot of love and care both grew to be fairly normal until they were about two years old. At that time Charlie's human family had a new baby. Charlie became overly aggressive and a fear biter, and the family, fearing for their new baby, finally had to give him up. Also around that time Gorgeous' family moved into a new house, and she suddenly became vicious. Her owners likewise had to give her up.

Misbreeding

Some neuroticism in dogs stem directly from improper breeding by unscrupulous persons seeking quick dollars. If Silver Toy Poodles are selling well, some breeders will turn out litter after litter of Silver Toy Poodles, giving no thought to the parents' temperaments or the health of the mother, who is being overtaxed. The result of such careless breeding of closely related unstable dogs is highly neurotic offspring.

In years past many fine breeds were almost destroyed by this practice. I remember when some German Shepherd and Doberman Pinscher breeders had one main goal—to produce as many ill-tempered watchdogs as possible. It didn't take long for both breeds to acquire a bad reputation. People became afraid of them. The Collie, that beautiful animal, was inbred so that he might develop a long, narrow head. Show people and many breeders fell so in love with the longer and narrower head that in a few years they had almost bred the Collie out of brains. Also, Collies became subject to congenital eye diseases. Fortunately for Dobermans, German Shepherds, and Collies, concerned show and kennel people have brought about improvements in the breeding of these particular animals.

Abnormal and Neurotic Behavior ——————

But there is still too much indiscriminate breeding for profit among commercial dog breeders. And I am not surprised to see so many nervous, finicky dogs being brought into my hospital by well-meaning owners who couldn't resist buying that cute little doggie in the window of the pet store.

"Beautiful misfits" is often an apt description for these dogs—physically admirable but mentally and emotionally crippled.

I must emphasize here that heredity does not always prevail. Just as brown-eyed human parents can have blue-eyed children, even though brown is the dominant gene, so it is also with emotional disorders. An undesirable trait does not always carry over into the offspring, and the environment is such an important influence, if good, can sometimes mollify the tendency for a bad disposition. I only want to indicate that heredity must be considered when searching for the cause of neurotic behavior and that the tendency for such behavior can be present latently.

Inherited Instinctual Causes

Every dog secretes a substance that plays an important part in his behavior with other animals. Called pheromone, it is secreted by various glands in the body, including the anal sac, and its particular odor provides an individual personal signature for such animal. This odor is believed to trigger aggressive behavior in some dogs and may explain why dogs smell a strange dog carefully, to see if he is friend or foe. It may also explain why some dogs seem destined for repeated battles with other dogs.

PEOPLE AND OTHER ENVIRONMENTAL CAUSES OF NEUROTIC BEHAVIOR

People Problems

The biggest cause of neuroses in dogs is people. Man's best friend is often a helpless victim of that very friendship. And people can have their most damaging influence when their animal is most vulnerable—in the early months of his life.

Improper Early Handling

A puppy reared in an unsuitable environment, particularly where he is deprived of affection, is likely to become unhappy,

nervous, too aggressive, or timid when he matures. He will not know how to cope with problems. He will often go to pieces when confronted with a new situation. If he is under three months of age, he can still usually be taught to deal properly with crises, but the older he is the more difficult adjustment will be and the slower his response to treatment.

Susie, a Wire-Haired Terrier, was five months old when she was flown from her kennel in South Carolina to her new home in Durham, North Carolina. The kennel owner had been delighted at the sale, made over the telephone, for Susie was the runt of a litter, the one who remained in the kennel when all the other pups had been chosen.

Two months after Susie's arrival, her new owners, the MacDougalls, brought her to me. Mrs. MacDougall, who loved all dogs, was almost in tears.

"I've never known a pup like this one," she said. "We want to love her, and she simply won't have a thing to do with anyone."

I examined Susie, but there was nothing physically wrong with her. I could only conclude that the time she spent alone in the kennel, deprived of human affection and support, had brought about her present condition.

33

Abnormal and Neurotic Behavior ───────

Eventually, through the occasional use of tranquilizers and continued loving care over many months, and the arrival of a new puppy—which stimulated some latent proprietary feeling in her—Susie became a different dog. She was still shy, still uneasy with other family members, but she gave unstinting love to Mrs. MacDougall—whom she had chose as her one-person-in-the-world. Mrs. MacDougall returned that affection in full measure. Years later, after Susie died, Mrs. MacDougall and I talked about the unnecessary torment endured by so many neurotic dogs. "They're like some people," she told me. "All they need is a little more love and understanding. But how very much they repay you for that extra attention."

People unknowingly affect their dog's behavior in many ways. One Beagle Hound suffered emotionally because his owner drove him to the brink every day while practicing his trombone.

Animal behavior is often influenced by the actions of their owners. Dogs mimic their owner's behavior.

————Abnormal and Neurotic Behavior

Two ladies who were good friends and drinking buddies would meet at the local bar a couple of times a week. Their dogs always accompanied them and played together while the ladies drank. On one occasion, the women got into an argument which ended in a hair-pulling brawl. Sure enough, the dogs started fighting too which goes to show that dogs often imitate their owners.

A few days later when the women met at the bar and were friends once again, their dogs played with each other as if nothing, had happened.

Humanization

One mistake people often make is imposing human standards on a dog. If the forced behavior is contrary to normal canine behavior, the dog will become a misfit. There are many human expectations that cannot be imposed on a dog without bad results, as in the case of Stormy, a Boston Bull Terrier, who slept in his owner's bedroom, but his snoring kept waking the owner. The owner would wake the dog to tell him to keep quiet. Stormy started becoming excitable and nervous. Not only did

he not understand the owner's impatience, but the owner was actually interfering with a normal physiological phenomenon, snoring. By doing so he was making the dog neurotic.

Treatment was simple. Let the dog sleep and snore or move him to other sleeping quarters.

Humanizing has caused many dogs to lose their natural instincts and literally forget they are dogs. They begin to prefer the company of humans and refuse to accept any biological links with other dogs. Fearful and aggressive with other dogs, they refuse to mate. If a bitch does become pregnant, her humanization may win out over her maternal instincts and she may ignore her puppies. Some dogs refuse to be housebroken. Many of these dogs are expected to fill the role of family members, to become child substitutes. As a consequence, many become "problem children."

Some peole want their pets to be completely dependent on them. They have to feel needed by someone and their dogs offer a solution. Usually these people have dogs who rely on them for survival. They are not allowed to associate with other dogs or cats and are usually kept away from people. The dogs and their owners live an isolated and sheltered life. Some of these dogs never touch their feet outdoors. They are carried everywhere.

Whenever these dogs face other animals or people, they freak out. A trip to the veterinarian really shakes then up and they have to be tranquilized before and after treatment.

Some of the dogs feel and act like people. Man's best friend can be a victim of that close friendship.

Neurotic Family Members

Another major cause of undesirable canine behavior is a neurotic owner or family member. Dogs do not naturally act like people, but in the home environment, where dogs are dependent on humans for food, shelter, and affection, they will often emulate members of their human family.

A friend with a Cocker Spaniel named Josephine came to me distressed about the dog's behavior during thunderstorms. Josephine practically went into convulsions at the first sound of thunder. I was able to explain Josephine's behavior when my friend told me that her sister-in-law, who lives with the family, is so terrified of storms that she goes into a closet to sit them out.

Abnormal and Neurotic Behavior

Josephine was mimicking that woman's actions. Now Josephine is given a tranquilizer at the first sign of a storm, and the timid sister-in-law and dog share the closet, or under the bed, for the duration of the storm.

Josephine also sensed the sister-in-law's fear and apprehension, which introduces another factor, explainable only by the fact that dogs seem to possess ESP. Dogs somehow perceive what a human feels, and they respond accordingly. These feelings can be conveyed on a conscious or subconscious level. An example of the latter is a dog's ostensibly inexplicable hostility toward a neighbor. The dog's owner does not realize the suppressed grudge he had against the neighbor, but the dog picks up on the feeling and acts. He bites the neighbor every chance he gets.

A human being is a dog's most respected and influential companion. This is why so often the real cause of a dog's problem is a human companion.

Abnormal and Neurotic Behavior ──────

One of the saddest examples I know involved a Seeing Eye Dog named Sally and her blind owner, Marie. This woman had come to hate her life, the world about her, and even the dog that guided and protected her. She treated Sally very badly. Harsh words and blows had their effect on the dog, who became almost as neurotic as her owner. The hostility she felt for Marie was transferred to other humans. She lunged at me with teeth bared when I first tried to treat her for a cyst on her back.

"She needs a good beating," Marie said. Later, after Sally had been sedated and treated, I asked if the dog had had a bad early experience with a veterinarian.

"Not that I know of," Marie said. "I think she was just born mean."

I shook my head. Then, realizing she couldn't see me, I said, "No, I don't think so. Dogs are like people. They're not born mean. Somewhere along the line circumstances or people, or both, are responsible."

Boredom and Loneliness

A puppy who must be left alone all day is bound to develop neurotic behavior. Ideally, a dog should not be penned up alone, inside or outside, for more than an hour or two at a time. Prolonged isolation is especially bad for a puppy between three and twelve weeks of age. Behavior problems are likely to emerge, and if no one is around to correct them, the misbehavior usually becomes habitual. A simple solution to loneliness is to provide a playmate, preferably another canine. If this is not feasible, a cat, a turtle, a rabbit, or any number of other pets can help, such a companion gives the dog another living thing to communicate with. I have known dogs to accept the following animals as companions: cats, rabbits, birds, skunks, porcupines, snakes, horses, pigs, and even a full-grown bear. If the dog must remain alone, even a television set or a radio can provide some solace for a lonesome or bored dog.

Overprotectiveness

Overindulgent and smothering love often leads to dog neuroses. An owner's excessive love may cause a dog to end up a nervous wreck. Overprotectiveness leaves a dog especially vulnerable to stressful conditions, for example, when he must

Kate Salley Palmer

be left alone or sent to a kennel for boarding or medical purposes. Such a pet is particularly vulnerable to the death of a beloved owner.

Overpermissiveness

Dogs, like children, are adept at making people do what they want. But letting dogs have their own way usually leads to intolerable behavior that is difficult to correct when an owner makes the effort too late.

Such a dog may throw a temper tantrum or sulk when punished. Usually the owner feels guilty and appeases the pet. I have seen dogs have epileptic-type seizures after being verbally admonished. Their feelings have been hurt and they want to let their owners know it. They know their owners will pet them and give them tidbits. When this happens, the canine has won the war of wits.

Some overindulged dogs, after those rare occasions when they are reprimanded for misbehavior, will refuse food until their owners seek forgiveness by cajoling and fondling them. Serious neurotic problems can result from this kind of canine and human behavior.

Abnormal and Neurotic Behavior —————

Beauregard Bonaparte Simmons was one of the handsomest French Poodles I have ever seen. He was a perfect physical specimen too. I told his owner so.

"It's his mind I'm worried about," she said. And while Beauregard sat at her feet, his intelligent eyes watching her every moment, she added, "He tears up all the curtains and chews my Oriental rugs, and last night he almost gnawed through a table leg."

She explained that the dog recently became destructive whenever she left him alone at night, something she did only occasionally, since she started dating her new boyfriend. During, the day she worked in a hospital as a speech therapist. Beauregard, allowed the run of the house, was apparently content with that arrangement as long as she came home at noon to feed him. He did not have the look of a dog who is a victim of separation anxiety. After questioning the owner a bit more, I thought I knew what the problem was.

"As I see it," I told Beau's owner, "you have a very exacting job where you cannot relax your discipline. You must impose strict standards on your patients in order to help them." She agreed.

"Yet," I went on, "when you got this puppy, this small helpless, adorable creature, you leaned over backward to do just the opposite. No matter what mischief he got into, he got away with it, didn't he?"

She nodded her head.

"You know as well as I do," I said, "that any young creature needs to have the security that only discipline gives. He has to be guided. Otherwise he becomes confused and expresses his confusion in various ways. You've given Beau a good home, the best food and medical care, and you've indulged him. But a dog needs more than that. He needs to be treated as a responsible member of the family. Only then can he learn how to behave in an acceptable manner."

Beau's owner got to her feet. For a moment I thought I'd offended her.

"What a fool I've been," she said. "I give people the help they need, but when it came to Beau, I couldn't even see what was as plain as the nose on my face. I'm going to take him home and enter both of us in an obedience class."

Beauregard was perfectly content with the new arrangement. And the mistress arranged to have the boyfriend visit her at

night instead of leaving Beau at home alone. Now the three of them sit together and watch television.

The most serious danger of overpermissiveness is that it can upset the normal, or at least desirable, relationship between owner and pet. It can encourage the dog to see himself as the leader of the pack (the family). Ideally the owner should be the leader, a substitute in the dog's psyche for the primitive canine pack leader. If he does not exert his authority, the owner becomes submissive to the dog, and the dog becomes unresponsive to the owner's wishes. This distorted relationship is a major cause of the most severe neurosis in dogs—overaggression.

Mistraining

Some psychologists think that dogs behave, the way their owners, perhaps subconsciously, want them to behave: That is, adults who complain about a dog's house-soiling problems, for example, often have children who are bedwetters; thus the house soiling may be a desired occurrence.

Abnormal and Neurotic Behavior —————

I disagree with this theory. I feel that such owners simply lack the ability to train their dogs. They may not know the proper training techniques or, at the other extreme, they may be too harsh in disciplining their dogs.

Dogs react acutely to handling. Rough handling usually brings on aggressiveness in highly active dogs. Gentle handling has a calming effect on all dogs. Usually the owner's handling technique lies somewhere between these two extremes. They know in theory how to train their dogs, and they want their dogs to be well adjusted and mannerly; but they are inconsistent. Sometimes owners reprimand their dogs for misbehavior, and sometimes they don't.

A "sometimes-training" program is not good enough for most dogs (or children, I might add). Every misdeed must be dealt with promptly, even if it means the owner must get up after having settled into a favorite chair, or interrupt an interesting phone conversation, or chase the dog halfway across the county. Action must be taken as soon as a misdeed or lapse in training has occurred. A dog must not be allowed to get away with misbehavior. If he does, he may come to think that he, not the owner, is the leader.

Cruelty

I have never understood how a human being can abuse a dog, a creature so filled with affection for our species. Yet cruelty to dogs (to all animals, for that matter) is a fact of life and an obvious source of neurotic behavior.

Some people get a dog as a status symbol, and then behind closed doors they treat the dog miserably. Other people get a dog purely and simply as a whipping boy. They have something to take out their anger on and to abuse. Such treatment causes its victims anxiety, fear and often hysteria.

In some families there may be a personality clash, for example, a member of the family may resent the dog and mistreat it when the rest of the family is absent.

Sometimes the cruelty is a result of callousness. For example, Samantha is a Dachshund belonging to a well-educated, moderately well-off owner who keeps the dog outside in an unheated doghouse even during the coldest days of winter. Samantha has repeatedly come down with pneumonia and other illnesses that decent treatment would have prevented.

Curiously, her affection for humans has remained strong. She approaches people she knows with a wagging tail and a bid for affection, but she falls over on her back when anyone reaches to pet her. She has reserved whatever hostility she feels for members of her own species. She will have nothing to do with other dogs, barking fiercely at smaller ones who seek her friendship and retreating into her doghouse when larger ones come near.

Sometimes the cruelty springs from ignorance as well as callousness. One day a farmhand brought in a young hound who was obviously terrified. When I bent over to look at the dog, whose name was Buck, he shied away so violently that he fell on the floor. The man picked him up and threw him roughly on the table.

"That's enough of that," I told the man. "This dog's frightened to death. What have you done to him?" As I spoke, I noticed that the end of Buck's tail was raw and sore.

"He won't eat, Doc. Something is wrong with his stomach."

"You work for old man Peters, don't you?" I asked "What has he done to this dog?"

"Well, he wanted to make him a good strong, smart huntin' dog, so he fed him some gunpowder and cut off his tail. That does it every time. You know that, Doc."

"Damn him!" I exploded. "What kind of superstition is that?"

"Taint no superstition; it's fact," the man said. "People from way back's done that all their lives."

"Yes, and killed more good dogs than all the diseases in the book," I said. "Look, go on back and tell Peters I'm keeping this dog here. Gunpowder! He ought to use it to shoot himself with, instead of killing a fine dog like this."

Problems with Other Animals

A dog's behavior may become neurotic if he has to share the family's affection with another pet who has behavior problems. Here is a typical story of how one animal may be influenced by another.

An owner had two dogs, one a Great Pyrenees and the other a small mongrel terrier. Both dogs became very aggressive with other people, and eventually the Pyrenees turned on his owners, growling at them and biting them. The two dogs were castrated, but that did not solve the problem.

Abnormal and Neurotic Behavior ————

Eventually the Pyrenees became so aggressive that he was put to sleep. After his death the other dog's behavior changed. He calmed down and was no longer aggressive. With the bad influence gone, he acted like a different dog.

Other animals in the neighborhood can also cause a dog to become neurotic. An example is the dog who was terrorized by the neighborhood cats. The dog's initial attempts to play with the cats brought her several stinging smacks on the nose. She quickly gave up her pursuit of their friendship, but they did not give up their idea of revenge for her improper intrusions. Each day, wherever the dog might go, a cat would be waiting, hissing and teasing the dog. Losing face with one cat, the dog would set out upon a different path—only to be met again by another cat waiting to continue the game. The cats were having a grand time driving the dog crazy.

A Dog's-Eye View of Behavior Problems

Most dogs will try to adapt to almost any domestic situation because they, like most owners, want to establish a mutually enjoyable and harmonious relationship. But as an owner you must fulfill your part of the bargain. You must choose a suitable dog and then proceed to socialize and train him properly. This is easier if you get the dog when he is young. It is much easier to keep a young puppy from developing bad habits than it is to try to cure him once the bad habits have developed.

————Abnormal and Neurotic Behavior

In every household the role of the dog is different, depending on the family's life-style. Many dog misbehaviors are, in fact, normal canine behaviors that simply occur at inappropriate, times and places. A dog may soil the carpet because his owner has inadvertently tracked dog feces through the house on the soles of his shoes. He may chew because he is teething. He may bark at a mouse under the floorboards. And he may dig a hole in the garden during a spell of hot weather to lie down on the cool earth. From his point of view; defecating, chewing, barking, and digging are quite normal.

You must remember that it is unfair to punish a dog for normal canine behaviors without providing some acceptable alternatives, a prompt trip outside for voiding chew bones, plenty of companionship, and lots of loving care. Further, many stressful events can be prevented by not allowing the dog to be isolated, lonely, or bored, for such problems often result from the dog's efforts to get attention or to relieve the anxieties created by separation and loneliness.

A dog should neither be treated with overindulgence nor ignored, and he should never be abandoned. Improperly treated dogs (as well as people) become depressed and develop into neurotic creatures.

When given the slightest measure of affection, most dogs will return it with wags of the tail and undying loyalty. Affection also makes for normal-behavior dogs, free of any neurotic tendency, because they believe they are loved as much as they love you. Being neglected only breeds misbehavior.

People who get annoyed with hair on the rugs, inconvenient

walks, and messed-up houses should never get a dog. True, dogs may be an inconvenience sometimes; but they give in love, loyalty, and companionship much more than they receive.

Dogs are our most unselfish friends.

The Neurotic Dog

COMMON NEUROTICISMS

The number of neurotic dogs is increasing. While some owe their neuroses to physical malfunctions or to inherited faults of temperament, the problems of most are due to a variety of environmental conditions. We have changed dogs' normal behavior patterns so much in recent years that it is a small wonder their neuroses are increasing apace. Today's neurotic dogs are mainly the result of easy living, overfeeding, overcoddling, lack of proper training, lack of exercise, and, in many cases, loneliness and boredom. Also, because dogs imitate their owners, they acquire many of the neuroses and mental ailments from the human race.

General Signs of Neuroses

How do we tell when a dog is neurotic? Neurotic dogs differ widely, but there are certain general behavioral signs that should alert you, the owner, to the need for help. Neurotic dogs are often extremely restless. Such dogs whine and whimper and bark excessively. They are not dependable with strangers and are apt to snap or bite without warning. But some neurotic dogs can be quiet, too quiet—sneaking and slinking around. These dogs generally run from strangers and seek hiding places. They tend to be easily frightened and will often urinate at the sight of a stranger. Most neurotic dogs are scared of new or loud noises. They are mistrustful of humans and will bite if frightened or if the human shows extreme fear.

Each dog has his own way of expressing his neurotic illness. Some will be shy; others, aggressive. Some may steal, hiding and burying their illegal bounty; others will defecate on a prized Oriental carpet or on the owner's bed. Overt or covert, aggressive or withdrawn, lustily robust or withering and sick, neurotic dogs exhibit types of behavior that are not only extremely varied but, for the most part, unpredictable.

Stress is a favorite catch-all word nowadays for explaining all disorders, from rashes to cancer.

46

Stress is disturbing, and it triggers an immediate reaction, but it is not in itself the cause of neurotic behavior. A normal dog will be able to cope with stress; a neurotic one will not. Most dogs do not like loud noises, strangers, children who grab them, separation from their owners, or going to the veterinarian for a shot; but they can put up with these unpleasant events. A neurotic dog cannot. A stressful event will throw him, into a fit of melancholy or ferocious activity.

Neurosis is a broad term, covering a number of more or less distinct conditions. As indicated earlier, I use the term to denote abnormal (problem) behavior that is in some way linked to mental or emotional causes. Generally, except where inheritance plays a role, neurotic dogs have failed to adjust to certain situations. Because of an unresolved conflict, these dogs will show diverse manifestations of emotional illness: fear, aggression, submission, destructive behavior, depression, anxiety, in fact, the gamut of distressing symptoms afflicting neurotic humans.

In many cases, as we have seen, dog neuroses are learned from humans. Dogs act out their emotions in concert with their human companions. For this reason we must be especially sympathetic to their problems; for surely, like humans, these dogs suffer the pangs of misdirected feelings and are not happy with themselves.

Neurotic dogs can be helped, and if not completely cured, they can learn to adjust to our society's demand for conforming behavior. And for the dogs" peace of mind, bad and erratic behavior must not be allowed to become a way of life. They too must live by a set of values in harmony with those of others, at the same time being encouraged to retain that amount of independence that keeps their spirits unique and free.

The following sections describe some of the most common neuroticisms and give time-proven methods of dealing with them.

Depression

Depression is a major cause of canine illness. While it can be brought on by chemical changes in the body, the majority of cases can be traced to causes more obvious than these. Most instances of depression are found in very active dogs who have been isolated and severely punished. The change in environment associated with the punishment is too much for the animals, and they crack under the strain. But dogs may also experience depression, when they mourn the death of an owner, for instance, or that of another animal. They are also very sensitive to the emotional disturbances of their owners.

Siegfried, a beautiful German Shepherd, was brought to me in a deeply depressed state. He had no appetite, even when hand fed, was losing weight rapidly, and could not be distracted from his melancholy. During the physical examination I could find nothing wrong. I knew he was the "only child" of a young couple, and, suspecting an emotional disturbance, I questioned the owner and learned that she and her husband were in the process of getting, a divorce. It then dawned on the young woman that Siegfried had become disconsolate the day her husband had departed to take up separate quarters. Several days later I was delighted to hear that Siegfried had his appetite back and was making up for lost time. For the sake of their pet's mental and physical health, the couple had decided to give their marriage another try.

Kate Salley Palmer

The symptoms of depression include listless behavior and increased amounts of sleep, loss of appetite, and a marked decrease in sexual drive. A dog becomes difficult to handle and is generally irritable. The most effective treatment is a combination of antidepressant drugs (administered only under a veterinarian's supervision) and environmental therapy. However, it is important to ascertain the cause of the stress and resolve it.

I am reminded of a country-dog named Doodlebug, who moved with his family from a farm to a big city. Soon afterwards, the dog's appetite began failing. He hid under beds or in closets and resented being taken outdoors for his daily walks. He lost weight and began snapping at everyone.

When I was consulted, I realized what was causing his depression. The noises and bedlam of the big city were too much for him. The treatment was simple and uneventful. Doodlebug was sent back to the farm where he became a happy dog once again.

Pup-Uppers or Dog-Downers

Prozac™ is called the "Happy Drug" of the 90s. It helps people suffering from depression and other mental disorders. In recent years, however, it has also been used on a Polar Bear suffering from boredom, to pet dogs who have become neurotic because they have become humanized. Prozac has been used on dogs with excessive anxiety and/or aggression. This anti-depressant has helped some canines become calmer while on the drug. The scientists explain it by saying that it helps the imbalance of the brain's chemicals.

Other emotional disorders in dogs treated with Prozac include lick granuloma (excessive chewing), tail chewing, tail chasing, excessive barking, various phobias such as fear of noises, cars, people, etc. Some cases of emotional loss of appetite and sex drive are also helped by the use of Prozac.

Hyperactivity

Hyperactive dogs, like hyperactive children, are continually moving and running either in circles or aimlessly. Hyperactive dogs are also prone to temper tantrums, during which they scratch and bite.

The Neurotic Dog

They differ, however, from hyperkinetic dogs, for the latter are much more violent, hostile, and aggressive. The hyperactive condition is aggravated when these dogs are penned outdoors, given little attention, or punished for their frenzied activity. These dogs eat very fast and may vomit frequently because of the swallowed air. Often they will eat the vomited food. Although it may seem revolting, they should be allowed to do so because the food is still nutritious. I suggest feeding a hyperactive pet several small meals a day. Hand feeding small amounts of food will encourage the dog to eat more slowly.

Hyperactivity can be effectively treated if the animal has no psychological imbalances caused by inbreeding. In many cases a change in diet can modify the dog's behavior. Just as hyperactive children have been helped by eliminating processed foods and those with various synthetic additives from their diets, hyperactive dogs need a high-protein, low-sugar, low carbohydrate diet. Don't give hyperactive dogs candy and other sweets. White-flour products are also bad for them. (Both sugar and white flour go directly into the bloodstream and rapidly increase insulin, thus stimulating the hyperactivity. Fructose, on the other hand, goes through the liver first and enters the bloodstream slowly).

Hyperkinesis

While this behavior problem has long been observed in children, it has been studied in dogs only in the past few years. The symptoms noted in children—hyperactivity, short attention span, and unpredictable behavior—are similar to those found in canines.

Many times I have faced a snarling, vicious dog that had to be sedated before handling was possible. In the past, when a vicious dog was physically sound and there was testimony that the owner was not treating it cruelly, he was generally dismissed as "just plain mean" and relegated to the end of a chain or to the gas chamber as a favor to the entire neighborhood. Such dogs are now suspected of having hyperkinesis. Symptoms to look for, especially when the animal is isolated or confined, include excessive salivation, extreme nervousness, inability to sit still, overexcitability, and flunking out of obedience training school.

A test that can confirm hyperkinesis is the animal's response to a drug, Ritalin™, that is used in the treatment of children. Surprisingly, although this drug is a stimulant, it can sometimes transform a vicious, out-of-control canine into one with fairly normal behavior. But pills alone will not do the trick. A combination of drugs, psycho social therapy, and training are recommended for best results. The dogs may not end up as models of virtue, but such treatment can make a critical difference in their recovery.

Hysteria

Hysteria (unmanageable fear or distress) is common in nervous dogs. It is almost always exhibited when the dogs are under unusual stress. A prime example is fear of storms. I've known some dogs to practically take a house apart during a storm. Such a dog begins pacing and panting well in advance of the storm. The best treatment is to slip him a "Mickey Finn" (a tranquilizer or a sedative) at the first sign of an impending storm.

The threat of a bath, a pill that must be taken, or a manicure session will send some nervous dogs into hysterics. Such high-strung animals often chew on themselves, causing lesions on their bodies. Mass hysteria can be easily precipitated in a group of dogs. Usually all it takes is for one dog to become hysterical, whereupon they all lose control. Unfortunately, such a group will often attack one poor defenseless animal. Tranquilizers provide the most effective treatment for hysteria among dogs.

Kennelitis

Kennel-dog syndrome, or kennelitis, results from prolonged isolation during the critical months of puppy hood (three, to twelve weeks). Puppies raised in a cage, in a kennel, or pet shop without human companionship may suffer crippling emotional damage. The neurosis is characterized by extreme shyness, submissiveness, and introversion. The dog will withdraw into a dark corner, become increasingly fearful of humans, and pace in a weaving and circular manner. Some become fear biters or even develop autism. Susie, the MacDougalls neurotic Wire-Haired Terrier discussed earlier, was a victim of kennelitis.

The Neurotic Dog

Good kennel owners give their puppies daily individual care. In large colonies where dogs are kept for long periods of time, the dogs are moved at intervals to different cages.

Rehabilitation of an animal who has endured lengthy confinement requires prolonged treatment with mild tranquilizers, patience, and gentle handling—especially when the dog is first introduced to the outside world. Increased socialization for the dog should include new people and new signs and sounds—but they should be introduced slowly, for even normal household sounds from telephones, doorbells, radios, television sets, and refrigerator motors may send the dog into hysterics. Outside, in the natural environment, even the sound of rustling leaves may frighten a dog who has never seen a tree before.

The patient, whether puppy or older dog, should be introduced gradually to his new environment. Soothing talk and petting should reassure the animal that the foreign sounds will not hurt him. Soon he will get used to the new world, and a wagging tail will replace the fearful behavior.

One of my colleagues adopted a six-year-old German Shepherd named Dusty. For a year Dusty's only human contacts had been with the kennel owner (a brief salutation every two or three days) and with the kennel keepers (two meals a day and occasional grooming). She was to be an indoor dog, but the inside of a house was completely foreign to her—and terrifying. For the first few days all was bedlam. Each night my colleague would arrive home from work to find most of the drapes on the floor and Dusty a nervous wreck. She was not punished. On the contrary, she was spoken to gently, taken for a good walk on her leash, and fed a fine dinner. The drapes were patiently rehung. After the third day, Dusty began to settle in, but it took about three months for her to test her new environment and get over her insecurity. After three weeks, she was allowed to run outside, but she stayed within seeing distance of the house. Even after three months she was fearful of company and would disappear into a bedroom when guests appeared. Gradually, however, she became more acclimated to her new, environment and friends. Now, six months later, she enters a roomful of company with her tail wagging and is everything a Shepherd is expected to be.

Nervous Breakdown

A dog may also suffer a nervous breakdown, an emotional disorder that is being seen more and more in both pets and people. Among the causes animal psychologists have discovered are overexposure to large groups of people and the pressures of city living. Crowded trains, bustling shops, busy streets, and high-rise apartments are a far cry from a dog's natural outdoor environment; these things will make most animals edgy. Many of them suffer from headaches, as well.

Show dogs are especially susceptible to overexposure to people. When benched and on display, these dogs should be kept away from crowds of spectators, especially those who may poke at or tease them.

Guide dogs, however, must be able to tolerate city noises and confusion; thus they are very carefully screened for their stamina. Because German Shepherds are especially prone to nervous breakdowns when exposed to noisy, crowded environments, they are gradually being replaced as guide dogs by other breeds, including Labrador Retrievers and Golden Retrievers, who have more easy going temperaments.

I know of one German Shepherd, a fine Seeing Eye dog with an especially loving owner, who lived in New York City. All was well until new construction was begun in the neighborhood. The dog became nervous, hyperactive, shied away from strangers, and even snapped at them when they got too close. Rather than put the dog to sleep, the owner sent him back to the farm where he was born. After a few months in quiet and peaceful surroundings, the dog lost his nervousness and returned to the normal behavior of his puppy hood.

Similar problems exist for animals in zoos. The Japanese government, after puzzling over the upsurge in nervous breakdowns at a Tokyo zoo, ordered the zoo closed two days every month to give the animals a respite from people.

Treatment for animals suffering nervous breakdowns involves quiet and peaceful surroundings and plenty of loving care.

Nervous Urination

A dog who wets the floor from fear and apprehension may have nervous urination neurosis. Shouting, hitting, or scolding will only make matters worse. Before undertaking any regimen to correct this behavior, you should have the dog examined by a veterinarian for a possible underlying physical illness. Kidney disease may cause the troublesome urination. Or, in older dogs, prostatitis is common. It gives a dog an uncontrollable urge to urinate frequently. Behavior modification will not cure a physical ailment.

Of course, even when wetting is not a result of physical illness, it is not necessarily neurotic, although it may be considered abnormal. Completely housebroken dogs may wet curtains, floors, and furniture just to get even with their owners or others in their human family. Also, male dogs may wet the house and each other when carrying out the territorial instinct to mark off their property.

One day Jimmy, a six-month-old Lhasa Apso male, who for three months had been completely housebroken, wet his owner's bed. The next day, in sight of his owner, he wet the carpet in front of the bedroom. In Jimmy's case, this was not neurotic behavior. Jimmy was letting the two other dogs in his family know what he considered his territory to be.

Nervous urination, on the other hand, is caused by a wide variety of stressful experiences. Young dogs, for example, often piddle when a stranger or another dog approaches, or during the happy excitement of greeting the owner. To correct this, you should never look directly at your dog or act excited when greeting, him. Ignore him for a few minutes after you arrive home, even if he is jumping all over you in frenzied excitement. Pay attention to your dog only after he calms down.

Then, when he relaxes, greet him quietly and gently. Reassurance is a good way to correct nervous urination in a young pup. Also, young dogs usually outgrow this behavior.

For an older dog with this problem, special understanding and a patient approach are necessary.

Before they were domesticated, the younger or weaker dog would wet as a sign of submission to an older or stronger one. Nowadays an owner or a member of the family with too stern an approach is often the cause of a nervous, oversubmissive dog who dribbles. With a neurotic dog, you must find out what is triggering the reaction and work with him gently, gradually increasing his confidence in dealing with stressful situations.

Remember, the dog usually does not urinate deliberately; it is an involuntary reflex.

First, the person the dog seems afraid of must persuade the dog that he or she is not going to hurt him. The person should crouch down to pet the dog, and not place hands on his head, neck, or shoulders because this signifies dominance to the dog. Instead, the dog should be petted palms up, under his chin, throat, or chest, in a quietly reassuring manner. Four to six weeks of this therapy will usually correct the problem.

Remember that punishment will not correct nervous urination—it is the wrong tactic. The dog's confidence must be built up by praise for the correct responses. A calm, relaxed attitude and soft words are the best medicine.

Shyness

Shyness is usually an acquired trait, although some dogs are born with an introverted personality. In the female, if the shyness is not inherited, sometimes breeding her will help. Raising puppies may give her confidence. But in those cases where the shyness is inherited, it is doubtful that the dog can be trained to have an outgoing personality.

As mentioned earlier, the shy bitch will impart this behavior to her puppies if they stay with her for more than three weeks. The puppies will learn to act as she does— unfriendly and fearful of the world around them.

Shy dogs are usually submissive in nature, lacking self-confidence in themselves and in the human race. They panic easily, and when excited they will usually urinate or defecate. They will creep along the floor, ears back, tail between their legs. Such dogs will bite when cornered (typical behavior for a, fear biter). This reaction shows that a shy dog is not necessarily a coward. Cowardly dogs will fight only in packs. When faced alone, they put their tails between their legs and retreat. The coward is not necessarily a neurotic dog, but the shy dog usually is and will attack if fearful enough.

Some dogs display shyness only in the presence of their owners and are quite outgoing with other people. This indicates that the owners have broken their dogs' spirits by excessive punishment, and are feared by the animals.

Because of emotional instability and lack of self-confidence, a shy dog must be handled gently. He should never be approached too quickly, nor should anyone make a sudden movement toward him, because in his fear he might bite. Quiet talk in a kneeling position and petting under the chin or on the chest will reassure him. His confidence should be built by training him to respond to simple commands, such as "Sit," "Come," and "Down." When he performs well, praise him highly. Never scold.

People should always act happy and very friendly when with a shy dog. A pet is extremely sensitive to his owner's moods. If a person is in a bad mood and feeling cross, he or she should stay away from the shy dog. Dogs emulate their owners' emotional ups and downs.

The best way to help a shy dog is to build up his confidence. If not properly treated, he will be forever timid and retiring. Patience and loving care are the prime ingredients in the cure. The older the dog, the longer it will take; but generally a great deal of progress can be made in two to three weeks.

Although shyness can be inherited, the environment plays a significant role in its development. For example, a puppy who received too much love from one person can become fearful of all other humans. The puppy becomes so attached to that one person that he will growl at or bite anyone else. A puppy who distrusts other people doesn't have enough contact with the outside world. Conversely, a puppy who does not get any love and affection can also become shy and withdrawn. It is a known fact that a puppy that does not have human contact before the age of twelve weeks will usually become a shy and fearful dog.

To prevent shyness, I advise all dog owners to take their puppies with them on trips around town so that the puppies can see all shapes and sizes of human beings. It will show them that people are not out to harm them—that many people love dogs and will stop to compliment and pet them. Puppies should make friends with strangers, up to a point.

When shyness does develop, however, treatment consists of administering tranquilizers for at least two months while gradually exposing the dog to the outside environment. Gentle handling and patience are essential in helping these animals gain confidence in their surroundings and in the human race.

Wolf is a good example of a shy dog who has been successfully rehabilitated. A German Shepherd, he was rescued from euthanasia at a dog pound by a woman who felt sorry for him. Wolf was very shy; he was not vicious, but he was afraid of people, especially strangers.

After a few weeks of loving care, Wolf liked and trusted his new owner so much that he would not remain in a fenced yard or in the house away from her, breaking though window glass and even doors to be in her company. Finally after six months, although still fearful of other people, he would remain at home by himself.

One eventful evening a burglar attempted to climb in a window of the house. The terrified woman screamed, and Wolf attacked the man—his love for his mistress overcame his fear of people. His basic instinct to protect his beloved mistress was stronger than his shy nature.

Temper Tantrums

An owner may have difficulty recognizing a temper tantrum, and attribute the behavior to other causes. However, when a mature dog chews furniture, rugs, and clothing and destroys draperies and other property, the chances are good that he is having a temper tantrum.

The Neurotic Dog

Dogs display temper just like spoiled children do. When they are reprimanded for misconduct, they can be just as temperamental as the members of the family they are trying to imitate. And if they are petted and given treats in apology for having been yelled at, these canines have no reason to change their ways.

Displays of temper should be curbed immediately after the first demonstration; the dog must not be allowed to get away with such behavior.

One solution for temper tantrums came about by accident. A patient of mine, a setter named Trixie, overcame her problem because of an oversight on the part of her owner. The TV set had been left on, and when the owner returned from his office, Trixie had obviously become so engrossed in television that she hadn't gotten around to tearing up the house. After that, the owner would always leave on the TV whenever he expected to be away. Now, with her soap operas, Trixie is happy and nondestructive. Since I learned about Trixie, I have recommended the same solution to other owners. Often it does work. But one friend reports that he is careful to tune in only an FM radio station that has no commercials, because his dogs go crazy when the mail carrier rings the doorbell.

If your problem isn't this easily solved, you must take a sterner approach. You should leave the house as usual, and when the dog thinks he is alone, sneak back in and catch him in the act. Do not let him see you. Then you should impress him with his wrongdoing by setting off a loud alarm that will scare him.

If all else fails and a rebellious dog doesn't respond to punishment, he should be confined to areas where he can do no damage. Often a pet simply wants his own way and will be destructive, soil the house, or mutilate in any way he can devise to gain attention.

Separation Anxiety

When certain dependent dogs are separated from members of their human family, particularly those they love most, they develop an anxiety-caused neurosis. They become nervous, pant rapidly, and sometimes become ill. They bark excessively, they soil the house, or they destroy a book the owner has been reading, a favorite cushion, a rug, or something else. I know of one dog who chews on rugs and furniture if his mistress comes home from work later than the usual 5:30 p.m. Another, used to riding in the car with her owner every day, defecates in the study if the owner goes off for a long ride without her.

This kind of behavior is not a result of spite on the part of the dogs (dogs are rarely spiteful). Instead, such behavior is really a manifestation of separation anxiety, a serious and increasingly prevalent neurosis.

Lulu, a white Toy Poodle who just became my patient, presents a classic example of separation anxiety. When Lulu is left alone in the house even for a brief time, she becomes extremely nervous, pants excessively, and urinates or defecates wherever she may be. Lulu's anxiety is alleviated only by the presence of human beings, especially when she is in contact with them, that is, when she is held in their arms or lying next to them. This has made it necessary to get baby-sitters for Lulu when members of her human family cannot be with her. Of her human family, the two most important to Lulu are the husband and wife.

When they tried to keep her out of the bedroom at night, Lulu had an anxiety attack and defecated outside the closed door. As a result, Lulu was allowed into the bedroom, where she now

The Neurotic Dog

sleeps in the bed with the husband and wife. There Lulu is content. Efforts to alleviate Lulu's anxiety through the use of TV and radio failed. So did the addition of a new puppy as a companion for her. She rejected him as she does all other dogs.

Sickness in dogs caused by separation from loved ones, or sometimes even the anticipation of separation, may appear to be feigned. But it is not; it is as real as sickness from an organic cause.

Chinook is one of the most beautiful of the many fine Cocker Spaniels brought to me for treatment. He is high-strung, most intelligent, and a beloved member of his one-woman-in-the world's household. For four years I had to treat Chinook for a violently upset stomach often complicated by an equally violently upset intestinal tract. Each time the illness occurred was when his beloved mistress was about to go on a trip. When Chinook saw the luggage at the door, he would begin to vomit. I can vouch for the fact that he was really ill. His mistress would repeatedly call off the trip to stay home with her pet. One day when another planned trip was in danger of being called off, it occurred to me that if Chinook did not see the luggage, he might not get sick. I suggested that his mistress shut Chinook up in the kitchen and sneak the luggage out to the car.

Kate Salley Palmer

60

A little later she phoned me. "It worked," she exclaimed. "That darned little malingerer, to think of how he's pulled the wool over our eyes all this time."

"He didn't," I said in Chinook's defense. "He couldn't help himself."

Frequently a dog left with us to be boarded will absolutely refuse to eat. The moment his one special person disappears from view, he loses all interest in life. With the exception of the very worst of these cases, we can usually succeed in breaking the hunger strike through patience, kindness, and understanding. There is the exceptional dog, though, that we cannot move. He remains tense, unheeding of water or food, a silent, miserable creature. It is in this type of situation that I am especially grateful for the development of tranquilizers. Before these drugs came into use, it was necessary either to force-feed the unhappy dog or watch him literally starve to death. Now, with tranquilizers, it is relatively easy to reduce the tension and strain so that before long the dog will accept food and drink.

One of my clients has solved the problem in her own way. Whenever she leaves her dog for boarding, she also brings a large, oil painting of herself for me to hang in her dog's kennel.

The Neurotic Dog

Her theory is "Out of sight, out of mind." She is taking no chances.

Sometimes owners miss their beloved pets almost as much as the pets miss them. One day I received a telephone call from Italy.

"Dr. Vine," said an anxious voice, "I wonder if you would do me a great favor and put Shadow on the phone. I'm sure he must be as lonesome for me as I am for him." Shadow was a Sheltie who had been boarding with us for about three weeks while his mistress was in Europe. I rushed to the boarding kennel and carried Shadow back to the phone. While I held the receiver to his ear, his mistress talked to him. I think Shadow recognized her voice, for he wagged his tail continuously.

When a dog is afraid to be left alone, it is often due to the fact that he was alone much of the time as a puppy. Perhaps his owners worked during the day. The puppy was left by himself— well fed, probably, but still lonely and desperately needing to be loved. Even if conditions have changed and the dog has more companionship during the day, he may still be unhappy and ill at ease whenever his people are preparing to leave home.

Tranquilizers are the recommended treatment to alleviate anxiety. But gradual and prolonged socialization may be necessary to bring about lasting change.

Phobias

A phobia is an abnormal fear, one that is a learned conditioned reflex. Most of the time a phobia is simply the outcome of a frightening experience. It begins with fear of a particular situation and, with time, builds up to hysteria. Dogs are subject to the same sort of phobic reactions that afflict humans.

Sometimes phobias generalize. For example, some dogs have an abnormal fear of riding in a car. Their few early rides in a car ended up at the veterinary hospital. Later this dreaded experience generalized into a fear of all car trips. In general, treatment is directed toward substituting a pleasurable experience for the fear response.

Fear of Close Confinement (Claustrophobia)

Claustrophobic dogs go berserk when confined to small areas, and they literally climb the walls. They will pace and whine and will often succeed in getting through paned and screened windows and doors. As a matter of fact, I have seen dogs work their way through wooden doors by clawing and gnawing a hole. Most often, the damage the dog does to himself and the surrounding property seems hardly worth the effort to confine him.

I used to hate to see Trigger, a Labrador Retriever, come to my boarding kennel; his destructiveness cost me more than I received for his boarding fee. Not only did I suffer a loss, but Trigger himself would leave my kennel with his body bruised, his paws and gums bleeding, and his teeth broken.

Now, with his owner's consent, I tranquilize him deeply so that he is sleepy for the first day or two. Then he is kept on a lighter tranquilizer for the rest of his stay in the kennel. In his case, this is the only alternative to the injuries he used to sustain from trying to escape through wire and concrete.

During and after close confinement, a claustrophobic dog may exhibit other kinds of abnormal behavior. He may chase his tail continuously until he collapses from exhaustion. He may "attack" a spot on the floor, first staring rigidly at the spot

The Neurotic Dog

for minutes until he is convinced he can carry out a successful attack, whereupon he pounces on it. He may repeat this again and again, as long as he is confined.

Fear of confinement not only makes such dogs destructive, but it can cause such a state of hysteria that the dog ends up in shock. Discipline is not the answer. The only appropriate treatment is freedom and exercise—the reverse of the usual, training procedures. The entire house should be opened to the dog, with a gradual closing off of rooms as he becomes more secure and less nervous.

This treatment should be carried out with love and patience. The dog's basic fear may never be entirely eliminated, but it can be modified to a livable degree.

In some cases, claustrophobia is inherited, and such dogs should not be bred.

Fear of Thunderstorms

Most dogs can tell a thunderstorm is coming long before humans are aware of it. And, although they do not like loud noises, normal dogs can tolerate thunder. Even dogs most afraid of it will usually just crawl under a bed or into a closet for the duration of the dreaded sounds.

But phobic dogs will become hysterical. They will pace, pant, salivate, and even become uncontrollable in their terror, snapping and biting, hurtling through windowpanes, wooden or screen doors, and generally tearing up the house. A sedative or tranquilizer should be given to such dogs at the first sign of an impending storm.

The best way to alleviate the problem, however, is to desensitize the dog to the sound of thunder.

This can be done successfully with the use of a tape recorder. Tape the sound of a thunderstorm, and replay it to the dog. Remain by his side and speak to him gently in soothing tones; insist that he lie still. Do this in a room from which he cannot run. In the beginning, keep the volume low and reward him for a calm reaction with a tidbit. With further gentle reassurances and petting, increase the volume gradually until the dog can stand the sound at full volume. The next step is to leave the dog in the room alone with the tape recording at full volume. At the end of each of these sessions, the dog should be praised and given tidbits.

Since 1952, Tropical Fish Hobbyist has been the source of accurate, up-to-the-minute, and fascinating information on every facet of the aquarium hobby. Join the more than 60,000 devoted readers worldwide who wouldn't miss a single issue.

Subscribe right now so you don't miss a single copy!

Return To:

Tropical Fish Hobbyist, P.O. Box 427, Neptune, NJ 07753-0427

YES! Please enter my subscription to *Tropical Fish Hobbyist*.
Payment for the length I've selected is enclosed. U.S. funds only.

CHECK
ONE:

❑ 1 year-$40   ❑ 2 years-$75   ❑ 3 years-$100   ❑ 5 years-$160

12 ISSUES   24 ISSUES   36 ISSUES   60 ISSUES

(Please allow 4-6 weeks for your subscription to start.) *Prices subject to change without notice*

❑ LIFETIME SUBSCRIPTION (max. 30 Years) $695.

❑ SAMPLE ISSUE $4.50

❑ GIFT SUBSCRIPTION. Please send a card announcing this gift.
I would like the card to read: _____

❑ I don't want to subscribe right now, but I'd like to have one of your FREE catalogs listing books about pets. Please send catalog to:

SHIP TO:

Name _____

Street _____ Apt. No. _____

City _____ State _____ Zip _____

U.S. Funds Only. Canada and Mexico add $11.00 per year; Foreign add $20.00 per year.

Charge my: ❑ VISA   ❑ MASTER CHARGE   ❑ PAYMENT ENCLOSED

Card Number   Expiration Date

Cardholder's Name (if different from "Ship to:")

Cardholder's Address (if different from "Ship To:")

Cardholder's Signature

Reptile Hobbyist is the source for accurate, up-to-the-minute, practical information on *every* facet of the herpetological hobby. Join many thousands of devoted readers worldwide who wouldn't miss a single valuable issue.

Subscribe right now so you don't miss a single copy!

Return To:

Reptile Hobbyist, P.O. Box 427, Neptune, NJ 07753-0427

YES! Please enter my subscription to *Reptile Hobbyist*.
Payment for the length I've selected is enclosed. U.S. funds only.

CHECK ONE:
❑ 1 year-$40
12 ISSUES
❑ 2 years-$75
24 ISSUES
❑ 3 years-$100
36 ISSUES
❑ 5 years-$160
60 ISSUES

(Please allow 4-6 weeks for your subscription to start.) *Prices subject to change without notice*

❑ SAMPLE ISSUE $4.50
❑ GIFT SUBSCRIPTION. Please send a card announcing this gift.
I would like the card to read: _____
❑ I don't want to subscribe right now, but I'd like to have one of your
FREE catalogs listing books about pets. Please send catalog to:

SHIP TO:
Name _____
Street _____ Apt. No. _____
City _____ State _____ Zip _____

U.S. Funds Only. Canada and Mexico add $11.00 per year; Foreign add $20.00 per year.

Charge my: ❑ VISA ❑ MASTER CHARGE ❑ PAYMENT ENCLOSED

_____
Card Number   Expiration Date

_____
Cardholder's Name (if different from "Ship to:")

_____
Cardholder's Address (if different from "Ship To:")

                                          Cardholder's Signature

A common mistake made by some owners when trying to cure their dogs of the fear of thunderstorms is the use of food. They take a fearful, quivering animal and try to stuff it with food while the storm is in full force. This procedure will not lessen the dog's fear of the storm; on the contrary, it may adversely affect the dog in two ways. He might go into an act whenever a storm approaches in order to get food, or he might just as likely stop eating because he associates food with a distasteful experience such as a storm.

There is some feeling among animal psychologists that the actual stimulus for the fear reaction to storms may not be the noise itself, but the barometric pressure change that the dog can detect a long time before the noise of the storm is apparent.

Fear of Guns

One of the toughest phobias to cure in hunting dogs is gun-shyness. When training for the hunt begins, some dogs who have never seen a gun turn out to go gun-shy. In some cases these dogs are not suitable to become hunting dogs because children have scared them with firecrackers or loud toy guns.

With some dogs, however, excitement can override fear. One bird dog never paid any attention to thunder until lightning struck near his kennel. After that experience, he would come apart whenever he heard the slightest rumble, but never at the sound of a gun. The excitement of hunting overrode his fear of noises.

Other dogs are gun-shy only when hunting with a stranger. One dog that I know does not exhibit fright when the owner is shooting, but becomes nervous and trembles if a stranger shoots. The dog obviously has confidence only in his owner.

The neurosis is inbred in some dogs, but in most it is the result of human carelessness or callousness. An overzealous hunter, for example, who attempts to familiarize a young hunting dog with shotguns by shooting a gun over the animal's head will only scare a pup and ruin it for life as a hunting dog.

Complete rehabilitation is difficult. But veterinarians have found that the use of tranquilizers can lead to a relatively, successful rehabilitation in roughly three or four weeks. The tranquilizer increases the dog's resistance to the sound of the gun going off, but it does not affect the animal's alertness, sense of smell, or other bodily functions.

The Neurotic Dog

Because fear of guns is a difficult problem to cure, prevention is the most practical solution.

Getting a dog used to the sound of a gun should be a gradual process, starting with light noises such as the shooting of a cap pistol, administered along with soothing reassurances that the sounds will not hurt him.

Fear of People

In his studies, Konrad Lorenz has shown that young animals (of various species) tend to accept, as a parent, the first human on whom their eyes rest, provided the association continues. A puppy's earliest recollection is normally that of his mother's caressing tongue, the milky smell of her nipples, and the warmth and security of her body. And a puppy also remembers the first time a human holds and strokes him.

Regrettably, puppies raised without any human contact before the age of twelve weeks will usually have an abnormal fear of humans. This fear is a difficult neuroticism to treat. The difficulty is to identify not only which type of people elicit fear, but also the environmental surroundings that scare the dog. Places and people that frighten the dog must be carefully noted so that the dog can be kept clear of them during the desensitization process.

The rehabilitation program should begin with people and objects that do not stimulate fear in the dog. First, have practice sessions with a "friendly" person approaching the dog while you stand nearby ready to reward the dog for good behavior. The friendly person should approach the dog, stopping about ten feet away, and raise an arm toward the dog. If the dog shows no fear, you should reward him with a tidbit and praise. The friend should then gradually get closer, again raising an arm, and you should reward the dog each time for good behavior.

After the dog is accustomed to this type of socialization and shows no fear, the process should be repeated gradually in other places not so familiar to the dog. If the dog shows any fear of a person or a place, no reward should be given; and the procedure should be repeated until the dog responds without fear. If the dog shows fear toward a person who is standing, that person should crouch down to present less of a threat to the frightened dog.

The Neurotic Dog

It may take several days and much repetition for the dog to gain confidence and not show fear. The aim should be to make, these exercises fun for the dog. The training periods should not be too long, not over thirty minutes. And needless to say, you should never use physical or verbal punishment in any training program to eliminate fear.

Over time, as the dog shows less fear of people, he should be taken into bustling places where he will see lots of people, all the while being constantly reassured that none of these people are trying to harm him.

Fear of the Dark

Dusty, a Cocker Spaniel, loses her cool when left in a dark room alone. She can be very destructive unless a light is left on. Possibly she was frightened once in a dark room when she was a puppy, but no manner of rehabilitation will correct her misbehavior. If another person or a dog is present, or if a radio or TV is left on in the dark room, she is quite calm. Just hearing voices or seeing people on the television screen is very comforting to her.

Fear of Cars

Fear of cars is an acquired phobic reaction. The dog whose fear stems from going to the veterinary hospital is an example. He associates the car with fear of ending up on the veterinarian's examining table, and thus he has learned to avoid this unpleasant experience by avoiding cars.

With a little patience, this type of phobic reaction is, easily cured. Simply substitute another bodily feeling-preferably relaxation-for that fear. A dog who learns to relax in a car will lose his fear of cars.

If your dog has this phobia, begin treatment by placing him in the car with you. At first, the car should not be moving, no motor noise, just peace and quiet, just the two of you. Talk to the dog, encourage him, praise him, play with him, and eventually give him a choice tidbit. Let him realize that everything will be all right.

Do this for no more than 15 minutes at a time. Too much time might bore the dog and take his mind off the lesson of relaxation. You can relax your dog almost to the point of hypnosis by quiet, soothing talk while stroking him. If the dog seems tense, keep working with him until you feel his muscles relax and eventually he will become mentally relaxed.

After he has learned to relax with the motor off, repeat the petting, talking, and tidbits while the motor is running. Then, keeping the dog by your side, take him for short trips (letting someone else drive). Soon he will lose his fear of cars and look forward to traveling in one with you.

Tail Chasing or Circling Behavior

Compulsive tail chasing or circling has been reported predominately in Bull Terriers, German Shepherds, Australian Cattle Dogs and crosses of these breeds. However, it occasionally is seen in other breeds as well.

The affected dog is described as rushing in tight circles with the nose as close as possible to the base of the tail. This condition can vary from whirling in tight circles (tail chasing), walking in circles or in a figure eight pattern, prancing, fence line running, floor scratching, and digging, to freezing in a fixed position. Most veterinarians describe this condition as a psychosis and all agree that it is not caused by boredom.

The age of onset is early, sometimes beginning at three months up to one year of age. It is seen mostly in males, but females can also be affected. Castration, spaying, or tail amputation does not eliminate this behavior. All types of drugs, sedatives, tranquilizers, and hormones have been tried but none aid the dog on a permanent basis. Other home remedies have been tried such as obedience classes, distracting the dog with long walks, putting a bucket on its head, or bandages on the tail. None of these completely eliminated the behavior, which eventually becomes worse. Researchers have determined that the brain is genetically damaged with no hope of a complete recovery for the long-term.

Antisocial Tendencies

Some dogs will not associate with other dogs. Sometimes such disdain is merely feigned; sometimes it is real. Once truly antisocial behavior is ingrained in a dog, it may be impossible to cure. The only approach is to try to teach the dog that other dogs will not harm him. It may be a long and tedious process, and the cure may never be complete. But some dogs recover well enough to coexist with their peers and with people.

Kate Salley Palmer

Introversion

Introverted dogs stay close to home and will have nothing to do with strangers. They are shy, timid, and fearful. Aspects of introversion involve autism, kennelitis, and in some cases, fear biting.

Hallucinations

Under stress some dogs will snap and chase imaginary objects, for example, flies that are not around. Some dogs chase their shadows and jump at them as if to attack them. Tranquilizers will help in some cases.

Overdependency

The overdependent dog is one who is, reared as a perpetual puppy and develops close emotional bonds with his owner. Any disturbance in the daily routine—a visitor, the owner's absence, a visit to the veterinarian or boarding kennel will send the dog into hysterics and often trigger destructive behavior. Because these dogs cannot be left alone in a house, a babysitter often has to be hired, assuming the dog will tolerate one. If a human baby-sitter does not work, another

puppy, kitten, or even a television may help alleviate the dog's anxiety and depression. Tranquilizers may also help.

Runt of the Litter

Litter mates, sometimes with the aid of their mother, often will persecute one puppy in the litter. This usually occurs between the ninth and tenth week. This is one reason it is best to separate the litter at eight weeks of age. Whenever the persecuted puppy tries to return to the feeding area, the others harass it. Such a puppy will be timid, shy and undernourished, but it can be rehabilitated.

My advice to breeders is to remove the puppy from the litter, hand feed him until he can eat and drink on his own, and give him daily attention and body contact.

If you get a puppy who has come from such a hostile situation with the mother and other pups and who exhibits neurotic behavior, you will have to be exceedingly kind to him. To rehabilitate him, you should try the same methods of socialization recommended for the shy dog.

Psychoses

Psychoses are the most extreme forms of pathological behavior. Although neuroses are serious emotional disturbances, neurotic dogs can be helped, and in most cases they can learn to adjust.

Psychotic personalities are seriously disorganized. Their contact with reality is poor. They tend to be either very depressed or overstimulated. They are incorrigible, unmanageable, and unpredictable. Usually they cannot be helped.

Mainly, psychosis in canines is inherited. But it can also be the result of a brain disorder caused by disease (for example, distemper), a head injury, severe worm infestation (migrating worms affecting the brain), or drug toxicity.

Tranquilizers can be used to calm some psychotic dogs, but complete rehabilitation is usually impossible.

Drug Addiction

Some dogs become addicted to certain narcotics or sedatives, either becoming dependent on the drugs or on the attention they receive when the drug is administered. One of my patients became so used to getting phenobarbital for his twitching (chorea, following distemper) that every night at ten o'clock he sat up and begged for his pill. He refused to go to sleep without his medicine. Finally, after months of barbiturates, we changed the drug to aspirin. He seemed just as satisfied with aspirin and slept like a baby. Eventually, a sugar pill was substituted for the aspirin, and the result was the same—a thorough and sound sleep.

An important precaution: Never administer unprescribed drugs to a dog. Besides introducing the danger of addiction, some drugs may cause serious side effects. A veterinarian should always supervise the prescribing, dosage, and follow-up of all drugs given to a pet.

Unfortunately, some people let their dogs have upper and downer drugs while they are "enjoying" their own. Many dogs have become hooked on their owners drugs, showing behavior just as erratic.

SEXUAL DISORDERS

Sexual abnormalities are common in dogs of all ages and both sexes. Often the female, for instance, will mount other dogs, male or female, and even children, in the manner of the male and try to perform the sex act. If the bitch is in heat, this is not abnormal. As some females, however, show signs of heat every three or four months instead of every six months, this type of behavior can become a nuisance. The increased number of heat periods are due to cystic ovaries that produce an overabundance of female hormones. An injection of male hormones may counteract this condition; but if not, spaying is recommended, as these bitches are difficult to breed.

Male dogs often also try to ride legs or mount children. While this is not uncommon during the breeding season, some dogs who are confined and not allowed to roam develop the habit from sexual frustration. It can become intolerable and dangerous to children. I use female hormones to try to counteract the condition. If they are not successful, castration may be required.

There are many neurotic canine sexual disorders. Even, with two normal dogs, the mating process may be a strained one for home-grown pets—those who do not roam the streets breeding with any dog who comes along. In some planned breedings, tension and excitement occasionally prevent dogs from getting together. Some emotionally disturbed pets—for example, those spoiled by over permissive owners—show little inclination to mate; such females, often make poor mothers even when they are bred.

Miscarriages can occur because of emotional trauma. In highly excitable dogs, almost any disturbing event can cause premature whelping. In such cases, puppies sometimes arrive without the accompanying flow of milk. The mother sometimes will refuse to care for her puppies and may even kill and eat them. The usual explanation for this is that she fears someone will hurt her puppies. In my opinion, it is possible that she feels disdain for her puppies and an unwillingness to share family affection with them.

Bestiality

A dog provides a convenient outlet for the owners need to display affection. Although it is taboo for two humans to show intimate affection in public, it is perfectly all right for a person to fondle and pet a dog in public. Many people ignore the fact that dogs can become sexually aroused, that they can "fall in love" also.

The Neurotic Dog

Severe problems develop when dogs develop hypersexuality toward their owners. These dogs become jealous of all human contacts of their owners, and this jealousy can result in disobedience, overaggressiveness, overprotectiveness, and husbands, wives, lovers, and friends with severely bitten parts of their anatomy.

Sexual feeling between humans and animals is often a result of frustrated emotions. An individual can fondle, pamper, and "mother" his dog until the dog finally resorts to sexual love. In his report on the sexual behavior of humans, Dr. Kinsey cites a small percentage of people admitting to overt sexual experiences with animals. The intent to arouse and to engage in sexual experiences with animals is called bestiality.

Some owners, misguided or neurotic, will deliberately encourage a pet to express his sexual feelings toward them without themselves experiencing such feelings. A veterinarian friend told me of one such owner who once a week, every Saturday night, allows his dog to mount his leg.

Some owners have no intention of arousing sexual feelings in their pets, but they are too permissive and do not recognize the developing feelings until they are outrageously apparent.

Human affection is important in producing a well-balanced dog, but it must not be overdone. When it is, treatment consists of a training program to end overpermissiveness and establish the owner's leadership. Correction of sexually motivated problems must be nonphysical in nature because such disturbed dogs can be vicious. Some male dogs must be castrated to reduce the male instinct, but even this may not help when the problem has been allowed to develop over a long period of time.

Homosexuality

Homosexuality is common in the animal kingdom. Males ride males, females ride females. For a male, the pleasure is derived from rubbing the penis against the body of the other animal. A male may also penetrate the anus of another male dog. The female (often one in heat) receives a clitoral orgasm when she rides another female. A certain amount of homosexual interest is normal in adolescence, but if it continues into adulthood, the only way to end it may be castration or spaying.

The Neurotic Dog

Homosexual behavior is often caused by physiological abnormalities such as pseudohermaphrodism, cryptochidism, and sertoli cell tumors.

Pseudohermaphroditism

Pseudohermaphrodites are dogs having both male and female sex organs, but one is usually predominant. With such mixed sexual features and hormonal imbalances their behavior is distinctly abnormal. These dogs usually will not mate with the opposite sex. Castration or spaying is the only cure for these animals.

Upon closer examination of one Boxer female, whose sexual organs appeared normal, I found signs of a penis inside the vagina. This male organ would enlarge upon stimulation. The dog would allow herself to be mounted or would mount a female and attempt to copulate, depending on her mood or the stage of her irregular estrus cycle. She attracted males but would not let them penetrate her.

Cryptorchidism

Some male dogs have no descended testicles, or only one. As this condition is inherited and can cause emotional and physical problems, even if the dog would breed normally, geneticists advise against it. An undescended testicle in the abdomen may form a cancerous tumor. It can also cause the dog to become feminized and sexually attractive to other males. Cryptorchid dogs can be temperamental, aggressive, and difficult to handle. They are disqualified from the show ring. Surgery to remove the testicle from the abdomen is recommended.

Male Feminizing Syndrome

This condition occurs because of a tumor in the sertoli cell of the testis. The male dog shows feminine characteristics. The problem may occur in a cryptorchid dog, but not always. Physical changes may include chronic skin infection, enlarged nipples, and enlarged, pendulous testicles. Behavioral changes include overaggressiveness, disobedience, irritability, and sometimes homosexual behavior. Because of their physiological abnormality, these dogs may secrete a female odor that attracts other male dogs. The only cure is to surgically remove both testicles. If one testicle has not descended, it must be removed from the abdomen to correct the physical and behavioral abnormalities that occur with this syndrome.

A story that accentuates how behavior is affected by hormones concerns a Boxer named Elvis. He was a well-behaved dog until the owner noticed a change in his physical appearance. His breasts and nipples were enlarging as well as his scrotal area. Male dogs were attracted to him, trying to mount him and engage in sex. The dog became depressed, hiding whenever possible, and especially when his owners called him Eloise instead of Elvis. When I was consulted, I realized that his altered behavioral antics were due to the sex change caused by the tumor in his testicles. Castration cured his feminizing condition and Elvis was a happy, normal dog once again.

Masturbation

Both male and female dogs masturbate, either by licking their sex organ or by mounting objects such as pillows, people's legs, furniture, or an article of clothing belonging to the owner. These dogs are generally unresponsive to their owners during the mating season. This behavior is common in adolescence , but if it continues into adulthood, these seemingly oversexed dogs are prime subjects for castration or spaying.

Some physical abnormalities, such as cystic ovaries or other physical abnormalities, may cause a dog to masturbate. The cures for these conditions are either hormone therapy or sterilization. But even some apparently healthy dogs will resort to masturbation out of frustration. Often such dogs have "fallen for" a member of their human family and sublimate their desires with articles of clothing belonging to that person. Or the behavior may occur in dogs who are confined to the home or kennel with no normal outlets for their sexual feelings. In either of these cases, you should give your dog obedience training and remove the personal articles that sexually excite him. When you catch a dog masturbating, you should distract him by giving him chew bones or playing games with him (for example, tossing a ball).

If nothing else works, surgical neutering (spaying or castrating) is recommended.

An interesting case comes to mind. A client of mine bragged to me how well-trained her Pomeranian, Louie, was. Upon command, he would fetch his stuffed teddy bear and make love to it until he reached an orgasm. She told me that Louie was the life of the party when he went into his act in front of her friends.

Shakespeare was right. "What fools we mortals be!"

Nymphomania

Females who show more or less constant signs of heat—mounting other animals, riding legs, and masturbating—are often victims of nymphomania. These dogs can achieve orgasm by rubbing their vaginas against objects. Most of the time these females are high-strung, ill-tempered, and inclined to fight both males and other bitches.

Nymphomania is usually caused by ovarian cysts, which produce false heat periods accompanied by enlarged vaginas. Dogs with this condition will attempt to copulate even though they are not in season. But, because ovulation does not occur, these dogs do not conceive.

The use of hormones can sometimes correct the cystic ovaries, but in severe cases, spaying is required.

In some male dogs, as in some humans, sexual activity is their overwhelming purpose in life. We call them oversexed because they exhibit excessive libido.

There is one dog in particular who roamed far and wide each day looking for a female dog to romance. He was aptly named "Casanova," and no bitch was safe in the neighborhood from his advances. No fence was too high for him to climb nor were there any doors or windows that could keep him out. As a result of his amorous escapades, there were many puppies in the neighborhood that resembled him.

If these "sex maniacs" get out of control, hormones or castration can slow them down.

Mating Problems

Dogs, like humans, have their preferences, courting some and rejecting others, but most need no help in their lovemaking. Yet veterinarians are seeing more and more dogs who show no interest in the opposite sex. Usually this is due to the sheltered lives the dogs have led with their human families and their inexperience in courting or being courted by dogs of the opposite sex. And often owners are at fault for teaching their dogs that any kind of sexual behavior is wrong. When this happens, a household male dog may never learn how to mate with a female.

Occasionally female dogs will not accept one stud while readily giving themselves to another. These unwilling females have to be tranquilized to allow the stud to get near them.

Frigidity

Frigidity in females is caused by the owner's overprotectiveness. Many overdependent females are so attached to their human owners that they are a real danger to an amorous suitor; they will growl, bark, bite, and even scream in fear if a male dog approaches and tries to flirt. If they are bred artificially, they make very poor mothers because they tend to refuse to nurse their puppies and many even kill and eat them. This is usually an expression of unwillingness to share their human family's affection with the pups.

In my experience, some problem matings are a result of human error in calculating when the female is ovulating and ready to receive her mate.

The Neurotic Dog

Impotence

When a male dog refuses to mate, part of the problem may be the breeding atmosphere. Some dogs will not breed in a new or unfamiliar setting. Home security is psychologically necessary for them. Therefore, the female is frequently brought to the stud's home grounds. In other cases, the presence of a member of the human family may be a deterrent. Either the dog is afraid he might be punished for sexual activity, or his love for some member of his human family is greater than any sexual desire he might have for a female in season. Although most males will breed in the middle of main street at high noon, some sensitive males will not breed unless all the conditions are to their liking.

When a male dog is timid, an overly aggressive female may inhibit his sexual advances and turn him off. If he has been raised with an aggressive female, he may be unable or unwilling to mate at all.

An injection of the male hormone, testosterone, helps increase the sexual ambition of some male dogs. Dogs who experience premature ejaculation and other physical problems have to be bred artificially. With those who simply do not know how to breed, especially young or physically awkward dogs (such as Basset Hounds or English Bulldogs), help may be needed to insert the penis into the vagina.

There is an English Bulldog by the name of Winston who could not breed a dog by himself. Because he is a champion, he's in great demand for breeding. But he has a problem mounting the females, and for the past five years I've been helping Winston with his lady friends. He has gotten so accustomed to my help that he will not even attempt to mount a female unless I'm there. In fact he has become so attached to me that he licks my face at the same time of his ejaculation. I believe he has fallen "in love" with me. He associates me with his pleasurable experiences.

The Effects of Spaying

There are many fallacies about spaying. Proper spaying does not make a female dog less feminine. It just stops the heat periods. It will not affect her female behavior patterns. She will not develop bad habits or become aggressive because of spaying.

Spaying at too early an age, however, does contribute to excessive urination, aggression, and masculine traits. Even, though these unwelcome traits can be treated by hormones and obedience training, it is far better to allow the dog's female organs to mature in order to supply the necessary female hormones. Therefore, I advise spaying a dog between six and eight months of age—six months in a small breed, eight months in a larger breed—which is before her first heat period. However, some people prefer to wait until after the first heat period. If this is done, I would advise a wait of at least two months. Spaying within one month after a heat period may cause the female to become irritable from too rapid a loss of the hormone progesterone. This spaying too close to a heat period is what started the old wives' tale that a spayed dog changes personality and gets more irritable.

Estrogen (female hormones) decrease body weight; therefore, a spayed female will tend to gain weight, but not if the owner carefully supervises the dog's diet. Sometimes a spayed female should be given prophylactic doses of estrogen in the same manner a woman is given the hormones after a hysterectomy. The notion that all spayed females get fat and lazy need not be valid.

The Neurotic Dog

Normal Effects of Heat Period on Behavior

When a female is in heat, she behaves a little differently than she does the rest of the time. One of the first signs of an impending heat period is the female's excessive cleansing of the enlarging genital area. This licking precedes the actual discharge of blood-stained fluid that marks the beginning of the heat period.

The female's behavior begins to change during the proestrus, or first signs of heat. She has an irregular appetite, appears nervous and moody, is more active and vocal, shows less affection, and seeks privacy. But in the middle of her heat period when she is ovulating and willing to accept a male, she is more affectionate and cuddly with her human family as well.

Some bitches in heat become very nervous and undergo a change in personality from quiet and friendly to excitable and biting. These "frustrated" females should indeed be spayed.

The Effects of Castration

Most owners are well satisfied after their dogs are castrated, for these dogs are more affectionate with children and other members of the family. But not all bad habits are cured by castration, and about 10 percent of castrated dogs do not change their behavior at all.

Where bad habits are sexually motivated, however, remarkable improvements in behavior occur after castration. Roaming (normally caused by sexual instincts) is reduced in 90 percent of castrated dogs.

Likewise, fighting with other males, urinating in the house, masturbating, and mounting dogs or people is either reduced or stopped in 50 to 75 percent of dogs castrated. Castration is also effective in reducing hyperactivity, hyperexcitability, and destructive behavior.

In some dogs the change is rapid as the male hormone, testosterone, begins to disappear from the blood within 24 hours after castration. In others, the change is much more gradual, over a period of a month or more.

For the dog with behavioral problems, the age castration takes place usually does not affect the response rate. Whether he is castrated when under six months or when he is older, the results are usually the same—with one exception: fear biters. In some cases, fear biters may be helped if the castration is done before puberty, but not if it is done later.

In cases where castration does not help an aggressive dog, injections of progestin (a hormone) may help cure such bad habits as intermale fighting, urine marking at home, and roaming. Urine marking at home is due to some disturbing condition existing there. It could be jealousy, resentment against a member of the family, or just the fact that the dog doesn't get his own way.

Instinctual behavior (excluding sexual drive) is not affected by castration. A castrated dog still has a male brain and will exhibit male behavior. He will still urine mark his territory outside the home, and he will still show territorial and fear-induced aggression. Therefore, he will remain a good watchdog.

Some misconceptions about castration are that it will ruin a dog's hunting ability or make him fat and lazy. These are simply not true. Hunting ability will not be affected by castrating or neutering an animal. Castration or spaying, will not cause obesity and laziness. Neutered animals who gain weight usually do so from lack of exercise or too much food. It is the owner's responsibility to monitor his pet's diet and to ensure proper daily exercise. Another misconception is that different breeds react differently to castration. Not so. Some people have aesthetic objections to castration and spaying because of the identification they have with their animals. Some men, in particular, are reluctant to castrate their dogs. They feel they are emasculating themselves when they do so.

It is important to remember that castration does not affect secondary male characteristics very much because other organs in the body produce hormones. In other words, a castrated dog will not look and act like a female dog, nor will it turn into a weak-looking and weak-acting dog.

There is one patient of mine whom castration has affected in a curious way. Siroux, a Saint Bernard will usually squat like a female dog while urinating. However, if there is another dog in the vicinity, either male or female, he will lift his leg like a normal male dog. I guess his male ego will not allow him to squat in front of other dogs.

The Neurotic Dog

PSYCHOSOMATIC NEUROTICISMS

Psychosomatic ailments are a form of neurotic behavior. They are usually allied to emotional reactions and are resorted to as a means of gaining attention. Although various emotions are responsible for psychosomatic illnesses (dogs, experience love, hate, envy, spite, boredom, etc.), the basic one seems to be jealousy. Since true psychosomatic disorders are actual organic ailments caused by emotional problems, these animals are not faking a sickness—they are actually ill. Of course, some dogs do fake illness. Such pretended illness is not psychosomatic unless it is something the dog cannot help doing or it leads to organic changes.

Jealousy

Jealousy generally develops in overdependent and pampered dogs when they are not the center of attention. For such dogs, some of the factors that can cause psychosomatic ailments include: a new pet, or too much attention paid to other pets in the household; a new human mate, or the owner's new boyfriend or girl friend; a new baby; or many parties and house guests, with the dog relegated to the backyard or a separate room during the festivities.

The Neurotic Dog

A male shepherd, Hans, picked a rather symbolic way of showing his jealous displeasure toward the boyfriend of a young lady I know. One night, while the couple slept, Hans jumped on the bed, lifted his leg, and urinated on the man.

One client told me that he was unable to hug or kiss his wife while their dog was with them. The dog was so attached to the man that he could not bear to see him giving affection to another person, even his wife. When the husband and wife danced together, the dog growled and tried to jump on the wife to push her away from the one -person-in-the-world he loved.

Another jealous dog that I know, Poochie, would not let the husband onto the bed if the wife was there first. He would snarl and show his teeth if the husband made the attempt to join his wife.

It seemed a coincidence, but whenever the husband was at home (which was very infrequent because of his job), Poochie seemed to be ailing. The lady of the house then gave Poochie her undivided attention, much to the chagrin of the husband. When I was consulted I finally realized that Poochie's jealousy precipitated all of his stomach ailments.

The Neurotic Dog

Kate Salley Palmer

Another family had four dogs of the same breed, two male and two female. The younger male, Nikki, was devoted to the wife. He was so possessive that he would not allow the other dogs to sit close to her. The older male, Mr. Mac, was a gentle, affectionate dog. Often in the evening, when the husband and wife and the dogs were sitting quietly in the living room, Mr. Mac would get up and cross the room to sit at the woman's feet. Nikki would watch until Mr. Mac got within a few feet of the desired spot. Then, quick as a snake, he'd get between Mr. Mac and the wife. Time and again this occurred. The older dog could go wherever he pleased except to Nikki's one-person-in-the-world. Nikki never showed jealousy when Mr. Mac approached one of the female dogs or the man of the house.

I have known dogs who were extremely jealous of another pet brought into the household. A Kerry Blue Terrier I know will not tolerate parakeets, for example, that have been brought to the children in the home. She watches with resentment when the youngsters play with the birds. Then, just as soon as she finds opportunity—and she always does— she kills the birds.

Psychosomatic medicine is a fairly new field in veterinary practice, but in certain cases of emotionally caused physical disabilities, therapy can now be effective. Discovering the cause of each emotional ailment is the first step in treatment.

Attention-Seeking Behavior

Dogs crave love and attention more than anything else. To ignore them is the worst punishment that you can give them. When a dog feels neglected, he resorts to various methods of gaining sympathy from the family.

I have seen dogs using asthmatic wheezing, coughing, lameness, vomiting, diarrhea, aggressive behavior, ear and eye problems, and even muscular spasms to gain their owner's undivided attention.

One Cocker Spaniel I know chewed his tail to the point of mutilation to gain attention. Gimpy, a mongrel terrier, limped on one foot for years, carrying her other front foot raised off the floor-that's how she got her name. Then she accidentally got her good front paw caught in a door. She started carrying the newly injured paw off the floor, and sure enough, began walking perfectly well on the previously lame one. After a week, when the paw was healed, she started holding up the original "lame" one. Obviously, she enjoyed all the attention she received.

The Neurotic Dog

Some dogs who fake an illness have a practical reason for doing so. For example, the "illness" might allow them to stay inside a warm or air-conditioned house rather than be relegated to the backyard.

Of course, all attention-seeking behavior must first be checked for medical dysfunction. The dog may not be faking an illness; he may actually be a sick dog with a problem. Before the pet is labeled a pretender, he should be checked thoroughly by a veterinarian.

Some dogs develop bad habits just for the attention they receive, even if it means being yelled at or punished. At least they are being noticed by their owner. One of my patients, a Toy Poodle named Toodles, has epileptic-type seizures whenever he gets emotionally upset. These seizures usually come after a verbal admonishment. Toodles knows that his owner will always pick him up and pet him after a seizure. Another dog, a shepherd, would get aggressive with his companion, a little terrier, whenever the doorbell rang. The shepherd was apparently unwilling to share the attention of new arrivals-guests or family members-with the terrier. He would only attack the little terrier when the doorbell rang; otherwise they were good friends.

Some dogs have a more direct approach to attention seeking. My own dog, Bridget McGuire, a beautiful Irish Setter, keeps me busy being a doorman for her. I made a doggie door for her, which she refuses to use. Instead, whenever she wants to enter the house, no matter what time, day or night, she scratches on the regular door. She knows that I will soon come running to let her in.

Another dog, Tico, a Lhasa Apso, imitates his human masters in order to get attention. Whenever he is left in the car alone, he will press on the steering wheel until the horn blows. He doesn't give one long blast but rather two or three short honks, just as a person would do.

The secret of finding out whether the behavior of the dogs is legitimate or not is to see what they do when family members are not present. If they go into their act only when people are around, they are just seeking attention, warmth, and love. The treatment of a psychosomatic case of attention-seeking behavior is to divert the dog to a desirable form of play, and reward him when he does something worthwhile. Play periods with rewards will work wonders with pets as well as with humans. No one, animal or human, wants to be neglected.

I should add here that I see nothing wrong in attending to your dog's whims as long as you don't overdo it. *There is nothing wrong in spoiling someone you love, be it a person or a dog.* Also, I disagree with people, both professional and nonprofessional, who warn you not to dote excessively on a pet when he is sick.

Personally, I think an owner's love and concern for a sick pet is very helpful in overcoming the illness.

Asthmatic Seizures

Certain types of asthma are psychosomatic. I have seen dogs jealous of either a human or another dog (or cat) go into loud asthmatic wheezing when things were not going their way and they wanted attention. But they were not pretending. Their asthma was real. Some excitable dogs will have a seizure when the doorbell rings or when strangers enter the house.

During a seizure, the dogs work themselves into a frenzy, panting and gasping. Their tongues may turn blue, and some dogs faint from lack of oxygen. Because the bronchial tubes become constricted, the dogs cannot get enough oxygen into their lungs. The best treatment for a dog in this state is to pick him up and relax him with soothing talk and petting; soon the breathing will return to normal. Because such attacks can prove fatal to a dog with a weak heart, some animals have to be kept on respiratory sedatives or tranquilizers to prevent recurrence. To prevent attacks when upsetting people or events are anticipated, the animal should be given a tranquilizer.

The short-nosed breeds, such as the Bulldog, Boston Terrier, Pug, and Pekingese, are the prime victims of this ailment. I know a Pekingese, Susie, who goes into a severe asthmatic wheezing when she wants attention. All she has to do is commence wheezing as if she were losing her breath and everybody in the house comes running to her. She becomes the center of attention. Her attacks will disappear soon after she has been picked up, kissed, and stroked with loving words of endearment.

A Pug named Wilfred would have an asthmatic seizure before each meal. While the owner prepared the food, Wilfred would work himself into a frenzy of excitement that brought on

SNORT GASP!

H"WHE·E·E·E·ZE!
WHEEEEZE
WHEEEEEEZE

severe wheezing attacks. The only solution to this problem was not to allow the dog to anticipate the food. For Wilfred and other dogs with this problem, the food should be prepared in secret and given to them before they get excited.

Car Sickness

Although car sickness can be caused by an inner-ear disturbance, in most cases in dogs, it is due to emotional problems. It can be classified as psychosomatic in origin when the dogs begin to drool and appear nauseous before they get into a car. (Motion sickness per se is rare in dogs). As I have mentioned before, because some dogs are taken in the car only to the veterinarian or to the boarding kennel, that association can be unfortunate and traumatic.

Car sickness can be controlled with a tranquilizer, which will calm the dog before he gets into the car. The tranquilizer is usually effective.In most cases it is the fear of the car that makes the animal sick. Also, intake of food and water should be limited prior to travel.

Steps should be taken to cure an animal of its fear of travel. Of course, it is easier if done in early puppy hood. Try taking the puppy for short rides for pure enjoyment, with a destination that includes a run in the woods or a food treat. The dog should soon have confidence in the car and lose its fear.

False Pregnancy

False pregnancy is a fairly common psychosomatic ailment, one that is frustrating to both dog and owner. The dog is definitely affected physically; she becomes very uncomfortable, with large swollen breasts.

At the supposed time of delivery some females give all the signs of impending whelping. The vagina becomes enlarged, and there is a discharge. I've seen them go through false labor pains and tear up newspapers to make a bed just as if they were preparing for puppies. During the period when (had they really given birth) they would have been nursing their puppies, they usually stay in bed or lie under chairs or other objects, and even refuse to eat. Some females actually drip milk and continue lactation during the four-to-six-week normal nursing period. They have the maternal instincts of a nursing mother and will frequently carry objects (toys, shoes, pillows) around in their mouth and snuggle them close to their breasts to simulate actual puppies. They are suspicious, protective, and disagreeable to anyone who goes near. At times they get upset and depressed, looking for their imaginary puppies.

In one case a setter, Mimi, apparently became so jealous of a new baby in the household that she developed a false pregnancy and became heavy with milk in her breasts. She went out and found a nest of baby rabbits, brought them home, made a bed for them, and nursed them. The rabbits were treated just like her offspring, and her maternal instincts and jealousy were satisfied. Fortunately, jealousy of a new baby generally works itself out, and the dog ends up lying by the crib protecting the infant.

No one knows exactly how female dogs bring about false pregnancies. There is disagreement among veterinarians and research scientists as to whether false pregnancy is an emotional disorder or strictly a hormonal malfunction. Some breeders feel that environment can also be a cause. I believe that there is a hormone imbalance in the body that causes an emotional change in the animal. There is no evidence supporting the idea that false pregnancy is hereditary. Fortunately, we do know how to relieve the poor bitch of her swollen breasts, her anxiety over her "puppies," and her depressed state.

We can treat her with hormones; if there is fever, with antibiotics; and if she is emotionally upset, with tranquilizers.

Labor Pains in the Male

It is not unusual for a bitch to go through false labor pains during a false pregnancy. It is, however, quite unusual for a male, nevertheless, I have seen a male dog go into false labor when the female with whom he was bred started the whelping process.

The dog was a Dachshund named Hans, and his was one of the strangest cases of jealousy that I have ever encountered. He and his mate, Hilda, produced a litter of puppies once a year. Once Hilda became pregnant, Hans was forced to play second fiddle while Hilda got all the attention from the family. His jealousy became so overwhelming that whenever she commenced labor pains for the impending delivery, Hans would jump into the whelping box and grunt and strain alongside her. As each puppy came, he would help Hilda lick and take care of it. However, as soon as the delivery was completed, Hilda would give a growl and Hans had to leave the area for the remainder of the postnatal period until weaning. It was a very strange sight indeed, to see both male and female delivering a litter of puppies together.

Lameness

Lameness can be a psychosomatic ailment that sometimes arises in overindulged dogs when they are jealous or seeking attention. Even temporary paralysis of the legs can be caused by emotional distress. Of course, veterinarians should examine such legs and X-ray them, if necessary, to make sure there is no actual physical abnormality.

When dealing with psychosomatic lameness, do not pet the dog or give it sympathy. The best solution is simply to give the dog a lot of attention and keep him busy-with games and walks. In the joy of playing and running, the dog will soon forget his lameness.

A Kerry Blue Terrier named Frenzie presented a challenge to me. She would be brought to my hospital for treatment of her intermittent lameness. Frenzie seemed to enjoy the visits and the treatments she was given. On several occasions she came to the hospital, about a mile form her home, by herself, expecting, and receiving treatment. Usually I would put a bandage on the lame leg and she would proudly limp out of the hospital holding up her bandaged paw. But X-rays revealed no sign of injury. I decided to try a new approach the next time she came to the hospital holding up her right front paw. I bandaged her left front paw. She proceeded to limp out of the hospital holding up the newly bandaged paw while walking perfectly well on her previously lame leg. Since I believed she was faking leg injuries to gain sympathy and attention, I advised her owners to play with her and give her more of their time.

The Neurotic Dog

Another case of psychosomatic lameness caused by jealousy was quite easy to detect. A Corgi, Patrick, began limping about the same time a new puppy was introduced into the household. After a thorough examination revealed no evidence of pathology, a tranquilizer was prescribed. While Patrick was on the drug, the limp disappeared; as soon as the drug was withdrawn, the limp came back. A new regimen was implemented; realizing that they were dwelling too much on the puppy, Patrick's owners began showering him with affection and play periods, which he needed to overcome his sudden sense of insecurity. Patrick's limp promptly disappeared. Within several weeks, Patrick felt much better about the new puppy, and the lameness never returned.

Loss of Appetite

Loss of appetite can be a psychosomatic ailment, when, for instance, a dog is on the canine equivalent of a hunger strike. In new surroundings almost any dog may refrain from eating for the first day or two. However, if after two or three days the animal is still not eating, and has no physical ailment, the cause is usually some emotional trauma. For example, a dog's feelings can be hurt if he is put in a boarding kennel when his owners go off on a trip. The dog feels left out, unwanted, and unloved.

Some pets are more sensitive to humans than others. I have known dogs to stop eating when a member of the family was absent, either for short periods or permanently. Other dogs will go on a hunger strike if a companion—either dog, cat, or human—dies.

The psychosomatic dog who will not eat usually shows other symptoms, such as involuntary urination and defecation, resistance to handling or walking with new sitters, and a fearful attitude, with the whites of his eyes showing.

It is essential to find out what is causing the animal such distress and to try to correct it. Luckily, certain long-acting hormones, such as progestin, can help restore appetite. This or any other treatment should be administered together with a lot of loving care.

Loss of Bladder and Bowel Control

Severe emotional stress, anxiety, or shock can produce loss of urine or bowel control in almost any animal. This is normal and to be expected. However, there are psychosomatic dogs who lose control without any apparent cause. A Toy Poodle, Doodlebug, often loses control of herself both emotionally and physically whenever anything disturbs her. If she is left alone too long, if something upsets her—such as too many strangers in the house or too many loud noises—or if her feelings have been hurt by some member of the family, she lets loose, either accidentally or purposely.

Nervous Diarrhea and Vomiting

Although overfeeding or incomplete digestion, due to a physical ailment, is the most common cause of diarrhea or vomiting, some dogs exhibit these symptoms because of emotional problems. Too much excitement, jealousy, strangers, or other disturbing factors can trigger psychosomatic diarrhea or vomiting in such pets.

Dogs can vomit at will, and whenever they are emotionally disturbed about a person, place, or thing, they can evoke the vomiting response. But this vomiting is not always done on purpose. Many dogs, when emotionally aroused—either elated or depressed—will get sick to their stomach, very much as humans do.

A nervous dog with this problem should not be fed within an hour of anticipated excitement. In addition, the dog should be given a tranquilizer or an intestinal sedative.

Skin Disorders

Some dogs, particularly if they are jealous of another pet or feel unloved or neglected, will bite and lick themselves excessively. This is a spoiled dog's way of attracting attention. But this licking and biting can produce a skin irritation and infection called neurodermatitis, which is definitely a psychosomatic ailment.

Some dogs go crazy with boredom when left alone too long. They are not only destructive in the house but also chew on themselves. Some dogs will chew on one spot until the hair is gone at the site of the licking, and a skin ulcer or wound is produced (called a lick granuloma).

Susie is a Toy Poodle whom I treated for several months for a chronic skin ulceration on the top of her head. I tried every known drug for skin lesions, both internally and externally.

The Neurotic Dog ────────────────

Her head was bandaged continually. Finally I resorted to surgery to remove the ulceration. Healing was perfect. As soon as the bandages and stitches were removed, however, Susie commenced scratching again, opening up a new sore. Finally, in desperation I questioned the owners at length about the history of the dog's skin trouble. I learned from them that the first sore appeared on the dog's head after they began locking her in the bathroom to keep her off a new rug. The cure was simple. I told them never to lock Susie in a room again. Once she had complete freedom of the house, the chronic scratching stopped almost immediately. The skin healed completely in one week without medication of any kind. Susie had felt neglected and unloved when her owners locked her up. She scratched her head to gain sympathy and attention.

Other dogs dislike being tied up—either to a post or to a tree—and will go berserk and chew on themselves. These skin lesions will not clear up until the cause of the problem is alleviated.

For some bored dogs, the introduction of another pet is recommended, even a bird or turtle—or another dog to keep them company. But this solution can backfire.

Kate Salley Palmer

One of my patients, a Dalmatian named Fancy, had an "incurable" skin itch. Almost every remedy, based on both professional and neighborly advice, had been used on the dog to stop the incessant scratching and biting. Nothing seemed to work. Upon questioning the owner, I found out that the skin problem started about the time that a new cat was brought into the household. I thought we had the answer—an allergy to cat hair. But after the skin test proved negative, I realized what had caused the problem; Fancy was jealous of the new cat and started chewing and biting on herself to gain attention. She succeeded, because she was medicated continually. The treatment was simple: Get rid of the cat. The cure was miraculous. Fancy's skin healed completely within a matter of days, without any medication.

OVERAGGRESSION

At the renowned Sorensen Clinic in Denmark, more than 5,000 mentally disturbed dogs from all over Europe received treatment last year. A high proportion of these dogs were sent to the clinic to be cured of biting people. This kind of overaggressiveness is the most widespread and serious canine neurosis.

Normal Aggression

A certain amount of aggressiveness is normal in a dog, especially when the dog is engaged in competition or territorial defense, fulfilling predatory instincts (for example, chasing birds), courting, feeling pain or, in the female, acting out maternal instincts. Even aggression that causes injury to humans, however regrettable it may be, may not be neurotic but the normal expression of instinct and breeding.

A newspaper account told of a Doberman Pinscher whose mistress came home from shopping to find him coughing and choking. She rushed the dog to a veterinary hospital, where she was instructed to leave him while the doctor probed the throat for a possible obstruction or sought some other cause of the problem.

When she arrived home, the phone was ringing. It was the veterinarian calling. He told her to come back to the hospital immediately. She rushed back, and the doctor told her what had happened. Upon probing the throat, he had found three fingers from a man's hand. He surmised that the dog must have attacked an intruder in the house and that the intruder might still be there. He had urged her to leave the house immediately while he phoned the police and sent them there. The police found a man hiding in a closet, unconscious from the loss of blood from his badly wounded hand.

Normal dogs show curiosity, too, which is closely akin to aggressiveness. These two traits, aggressiveness and curiosity aid learning and survival in both dogs and humans. A sign of strength and character, a little aggression is preferable to the spineless, submissive behavior that is indeed abnormal.

With this in mind, as an owner you must be careful to discipline without damaging the normal instincts of aggression. For example, when a male puppy approaches puberty, he will become more aggressive because of the male hormone that is being produced in his body. He will likely become more prolific at marking his territory, more curious about the lady dogs in the neighborhood, and more protective of his human family. This behavior is healthy because it is part of his normal development. However, such behavior must always be kept within socially acceptable limits. Marking furniture is not okay, assaulting cats is out, and biting family friends is not to be overlooked.

Immediate castration is not the solution. Nor is cruelty. Some owners will reprimand too harshly every act of male aggression. These owners, through their unrelenting and stern approach to even normal signs of aggression, will damage their dog's self-esteem, making him so submissive and neurotic that he can no longer feel in tune with his natural instincts or his environment. Oddly enough, the perversely submissive dog can be very dangerous if he becomes a fear biter.

Misdirected Aggression

Some owners actually contribute to eventual misdirected aggression in an adult dog by overlooking or tolerating, with amusement, the swaggering overtures and misadventures of the developing male puppy. Then when the puppy grows into an obnoxious adult, they want to get rid of the monster. I am constantly called on to help young women troubled by their aggressive male dogs. When the dogs are brought home, they

generally seem to be quite gentle and manageable. The story that usually unfolds, however, involves a new boyfriend, from whom the dog is trying to protect his mistress.

Earlier it amused these women to be protected from someone—in one case, it suited the young woman to see the dog get upset when her sister teased her; but being protected from her new companion does not suit her at all. The couple can't even hold hands, let alone embrace, without the man being attacked. By the time I am consulted, the situation is usually desperate—the owner wants to get rid of the dog or even put it to sleep. Such an extreme solution is seldom necessary. Getting the new companion to feed and play with the dog usually solves the problem.

Like the male dog reacting to hormonal changes, the female dog, too, may have times when aggressiveness surfaces more readily. (Incidentally, the notion that spaying a bitch affects her personality and causes her to be mean is not true. In fact, it is the unspayed bitch who is more subject to mood swings). A female dog's heat period can make her more temperamental, and sexual frustration may cause her to perform some act of aggression. Also, a female mothering her puppies may show aggression toward strangers or those she thinks might harm her young.

The Neurotic Dog

Sometimes the desire to protect or guard is carried to an unwarranted extreme. The mother dog who snaps at the child approaching her puppies is an example. At these times, the owner must reproach the dog and also provide the child with a better understanding of the dog's nature. Allowances must be made for the dog's motives (to protect her young), but she must not be allowed to bite. The owner must mediate the dispute, with firm control over both dog and child. The same is true of the dog who attacks his owner's new boyfriend. Understanding and owner leadership must be established and the dog must be made to obey.

Redirected Aggression

When dogs get excited and aggressively aroused, they often redirect their behavior towards anyone near them, usually a companion dog, but sometimes a human.

Usually there is one troublemaker in a group of dogs who usually will start the fighting when provoked by a loud noise, the presence of a strange person, or a nearby barking dog. This agitator will attack anyone that is near him.

The Bully

Some dogs not disciplined at appropriate times start to enjoy being the bully. A friend of mine was walking his two Lhasa Apsos one evening. Both dogs, an old male and a young female, were on leashes. As they crossed a busy street, a large brown dog-apparently a Shepherd-Collie mix-came charging at the two Lhasas. He bowled over the female and nipped at her head; the male jumped to her defense, but was knocked off his feet by the larger dog. My friend tried frantically to push the assailant away with his feet, while holding tightly to the leashes to protect his dogs from the oncoming cars. He tried to hold both dogs in the air to get them away from their attacker, but the big dog had hold of the female and would not let go. At that moment three people leaving a corner restaurant saw what was happening and rushed to pull the big dog away. He did not resist them. Either he had his fun and was satisfied, or, like most bullies, he was at heart a coward.

Not only do such dogs bully other dogs around the neighborhood; at times they will try to scare and push people around too. Even though this behavior harks back, to some extent, to primitive times, when their instinct was to become leader of the pack, this behavior must not be allowed free reign. Just as the dog must obey the human family inside the house, so the dog must not be allowed to try to bully other animals in the neighborhood. In addition to other undesirable consequences, such behavior often leads to neighborhood dog fights to establish a leader. Several fights may occur before a leader is established. Then, inevitably, a hard-nosed contender appears who can't accept the leader, and the fights go on.

The Vicious Dog

Viciousness, extreme overaggressiveness directed against people and other dogs, is not an instinct; it is not usually an inherited trait (except among psychotic dogs). And although some cases of viciousness are due to brain damage or hyperkinesis, viciousness for its own sake is quite rare in the animal kingdom. Dogs normally do not perform acts of violence without provocation (defense of life, of mate, and so on). Even then, most dogs are reluctant to attack. Some German Shepherds and Dobermans trained for guard duty or police and military service (who are taught to attack) can't be induced to bite, regardless of training or provocation.

Most often, viciousness, like most overaggressive behavior, is the product of early environment-abuse, lack of training, or neglect. In almost all cases, overaggressive behavior could have been prevented by early supervision and proper training. Unfortunately, an overaggressive pet is not only one of the most common problems encountered, but it is also one of the most difficult to correct.

Early Signs of Aggressiveness in a Puppy

You should be aware that if you train a puppy to be aggressive for guarding purposes, the dog may not be able to discern friends from foes and may attack one of your friends, or even a family member. If a five- or six-week-old puppy barks or growls at a stranger without provocation, watch out! Without the proper early training, he will probably grow up to be vicious.

Early signs of the dominant dog—the overaggressive one who sees himself as leader—are excessive barking, forward ear position, bristling hair, curled lip, low throaty rumble, elevated tail, and erect body posture. The barking may be triggered by any number of things inside and outside the house—especially people, animals, cars, or bicycles passing the house. Some owners interpret this barking as a sign of protectiveness and do not discourage the puppy. In this way, the owner unconsciously contributes to uncontrollable outbursts of temper.

Since most dogs grow more aggressive as they get older and can become uncontrollable by the time they are one or two years old, the time for the owner to concentrate on training is at the puppy's first sign of aggressiveness. The dog should be taught tricks and commands that he will respond to. Play periods morning and night, 5 to 15 minutes long, will often help avert viciousness later on.

To correct territorial barking, you should give the dog a command to stop in a raised, disapproving voice. The dog should then be made to take a prone position. At this time, he should be spoken to in a soft, quiet voice and kept in the position for three to five minutes before allowed to get up.

Inherited Causes of Aggression

Although viciousness itself is not usually inherited, some dogs are born with the inherited tendency for some emotional disorder, which may unfortunately result in violent behavior. Because of such a dog's distorted perception of the world, he may revert to some primitive urge to protect, defend, or conquer that will manifest itself in violence.

Not all overaggressive dogs are vicious. I once treated a dog who would have periodic episodes of "going on a rampage." It always manifested itself in the same behavior. He would suddenly, and for no apparent reason, decide that day he would "conquer" the neighborhood children. Being a big, lumbering Labrador Retriever, he would successfully knock the children down and sit on them. The little ones were most vulnerable to his attacks. He never really hurt them or bit them, and most days he ignored them. But whenever one of his "bad" days rolled around, he would diligently head out to sit on the first conquerable child he encountered. Oblivious to the screams of terror, he staunchly, and in a very businesslike way, would hold his position until someone came to rescue the child.

Whenever a mental disorder does, however, manifest itself in vicious behavior, it is a serious and dangerous problem.

Abnormal Shyness and Fear

Fear biting is sometimes the result of inherited influences. The dog born with the tendency to bite out of fear grows up as a shy and timid creature who is irrational in the presence of strangers, no matter how much training or patience on the owner's part. If cornered by a stranger, human or animal, he will become vicious. To be able to chase away his tormentor is very rewarding to him. The fearful dog usually will warn a potential victim with a snarl and lowered eyes and ears. But if someone keeps coming at him, he will bite. It is best to heed the dog's warning. Owners of fear biters may try to soothe the dog with praise and reward. Lots of patience, is needed to win over a dog that is aggressive because of fear. Dogs born with this tendency are suspicious and fearful, are likely to remain insecure, and they can be dangerous.

Fear biters often result when an aggressive, dominant dog is bred with a timid dog. Owners of these dogs are breeding extreme opposites in hopes of getting desirable puppies. However, the worst traits from both animals can easily show up in the offspring, and a fear biter is produced.

Psychotic Dogs

Some truly vicious biting dogs can be classified as psychotic individuals. These animals are usually very insecure; and if they feel threatened by another animal or human being, they will attack. The difference between the fear biter and the psychotic biter is that the psychotic dog will attack almost every dog encountered. The sex or age of the victim makes no difference, and the attack is usually entirely unprovoked. A normal male dog will not fight a female dog unless attacked. A psychotic dog will.

One morning an elderly woman was walking her three Poodles (Miniatures) on a street. One of the Poodles was a new puppy. As he cavorted about her feet (the older Poodles walked more or less sedately at her side), she was aware of a large German Shepherd standing not ten feet away.

"The moment I saw his eyes, I was terrified," she told one of my clients. "They were not the eyes of a normal dog. There was something fierce and at the same time cold as ice in them. I tried to get the dogs away, but the puppy was playful and I had trouble moving him. Perhaps it wouldn't have mattered, for the Shepherd came so fast. Somehow I knew it was the puppy he was after. I grabbed the puppy in my arms. The Shepherd jumped, almost knocking me over, and I saw that one of the puppy's ears had been ripped. I began screaming and tried to protect the puppy by turning my back on the Shepherd, but he was in front of me again in a flash. In desperation, I held the puppy above my head. The Shepherd leaped, I saw his open mouth. I held on to the puppy as he grabbed it, pulling me to the ground as they fell. I was stunned for a moment, but when I opened my eyes I saw the Shepherd was gone. Then I saw the puppy. His head had been torn from his body."

Some psychotic dogs appear quite normal until the day they suddenly, and unexplainable start performing acts of violence, a phenomenon very similar to the nervous breakdown that some humans undergo.

Some psychotic dogs respond to medical therapy, high-protein diets, or castration. Others do not. These dogs are much like human criminals who seemingly cannot be rehabilitated.

Some dog breeders feel that psychotic aggressive behavior appears most often in large breeds such as: Saint Bernards, Doberman Pinschers, German Shepherds, and Bernese Mountain Dogs. But it can occur in any breed, however large or small. Any dog showing signs of uncontrollable aggression should not be bred.

For these dangerous dogs whom you cannot trust, I can, with a clear conscience, say that euthanasia is the only answer. I would rather see an uncontrollable dog be put to sleep than a child or adult injured. In such cases, euthanasia is performed for the safety of humans and for the canine kingdom.

Hyperkinetic Dogs

As we saw earlier, hyperkinesis is an inherited trait in dogs and is characterized by symptoms of hyperactivity, short attention span, and unpredictable behavior. Hyperkinetic dogs are usually raging, vicious beasts that are "just plain mean." There are no known causes for this condition, but in some cases, an amphetamine-like drug, Ritalin, is helpful in controlling it. Such stimulants (not tranquilizers) have a calming effect on hyperkinetic patients.

Physical Causes of Aggression

Various physical abnormalities can cause overaggression in dogs. Certain glands, when not functioning normally, can stimulate aggressiveness.

Poor nutrition can also be a factor. Too much starch or sugar in the diet might make a dog violent. In such cases, high-protein foods that lower the sugar content of the blood will restore normal behavior. An overaggressive dog should never be given a diet high in sugar or starch.

Some dogs with poor peripheral vision inadvertently bite people who get near them. This poor vision is commonly caused by profuse facial hair, a natural condition found in breeds such as Old English Sheep dogs and Lhasas Apsos. Older dogs with failing eyesight, usually the result of cataracts, will occasionally bite people who touch them before speaking and letting themselves be known. Glaucomas and ulcerations, too, bring about poor eyesight and sometimes cause a dog to bite.

In fact, any form of ill health can cause aggression. When a dog is ill his threshold for pain is lower, and he is more impatient with any annoyance. And some physical conditions cause real behavior changes in dogs. For instance, false pregnancy may sometimes make a bitch very disagreeable to live with. Because of the hormone imbalance in her body, she becomes temperamental and may bite. Therapy consists of the use of tranquilizers to calm her and hormones to counteract the false pregnancy.

There is an age-old fallacy that feeding gunpowder to a dog will make him more aggressive, and that feeding him raw, bloody meat will make him vicious. Gunpowder might give him an explosive personality, but it will not make him mean and ornery. And neither will raw meat.

People-Caused Aggression

Aggression begets aggression, and some people unwittingly stimulate it in their pets. Puppies handled improperly during the socialization period (3 to 12 weeks) can turn into overaggressive dogs.

The Neurotic Dog

Rough handling, tug-of-war games, and encouragement of biting and growling will teach a puppy to be aggressive. This kind of handling will also cause overexcitement and can turn a docile pet into a savage beast.

Not all people-caused aggression is unwitting. Some male owners take a curious macho pride in the aggressiveness of their dogs (usually, but not always, from breeds with fighting reputations, such as Pit Bulldogs, Dobermans, and shepherds). They do nothing to discourage their animals when they play the bully on city streets or in the neighborhood. Indeed, such owners often boast of how "tough" or "mean" their dogs are and recount stories of their conquering prowess. These owners resemble little children who boast that "my dad can whip your dad"—only in their case, dad is a dog who depends upon them for guidance. Such owners are storing up trouble, for themselves and for their dogs.

Even animals trained to be aggressive can be dangerous when they are overexcited. Some military guard dogs become so excited that they turn on their handlers. Their adrenal glands overproduce adrenaline, causing them to become so frustrated that they "lose their cool." Fortunately, this happens only in severe cases where attack dogs have been overtrained.

Another cause of aggression can be personality clashes with people in some families. One person may resent the dog and mistreat it when the rest are absent.

Trixie, a terrier, bit all the neighborhood children. A dog psychologist discovered that a child in the house was very mean to the dog because he believed that Trixie was getting more attention from the parents than he was. The jealous child abused the dog physically whenever the parents were absent. He'd kick the dog, pull his ears or tail, and throw things at Trixie, who then came to hate all children. The doctor stressed to the parents the importance of giving equal attention to the child and the dog—urged them to allow the child to feed and play with Trixie. They did this and Trixie soon became the favorite neighborhood pet.

Overindulgence

Overpermissiveness on the owner's part, allowing the dog to have his own way, can cause a pet to become too aggressive. Exaggerated affection by a "weak" owner, who lacks leadership or control, can open the way for the dog to take over and become dominant. The dog knows a "weak" owner and knows what he can get away with. He will test his masters often. If he finds he can take more liberties with the wife than he can with the husband, or vice versa, be sure he will do so. Like children, dogs are adept at testing the limits of permissiveness. The owner, however, can regain authority by proper training and the assumption of the dominant role.

As an owner, you can unintentionally stimulate aggression by rewarding the dog when he growls or barks at noises around the house, for instance, the doorbell, a passing car or animal, or approaching strangers. Some dogs have personality quirks and try to protect the entire neighborhood.

You should always investigate the situation. It could be that the neighbors or their children are provoking the dog by yelling and throwing objects at him. If he stays outside, a covered fence that the dog cannot see through will shield him from provocation. Many normal dogs have been prodded verbally and physically into becoming an outlaw. This is especially true in younger dogs in the critical periods of their lives. Unkind humans can cause a dog to become a juvenile delinquent.

Kate Salley Palmer

The Neurotic Dog

I cannot emphasize too much the importance of investigating the cause of overaggressive and other undesirable behavior. It is the only way that a reasonable treatment can be devised. A dog I know named Prissy, a Miniature Poodle, had to be confined constantly because she bit someone every time the telephone rang. She was brought to me for treatment of a skin ailment, caused by licking and chewing brought on by confinement. In questioning the owners, it came to light that as a puppy she had been accidentally stepped on and her leg injured while her mistress was answering the phone. A rehabilitation program cured the dog of associating a ringing telephone with pain.

Anger

Anger can cause aggression in dogs just as it does in humans, and the provocation are limitless. If someone other than the master, be it animal or human, tries to assume dominance over the dog, he may respond with aggression. When eating, a dog may bite to protect his food from another moocher or intruder, even sometimes the owner.

Confinement

Forced restraint on a chain or constant confinement to a small area can irritate a dog into aggressiveness. I know dogs who will bite anyone approaching their outdoor enclosed runs, even their owners. Outside the runs, they are friendly and peaceful. It may be territorial instinct operating, but I tend to think it is more the isolation and lack of freedom to socialize that causes these dogs to go wild. When penned-up dogs are allowed outside more and more each day, their aggressiveness tends to subside.

We must think a minute about what happens when a dog is confined. A dog is a creature of nature, a child of the wilderness. We take this creature who is by our intellectual standards, imperfectly developed, and we tame him, make him conform to our social mores. Then we thrust him into a pen or chain him to a tree. He has no language skills familiar to us; he can only bark, snarl, pull at the chain, or run circles in his pen. Prisoners exhibit the same characteristics, except they have language and can communicate with each other. But still, the hostility grows. The anger is there. When released, some of these dogs literally knock themselves down wagging their tails. Their relief is so great and their joy so apparent that it seems clear that their violence was only a product of their being cooped up.

If it is necessary to confine a dog, he should be provided with a companion or playthings and allowed daily periods of unconfined activity to relieve his boredom.

Barrier Psychosis

Confinement makes some dogs behave in a psychotic way. Psychologists call this barrier psychosis.

Zelda was a female black Labrador Retriever who was a garbage hound, scrounging in the neighbors' garbage cans at every opportunity. Finally, because of complaints from the neighbors, Zelda was compelled to stay in the house during the day when the owners were at work. When left alone, she would claw and chew at doors, eventually getting through any barricade that got in her way. To further show her anger at being confined at home by herself (when she had once been allowed to roam free with other dogs), she urinated on beds and in other places in the house. Then she started to chew up sofa cushions and velvet-covered chair seats. When she was banished to a fenced-in yard, she destroyed everything chewable that she could get her teeth into. When her owners could not find a suitable home in the country, where Zelda might have the freedom she craved, they reluctantly had the dog put to sleep. Tranquilization could possibly have helped this dog.

Temporary Isolation

Sometimes you can unwittingly aggravate a tendency for overaggression in your dog by temporarily isolating him when company comes. Most dogs are smart. They will associate being shut up with the visit. To the dog, being isolated is punishment; so he will take his anger out on the visitors. The goal is to get him to be friendly. Punishing him before he does anything wrong will not help achieve the goal, but only have the opposite effect.

Your dog must be trained to be tolerant of your friends, and he must be assured that the friends are not invading his territory. They are your guests, and both family and family dog must be nice to them. Remember: The tone of your voice will usually key the dog's reaction while guests are present. Instead of shutting him up when you are expecting visitors, try a different approach. Put the dog on a leash before the visitors arrive. Then when company comes, allow the leashed dog to approach the people. Show the dog that the guests are friends by petting and talking to him in a kind tone, encouraging the friends to also talk to him and after a few moments to scratch the dog's ear while still talking to him. All this should be done while you keep the dog under the closest scrutiny. At the slightest curl of the lip, backward movement of the ears, or growl, the dog should be reproached.

Getting a dog to adjust to visitors will avoid many unpleasant situations, such as a besieged young salesperson or a mauled charity volunteer. And the adjustment should include mailmen, garbage collectors, meter readers, and others who come to the home. You have to assure your dog that these strangers are not invading your property. If they will cooperate, have them give the dog food or tidbits while you introduce them to each other. Shake hands with these people in your dog's presence so that he is assured of their friendship. While this isn't always practical, the point is clear: The more strangers a dog learns to deal with, the better the dog.

Types of Aggression

Territorial Aggression

The territorial instinct usually shows itself in most dogs when they are six months old. Any hostility a puppy might show at this time toward strangers must be discouraged through training. Once the biting habit is established, it is difficult to eradicate. As an owner, you should catch the offender in his first act and not allow him to get worse with age.

Usually, at six to nine months of age a male dog will begin lifting his leg, which shows he is becoming interested in defining his territory by marking it with his urine.

The dog should not be allowed to become overprotective, because this will lead to overaggressiveness. Chaining a dog will make him more aggressive because he will defend the territory in which he is confined to the point of being obsessive about it. It is instinctive behavior to guard and to protect property. Most small dogs just bark, but a large dog may tear into an intruder.

Intermale Aggression

Male dogs will fight each other to assume dominance over the pack. Once the pack leader is determined and the pecking order is established, the fighting usually ceases until a new dog challenges the leader.

Females will fight each other, but a male will seldom fight a female, although a male will defend himself if the female gets too rough.

Competitive Aggression

Competitive fighting between males or between females is done to gain dominance in the family household that, to the dog, represents the pack.

Pain-induced Aggression

An injured dog will bite. It is a natural instinct to strike back at pain, whether it is inflicted by a stranger or an owner. Remember this when trying to give first aid to an injured dog. A stepped-on tail, ears pulled too hard, or an accidental kick may provoke a dog into biting what he sees, at the moment, as his antagonist. Sometimes a dog will get unruly because of an abscessed tooth, an earache, hip dysplasia, or a bad case of arthritis. Any pain can cause a dog to become more aggressive. In the case of Prissy, the Poodle, even the memory of pain, when stimulated by the ringing telephone, led to violent behavior.

Instinctive Aggression

Many dogs who behave aggressively are acting out an instinctive need to show dominance over the pack-canine and sometimes human. (Territorial aggression is also instinctive).

Such a dog will growl and display his teeth when his territory is challenged, and he may snap at anyone attempting to come toward it. These dogs are not necessarily asocial, neurotic, or psychotic; rather they are just behaving in an instinctive way.

Dogs retain the pack instincts of their ancestors and, if given the opportunity, will run together. This should not be allowed because a pack can be vicious. Mob psychology can transform packs of roaming pet s into biting dogs. They forget they are nice little pets and revert to biting. A dog pack is like a mob of humans out to hang the culprit or burn the witch. Individuals will do things in a group that they would never dream of doing by themselves. Mob behavior or mob psychology takes over, and dogs that individually would not attack become gripped by the pack mania of the chase.

Hormone-Influenced Aggression

The male dog is generally larger and stronger than the female and is usually more aggressive, owing in part to the stimulus of male hormones. Females given male hormones will begin fighting, and males who are castrated or given female hormones will become more peaceful and try to avoid fights.

Even though it is not seen as often, the aggressive tendency in females can become serious. Some females are exceptionally vicious with other females. I suggest using a muzzle on such females when they are let out of the house. Although a muzzle in not a cure for viciousness, but only a temporary restraint, it will slow up aggressiveness because of its obvious handicap in a fight.

Most aggressive female dogs become more so immediately before and during heat cycles. This is especially true when two or more female dogs are living together, although they tend to act hostile with any nearby bitches, too. This added aggressiveness is due to hormones in the bloodstream.

Hormone therapy can sometimes counteract these behavioral problems. And spaying can help by eliminating the heat periods and thus eliminating the females moody cycles.

Castration, too, although not a cure-all, definitely helps some aggressive dogs. Unfortunately, it does not help all of them. However, neutering a dog, whether male or female, usually reduces excitability, sexuality, and competitiveness. It has also been shown to reduce alarm-type barking and aggressiveness towards other dogs. In the male, urinating in the house can definitely be curbed by castration.

Maternal Aggression

Maternal aggression is an instinct of nursing females. They will defend their puppies against any intrusion and will give their lives, if necessary.

Predatory Aggression

Predatory aggression is seen in the wild state when dogs hunt for food. It is not seen in the trained hunting breeds because the dogs perform for the sport, not for food.

Aggression Caused by Mental Lapse (Schizophrenia)

Friendly, easily controlled, and well-mannered animals may, for no apparent reason, suddenly turn and viciously attack a person who may be a friend or even a member of the family. These dogs do not recognize familiar faces and appear dazed, with a distant look in their eyes. Often they will attack a person around the neck or face and afterward appear subdued or shaken. This condition is very similar to schizophrenia in people. Soon after the misdeed, the animal may revert back to his normal, happy self.

Frequently, these dogs are normal members of a family, but when they reach maturation, between one and a-half and two years of age, they undergo a sudden personality change. While this problem can occur in any breed of dog, unfortunately there are several breeds in which this aggression is more noticeable such as: Saint Bernards, Doberman Pinschers, Bernese Mountain Dogs, Pit Bulls, and German Shepherds. It is best not to breed these canine misfits.

At the present time, there is no effective medical treatment for this inherited behavioral problems. Some dogs have been helped through the use of anticonvulsant drugs, similar to the ones used in epilepsy. The reasoning behind this treatment is that these unprovoked attacks are a type of seizure.

But because these dogs can injure or, on occasion, kill human beings, I would advise that dogs who repeatedly have such mental lapses be euthanized.

Food Bowl Aggression

Combating food bowl aggression is especially important in households where there are small children. This type of aggression begins in puppies and builds up to intense proportions as the dog gets older. The dog will not let anybody, human or animal, near his food dish.

The best time for correction is in the puppy because good results can be obtained with a little training. In the grown dog, it is more difficult, but can be accomplished.

The Neurotic Dog

When a dog growls at you as you approach his food dish, talk to him in a soothing, calm voice, crouching down and offering him a delectable food treat. As he eats the tidbit, remove the bowl while petting him and talking to him. After a few sessions, he'll realize that he will receive a treat when you take his bowl away. When he doesn't growl at you, he should receive his food dish back again.

Jealousy and the New Baby

Many people are faced with the problem of what to do about their dog when a new (usually first) baby is expected. They fear that the dog will be jealous and perhaps endanger the baby. Although no one can guarantee how a dog will react, I feel that a properly handled dog will respond favorably to a new baby. First, as the owner, you must reassure the dog that he is still loved. You should show him extra affection and spend more time with him—throwing a ball or just taking a stroll. Talking to him also helps.

It is important that both husband and wife feel the same way about the dog. If they do not, the dog will be able to detect the antagonism or the apprehension that one member of the family has about him. This might create an emotional atmosphere that is not conducive to keeping an aggressive dog satisfied and calm, especially in the presence of someone he might see as a rival in the family.

If the dog is a fear biter, I would not allow him near a young child. The child might inadvertently scare the dog, provoking a bite.

An example of jealousy-induced aggression is that of the terrier who would attack the husband whenever the man and wife were engaged in sex. The treatment was simple: Close the bedroom door.

The Biting Dog

Every dog is still basically a wild animal conditioned to living with humans. The dog retains many primitive instincts and still exhibits an escape reaction by showing and using his main weapon of defense-his teeth. Large dogs may growl, show their teeth, or indulge in fierce barking. Small dogs will sometimes snap without warning.

For example, a long-jawed dog, such as a Corgi, whose ancestors were accustomed to snapping at the heels of cattle, may often bite without barking. On the other hand, a short-nosed breed such as a Pug or Boston Terrier may seek protection in friendly arms rather than exhibit active aggression. But there are no hard and fast rules. Any frightened dog may seek protection from his owner or instead use his teeth.

Of course, biting is an unacceptable practice and that, for the dog's sake as well as that of his actual and potential victims, it is essential to try to change. In many communities a dog can be put to death for repeated biting.

As there is usually a reason for biting, we should attempt to understand why a dog bites in order to better deal with the problem.

Three Types of Biters

Biting dogs belong to one of three basic types: fear biters, indiscriminate biters, and protective biters.

The **fear biter** is a product of his genes or of undersocialization with humans while a puppy. He is neurotic. A normal dog can, however, become a one-time fear biter if he is panic-stricken or otherwise under extreme stress. An injured dog, normally friendly, can become a temporary fear biter because of pain and fright. Fear biters will bite strangers or family members because they associate certain movements or gestures, such as raising a hand as if to spank, with pain and punishment. They will bite these uplifted hands in anticipation of the pain or punishment. Some dogs will bite strangers who wave their hands, yell, scream, or annoy them but will not bite their owners for doing the same thing.

The **indiscriminate biter** is usually the brat, spoiled as a puppy, who has grown up to be the boss in the household. He is the type of dog who merely allows his human family to coexist with him. Most dogs who bite their owners are indiscriminate biters who lack discipline. They don't respect their owner. They think they can get away with anything. They are usually dominant dogs who growl at their owner, and the owner backs away. These dogs have assumed pack leadership. This is the fault of owners who have failed to train their dogs.

The **protective biter** usually belongs to the working breeds (Shepherds, Collies, Dobermans, and so on). Usually he bites because he feels the need to protect something or someone. When such a dog becomes overaggressive, he is carrying out, in a distorted way, the mission for which he was bred. When protective biters turn neurotic, they not only chase but attack almost anything that moves in front of them. They will bite at cars, motorcycles, bicycles, or a running child. The pursuit and the biting are part of a wild game to them. They are attacking an enemy.

As I have pointed out earlier, all three types of biters can be stimulated to overaggressiveness by excessive roughness when playing as puppies. Some people tease puppies by poking them and throwing them over roughly. Others play tug-of-war games with them. They should not. The consequences of such rough play can be dangerous for dogs and humans. There are, of course, other causes of overaggressive behavior, including biting.

Sometimes a dog bites for reasons that make some sense. In one case that came to my attention, a certain mongrel dog would become aggressive toward his owner whenever the man had too much to drink. As the years went by, the normally gentle dog began to bite the owner if he so much as smelled alcohol on his breath. Perhaps the dog associated the odor with the change in the owner whenever he became inebriated. Or it could be that the dog felt there was a real need to take over the leadership to prevent these periodic binges.

A few dogs get openly belligerent when their sense of values is offended. For instance, Taffy, a Cocker Spaniel, although upset by his owners divorce, nevertheless seemed to adjust to living with the husband and, in time, to accept the absence of the wife, except when another woman entered the apartment. Then Taffy would openly attack and try to bite her. The husband, a firm and strict disciplinarian, reprimanded the dog for each of these upsetting episodes. Thereafter, Taffy would wait in ambush for the right time to arrive. At the most unexpected moment, Taffy would slide up to the lady visitor and adeptly sink his teeth into the nearest exposed part of her anatomy. It was abundantly evident that Taffy did not approve of the husband associating with other women. This man had a real problem and especially when he found a lady whom he wanted to marry. He loved the woman and the dog so I helped him with a plan to keep both.

We had his fiancee wear clothing from his first wife. Taffy was not fooled but confused and did not bite the lady. The woman, (while wearing the other wife's clothing) would feed the dog and play with him, taking him for several walks a day. Eventually it worked and the three of them lived happily ever after.

Reasons a Dog May Bite

- A mother dog will bite to protect her puppies if she thinks they are in danger.
- Loud noises or sudden movements may trigger a dog bite.
- Children are bitten most often because they tease a dog by pulling his hair, his ears, or his tail, or possibly by annoying him while he is eating, or trying to take away his food or toys.
- Trying to pat a strange dog may frighten him and cause him to bite.
- Keeping a dog isolated from human beings (for example, locked up in the backyard all by himself) may produce a biting dog.
- A sleeping dog may bite if he is awakened suddenly or disturbed or frightened.
- Mistreated dogs may bite in self-defense. People who hit or kick at dogs may expect to be bitten.
- A spoiled dog who is not controlled or disciplined may bite if he is forced to do something against his wishes.

People who are afraid of dogs sweat profusely when near them. The scent of the discharge makes the dogs wary. It is wise to stay away from dogs you are afraid of.

Correction of Overaggressive Behavior

Biting behavior should be corrected at once, before it is too deeply ingrained in a dog's mind. The punishment for biting in a very aggressive dog should be an immediate and sharp slap with a newspaper across the muzzle to show the dog that his mouth and the biting are most displeasing. This should be accompanied, of course, by a stern "Bad dog."

The amount of punishment is in proportion to the type of animal that you are chastising. A mild mannered dog needs only a loud voice reprimand, but a more stubborn dog needs a more severe punishment such as a newspaper on the snout (or muzzle). Hitting a dog across the nose is very strong punishment for the average dog and it should not be done. It should only be used in cases of very bad behavior in very aggressive dogs. Initially, always try to praise and reward, which reinforces the human-canine bond. Praise and reward will work for most dogs.

When walking a leashed dog who is biting and aggressive, always maintain some slack in his leash. If the lead is held tightly he will strain to bite a passersby. He acts bold because he feels you at the other end of the leash, and it gives him the confidence to attack.

Sometimes it is necessary to resort to a muzzle when turning an overaggressive dog loose in the neighborhood. There are certain cities and towns where muzzling the at-large dog is required by law. I don't believe muzzling is cruel. Comfortable muzzles are sold at pet shops, and sometimes such a device allows a dog to be kept who would otherwise have to be sent away or put to sleep.

Obedience Training

There are many specific ways to deal with overaggression and other canine behavior problems. But I must emphasize the importance of obedience training. It is your responsibility, as an owner, to train your dogs to be, at the least, acceptable members of the community. Overaggressive, biting dogs are not acceptable members. In many cases, obedience training (for both owners and dogs) can reform such animals and make them not only acceptable citizens but a pleasure to live with.

One reason that overaggressiveness is so difficult to correct is that most people allow this problem to exist for a long time before they attempt to get help from a trainer, a veterinarian, or a psychologist.

For months, and even years, the dog may have been attacking the mailman, the milkman, and the newspaper boy. The appropriate time for correction (when the dog was a puppy or adolescent) has already passed. The dog has seen that he can dominate "intruders" by growling and barking. His behavior pattern has been reinforced by his repeated aggressiveness.

The younger the dog, the easier it is to correct aggression. Prevention is the best answer, by properly rearing the puppy, but an older dog can be taught to control his aggression through various methods. In any corrective or rehabilitative procedure, it is important that you, the owner, carry out the training techniques yourself. In this way you assume dominance over the dog, while the dog becomes submissive. Professionals should provide advice but not perform, the actual corrective procedures.

Usually three to six weeks of intensive and persistent care is needed to rehabilitate an aggressive dog. During this period, you should spend more time playing with your dog and trying to find out what is making him so aggressive. As an owner, you might make use of the ideas in this chapter to evaluate the provocation that are causing your dog's aggression. And remember, your own relationship with the dog may be contributing to his problem.

You should try to make your dog happy by showing him you are happy. When he pleases you, praise him, pet him, rub his ear, tell him those little endearing compliments he loves to hear. Let him know you love him. But also let him know you dislike him when he terrorizes the playground and ambushes the garbage collector. The point is to communicate your feelings, whether good or bad, to your dog. He will understand.

The two most successful methods for correcting overaggression are the prone-position and time-out techniques. For mild to average overaggression, I recommend the prone-position technique; for more persistent cases, the time-out technique; and for very stubborn cases, a regimen that consists of both the prone-position and the time-out techniques.

Prone Position

Whenever the dog misbehaves, he should be made to lie down in a prone position for at least three minutes in a state of calmness. You may have to put the dog in the prone position and hold him there by force if necessary. He must not be allowed to stand during this time. At the end of this period, he should be praised and petted and then allowed to get up. If he attempts to get up during the three minutes, hand pressure should be increased on the scruff of the neck.

This procedure should be repeated each time the dog misbehaves, and at different locations in the house so that he does not feel that he must behave in only one location. If the dog acts very badly, he should be muzzled and then made to stay in the prone procedure. He should be muzzled until he behaves properly.

Time-out

This method is used only on stubborn dogs who do not respond to normal commands. It consists of removing the dog from the environment that is causing the overaggressiveness. For example, a dog growling and barking at a visitor in the living room should be removed to a room that is at some distance from the living room. It can be a large closet, a basement, a garage, a utility room, or a bathroom. All windows and doors should be shut and the dog kept in complete peace and quiet during the time-out period. No food, water, or toys.

The time-out period need not be long, only three to five minutes, or long enough to instill in the mind of the dog that he is being punished. You must not speak to the dog during the time-out. You should completely ignore him. If the dog misbehaves again after being released, you should say, "Bad dog," and then take the dog back to the room for three to five more minutes or longer. By the way, this method works well with children, too.

A good reinforcement position is the prone position, because if the dog is made to relax for three minutes, the aggressive behavior is more likely to be suppressed. Rehabilitation by this method usually takes from six days to six weeks.

Dominance Gentling

This method is used on an aggressive dog to establish the owner's dominance. It is very successful when employed by an assertive owner, but it does not work for an indulgent person. Such people should use the time-out method. (Never use dominance gentling on a fear biter. It will only make the dog's aggression and hostility worse).

For dominance gentling, you will need a collar that does not slip or slide around the dog's neck, but not a choke collar or chain. At the first sign of aggression, grab the collar, put the dog flat on the floor, and say "No" in a loud and forceful manner. With a large dog, it might take two people to throw him down on his side. Each time the dog is forced down, keep him down until he relaxes.

After he relaxes, begin releasing your grip, stroking him and talking gently to him. Repeat the process whenever he shows any signs of aggression.

Take care when doing this procedure, for some very aggressive dogs will attempt to bite. Such a dog might have to be muzzled, and you might need to wear gloves to safely perform this technique.

Physical Punishment

Nonphysical techniques will usually correct overaggressive behavior faster and with more long-lasting results than will physical punishment. Further, it is unwise and dangerous for you to attempt to correct an overaggressive act by your dog with extreme physical punishment, severe scolding, or yelling. If the dog is in a violent mood, he might turn on you. It is far better to wait until the dog calms down. Then you should talk to him, gently but firmly. If however, the dog needs a stronger reminder of his wrongdoing, I am not against a moderate form of physical punishment, but not with a two-by-four. What I mean by moderate is a rolled-up newspaper across the muzzle at the right time, accompanied by a verbal reprimand, calling him a "bad dog."

Firmness is the key along with consistency. Too many people add fuel to the aggression by showing weakness in the punishment, being wishy-washy, too meek, and not consistent in correcting the dog every time he gets out of line.

Other Corrective Measures to Use—or to Avoid

Unfamiliar Environment

Animals are less aggressive in a strange area, a factor useful in handling problem dogs. At home, the territorial instincts take over, the yard, house, and family are under the dog's domain of protection. When dogs get too assertive and arrogant in this role—in short, over aggressive—they should be taken to obedience classes away from home.

Exercise

When a dog has an overaggressive episode, calm him down with the techniques described above. Then give him strenuous exercise. This will help cool him off.

The Neurotic Dog

Kate Salley Palmer

Muzzles

In extreme cases where the owner cannot handle a dog without the possibility of being bitten, a muzzle may be used, preferably a wire-basket type. It should be left on continuously except during feeding. Muzzles, however, may aggravate some dogs and make them more violent.

The Halter

In recent years, a new humane halter has been developed that will help control even the most stubborn dog. It controls the neck and mouth of the dog and helps a pet owner learn how to communicate with his dog in a language that dogs understand. The dog will know that his owner is in control.

In extremely aggressive dogs, I would advise caution in using this halter as these head-strong dogs will resist the use of this system. Tranquilization may have to be used in conjunction with this halter.

Restrictive Urination

Restricting a dog's urination to a single area in his own yard tends to lower aggressiveness. Most aggressive dogs apparently need to urinate before commencing a fight. They are marking the territory to show that this is their land.

Shock Collars

Do not use shock collars on overaggressive dogs. Excitable animals will react violently to the electrical stimulation and might become more aggressive. (These collars are different from electric shock therapy).

Chain Restraints

Do not use chain restraints. They might prevent a stranger from being bitten, but they do not correct the overaggressive behavior. Chaining a dog only intensifies the aggression, just as isolation or being penned up for prolonged periods does.

Medical Treatment

In many cases of long-term aggressive behavior, a combination of chemotherapy (tranquilizers, hormones) and behavioral therapy is needed. During chemotherapy, behavioral correction (the prone position or the time-out method) is practiced several times a day. The collar and lead are kept on the dog during these periods to help enforce the corrective procedures.

Tranquilizers

Tranquilizers are generally effective in calming an overaggressive dog. They help the animal overcome the fears that are causing the aggressiveness; for instance, the dog whose day is "ruined" by the approach of the garbage collector. A tranquilizer one hour before the dreaded arrival may go a long way toward easing the dog out of this aggressive reaction to the garbage man. For more serious problems, large doses may be needed at first, with gradual reduction according to the dog's response. As the dosage is reduced; reward, praise, and affection have to be added.

Tranquilizers, however, are not a cure-all. Not all dogs respond to tranquilizer therapy, and some have a violent reaction and become hyperactive and even more vicious. Tranquilizers should always be used under the supervision of a veterinarian.

The Neurotic Dog

Hormones

Many overaggressive dogs have been helped by the use of hormones, either by injection or tablets. These dogs become calmer and more submissive during the treatment, for reasons not yet fully understood. Treatment should also include frequent handling and training. The goal is the owner's ultimate dominance over the dog. Hormones will also make a dog more tolerant of strangers.

As the dog shows more normal behavior, the dosage is reduced. Any sign of regression during the treatment period should be dealt with by discipline and training techniques. Hormones are also helpful in calming a male dog who is overprotective of a female dog living in the same house.

Castration and Spaying

Although castration reduces the aggressive drive in about 50 percent of the male dogs it is used on, it is not the ultimate answer. Obedience training and environmental changes are generally attempted first, but if not successful they may be tried again in combination with castration.

If the cause of aggressiveness is sexual frustration, then castration or spaying is definitely the answer; but I would not advise altering every dog, whether male or female, just because it has any overaggressive nature. The cause could be simply overprotectiveness or jealousy.

If the dog is neutered before the age of six months—that is, before sexual maturity—the chances of keeping him calmer are much greater. Once the aggressive habit is established, neutering may or may not help. Even though it is not a sure cure for aggressiveness, many dogs have been saved from euthanasia by the operation.

Treatment of aggressive dogs has come a long way in recent years. I shall mention some "old tried and true" methods that sound like they came from the Dark Ages— and probably did.

Shock Treatment

Electroconvulsive therapy (shock treatment) has been used on people since 1938. Its primary use has been in the treatment of depression, hyperexcitable conditions, and aggression. It was tried on severely aggressive dogs and helped in some cases. However, the successful use of drugs in calming dogs have nullified the need for shock treatment.

Pulling Teeth

It had been found that trimming or pulling teeth helped tame chronic aggressor. The veterinarian either pulls the four canine teeth, which are the most damaging in a bite wound, or trims the canine teeth below the incisors, giving them a blunt shape instead of the long, tapered cone used for puncturing and tearing. It was anticipated that after the operation is over the dog would realize that he lacks some of the tools needed to be mean and vicious.

Barbiturate Anesthesia

Chronic fighting between two dogs can be prevented by anesthetizing both dogs with barbiturates and allowing them to recover in the same cage. The peaceable effect is seen only if the animals are kept in the same cage during recovery. Also, dogs aggressive toward people can be made docile by petting them during their recovery from anesthesia.

Prefrontal Lobotomy

This is a surgical operation developed for humans but not widely used at the present time because of its side effects. In fact, it was supposed to rehabilitate vicious dogs who otherwise would have to be destroyed. Killer dogs became friendly. It had been especially useful in converting attack guard dogs trained to kill, into peaceful pets. However, it is too radical a treatment for the average pet.

Bloodletting

A severe treatment, and fortunately one not widely used, is bloodletting, or the removal of large amounts of blood from a vicious dog. Several pints of blood are removed from the dog, depending on this size. This leaves the dog in a weakened condition and supposedly drains out all "bad blood" in the dog. This treatment sounds as if it originated in the dark ages. I do not recommend it or any of the several previous treatments mentioned.

The Neurotic Dog

The Incorrigible Dog

Occasionally a dog is incorrigible and can quite easily be classified as a canine criminal. No amount of training or medical treatment will correct his biting. If he's a large dog, such as a German Shepherd or Doberman Pinscher, I would advise military service if possible. Such dogs might also be used for guard duty. I certainly would not advise keeping them as pets, as they are untrustworthy and the potential danger to neighborhood children is too great to take chances. Sometimes an acceptable home can be found for such animals in rural areas; but in drastic cases, they must be put to sleep.

How to Avoid Being Bitten by a Dog

If ever you are cornered by a vicious dog, and you do not know whether he is a fear biter, an indiscriminate biter, or a protective biter, do not try to find out. Instead, stand still. Turn the left side of your body toward the dog and wait.

Do not approach too rapidly. Keep a respectable distance from the dog. Watch his reaction to you. If the dog licks his lips, it is a sign of anxiety. Be careful, but kneel down, talking gently all the time. If the dog's name is known, it always helps to keep repeating his name while talking gently, smiling all the time. The dog will be watching your facial expressions, so be cheerful. Slowly extend you hand, palm up, and wait for the dog to make the next move.

While confronting the dog, always watch his face for the first signs of aggression. Excessive eye blink or movement of the snout or ears might be a signal to you to beware. Either he is actually warning you to stay away, not to make any further moves toward him, or he is trying to bluff you with his hairs on his back standing up, making him look more ferocious and unruly.

If the dog gives such warning signals (even if he is bluffing), back off slowly and leave him alone. If the dog bows his head, pulls his ears back, and licks you hand, the battle is won, and you have probably made a new friend.

Fear Biters

Dogs bite most frequently on their own property, and most of these dogs bite out of fear. But a fear biter is protecting nothing but himself.

The Neurotic Dog

When confronted by a fear biter, your first task is to try to make friends and reassure him that you are not going to hurt him. The best way is to kneel down so that you are on his level. Standing upright, hovering over him, just makes him more frightened of you. Do not advance toward the dog. Carefully hold out the palm of your hand below his head, never above, and let him come toward you and smell you. Do not hold a newspaper, stick, or anything else in yours hands. The fear biter may see such things as possible weapons.

Take lots of time to talk in a quiet, friendly, yet enthusiastic, tone. The dog will be able to tell by your voice that you are not angry and that you mean to be friendly. He doesn't want to bite or have a bad confrontation with you. Remember, he's the one who's afraid. But even if you are afraid, you must give the impression of calm authority and, above all, friendliness.

Never force your attention on a dog who is unwilling to come to you. And never put a hand on the head, neck, or shoulders of an agitated dog, or one you do not know. He might think you are trying to challenge him, and he may turn on you and bite.

Indiscriminate Biters

When you are confronted by a dominant dog, who is almost always an indiscriminate biter, you must be particularly careful. Dominant dogs stare at people, and other animals, but don't like to be stared at. Do not turn your head away when such a dog stares at you. Look him steadfastly in the eye. If you turn your eyes from his, he may see you as submissive and attack.

Protective Biters

One of the most dangerous things a person can do when confronted by a protective biter is to run. That act alone will trigger him into action. He will chase you; and if he catches you, he is almost certain to bite. Children are particularly vulnerable to such biting, for they usually run from barking or snarling dogs. If you stand your ground, the odds are that you won't be bitten.

The secret to not getting bitten by a dog is to allow the dog time to make friends—or to withdraw without losing face. Don't rush. Time is usually on your side. Let the dog come to you. Don't force your attentions on him. Meet him on his level.

Kneel down with your palm exposed for him to smell—if he chooses. And try to avoid dogs you fear.

How to Protect Children

There are dogs who consistently growl at, and on occasion, try to bite children, either a specific child in the family or neighborhood or all children. Most children try to grab a dog in a quick, hitting motion. And they want to hug the dog, which is frightening to some pets, especially to those who previously have been nearly strangled by a child's hug.

Fortunately, this behavior problem can be treated with fairly good results. But it takes conscientious work to teach a dog to have a friendly attitude toward a child and also to teach the child not to grasp and pull on a pet's skin or fur. The dog needs to associate pleasant activity with the child, not manhandling.

The temperament of both dog and child plays an important part in the success or failure of the treatment. A hyperactive or undisciplined dog or child lowers the chances of success.

For the duration of the treatment, the owner should keep the dog and child completely separated except during the training exercises. The dog should be trained to sit and stay, with food rewards given when he accomplishes this. Next, while the dog sits and stays, the child should be shown in slow stages how to approach the dog. If the dog shows any signs of fear, nervousness, or aggressiveness, he should be severely reprimanded verbally. The dog has to be conditioned to allow the child to move close to him. This is done by rewarding him with tidbits of food when he begins to accept the child. The child also has to be taught not to make any quick or loud movements toward the dog. Gradually, as both child and pet get used to one another, a closer relationship between the two can be allowed.

The dog and child should never be left alone during the training period. It might take weeks of daily sessions to accomplish good results. And results cannot always be 100% successful. This method does, however, greatly reduce the possibility that the dog will attack the child.

Another type of problem, which is the owner's dislike of children, sometimes provokes a dog to bite them. The dog will remember the owner yelling at children passing in front of their home, and he will begin to take up the chase, barking at and biting at the children, the least he can do is help in his own way, by barking and biting. To cure this behavior owners themselves have to set an example of good behavior and good manners so that their dogs will take the cue from them, we hope.

How to Break Up a Dog Fight

You should not attempt to separate fighting dogs by putting your hands near their heads. Use a leash, pull on the dog's rear legs or tail, or give a sharp oral command if the dogs have had obedience training. An oral command, however, will only work with a well-trained dog who has enough self-control so that your command to "Stay" will take precedence over his natural inclination to fight.

When dogs are fighting, they will usually bite whatever gets in their way, including people and animals. And a person who hits or shouts at the dogs will stimulate even more hostility in them. The easiest way to break up a fight is to douse the combatants with a pail of water or, better still, aim a hose at their faces.

How to Handle a Vicious Dog in a Veterinary Hospital

In my hospital, some badly behaving dogs are vicious in the presence of their owners but react much differently when their owners leave the examining room. Some overanxious owners unknowingly contribute to their pet's anxiety, and the pet feels he is protecting his owner from this intruder in a white lab coat. Because such an animal is unmanageable while the owner is present, I usually ask the owner to hand me the leash and leave the room. To get the leash, I do not approach the owner but let the owner come forward to me. As soon as the owner leaves the room, I start talking to the dog, very quietly and slowly, calling him by name, crouching down, but not advancing to him. I extend my hand, palm up, so that he sees it is empty. Gradually he will cautiously come to me, sniffing all the way, first smelling my fingers and then if he likes what he smells, more of my hand. I make no quick motions toward him, and I let him do all the advancing while I talk soothingly all the time, using his name frequently. Eventually he will see that I am not trying to hurt him, and he will let me pat him under his jaws and under his neck.

The Neurotic Dog

If his owner were present, I would not be able to handle him this diplomatically and peacefully. It could be that the dog does not want to lose face. With the owner present, he feels that he must keep up the ruse of the protector; but in a one-to-one confrontation with me, he is willing to be persuaded that I am not the foe. Veterinarians generally agree that most vicious dogs can be handled in a manner similar to mine. When this fails, however, the use of tranquilizers slows down the most vicious of dogs and saves a lot of bitten fingers and hands.

A rather strange case of overaggression concerns a German Shepherd Dog named Adolph. For years he came into my office with both his owners, husband and wife. He charged at me, showed me his teeth, and was very difficult to handle and treat. However, one day only the wife brought the dog to the hospital. He was docile and manageable, and seemed like a different dog. On Adolph's next visit to the hospital, I told his owners to let only the husband bring him in, to see if it made any difference in his behavior. Again the dog was docile, which meant he was only overprotective, and violent, when both owners were present.

The Nuisance Dog

BAD HABITS

What might seem a nuisance dog to one person might be classified as a mischievous or high-spirited one by another. And certainly a namby-pamby or broken-spirited dog is not what most dog owners prefer. Just as there is no "perfect" person, there can't possibly be a perfect dog, except in the eyes of a doting owner. But even that dog might be a nuisance to friends and neighbors.

Many of our urban dogs have been deprived of the normal use of their natural instincts. The herding breeds deem themselves lucky if they can find people, bicycles, or cars to chase. Many terriers have a hard time finding badgers or rats to catch. There are very few hares for Greyhounds to chase. Bull Terriers are expected to behave amiably in the company of other dogs instead of trying to kill them. Spaniels lie around in air-conditioned rooms instead of flushing birds. Countless pets are bored and frustrated into nuisance behavior while their absentee owners are out earning the bacon.

While most dogs are not neurotic or psychotic, many are a real aggravation because of their bad habits. Somewhere along the way, the owner must take control, or the bad habits can develop into full-blown neuroticisms. What was tolerated in the puppy may not be so acceptable in the adult dog. Or maybe what used to be an occasional slip-up is now an everyday occurrence, something to be stopped once and for all.

Once the bad habit is recognized as a problem, the method of getting rid of it follows the procedure: discover the cause, establish leadership, train with consistency, and give lots of attention and affection.

The causes for bad habits are many, and as with other behavioral problems, they deserve careful investigation. The cause should not be taken for granted. Ask the questions: When did it start? When does it happen? Where does it usually happen? Has the dog had obedience training, and does he obey? And so on. Once the cause is ascertained, treatment and corrective training can begin.

The Sweet Brat

There is one special type of dog that defies the usual methods of investigation. He has no problems, as far as he is concerned. He's not worried, anxious, spiteful, jealous, mean, or ornery. He's in good physical shape, eats fine, sleeps well, and loves everybody (with maybe a few idiosyncratic exceptions). His one problem (which he doesn't recognize) is that he has never been taught how to behave. He is not neurotic, but he is a brat.

In the house, the brat is everywhere and in everyone's way. He takes over the best chairs, carries his food from room to room, and sleeps where he pleases—often in doorways and on steps where the flow of traffic is thickest. Worst of all, he shows no sense of manners around guests. He jumps all over them, hangs on their legs, sits in their laps, licks their faces, begs for their food, and if he's in the mood and they smell just right, he may even sexually attack them.

Outside the house, he is just as unruly as he is inside. He'll take off with the paper boy and ignore you when you call. But if you open the car door, he'll be right there to prance around the driver's seat leaving dirty prints before you know what's happening. Public Enemy No. 1 leaps on joggers, chases cars, and "marks" the neighbor's yard as his own, greeting the neighbors' guests with unparalleled exuberance and an etiquette even Attila the Hun would consider uncivilized. He digs in their yards, naps in their flower beds, rummages through their trash, and rushes any open door. Most neighbors will succumb to a habitual caution and a quickness of step when entering and leaving their homes. And they will resignedly replace their boxwoods that had died from the daily doses of urine.

But an occasional neighbor, not so gently inclined, will take you to court. If you are hoping for the Mother-of-the-Year Award or if you plan to run for County Commissioner, don't. Your dog's reputation will precede you.

It is very difficult to punish these sweet brats, but the timing usually comes when a giant step must be taken to keep from losing good friends (like a wife or husband). Or maybe you acquired the dog by default (i.e., the owner moved away but the dog didn't), and you want to shape him up now that he is yours. Fortunately, these dogs are fairly easy to train. They are already eager to be accepted as one of the group, and a firm approach with consistent discipline, will make such a dog respect you and want to follow your leadership.

The Unruly Dog

An unruly dog differs from the sweet brat in that the unruly dog does not obey any commands and is completely out of control.

They bark incessantly and chase children and animals whenever they can. Unruly dogs are constantly pestering people, slobbering on their hands and clothing.

Unruly dogs are problems for the household and the entire neighborhood because they have never been disciplined. They are not mean or vicious, but are very active dogs who walk poorly on a leash and steal all kinds of objects from the house and garden.

Many owners unknowingly contribute to unruliness because they are not consistent with their discipline.

The Nuisance Dog

House Soiling

Whenever a completely housebroken dog starts urinating or defecating in the house, there is a medical, physiological, or psychological cause. First, look for a medical reason such as a kidney problem, diabetes, prostatitis, cystitis, worms, colitis, pancreatitis, or toxins. A complete examination by a veterinarian is in order.

The aging process usually leads to a relaxation in toilet training. The owner has to realize that the dog needs to go out more frequently. Scolding and shaming only make matters worse.

Sometimes a dog soils in the house because he is eating too much. A shepherd puppy, Abe, was still soiling the house at five months of age; his owners, friends of mine, were considering getting rid of him. The situation was getting progressively worse, so I visited them to see if we couldn't work something out. Abe's problem was all too apparent. And I'm surprised the six resident cats hadn't gotten around to a little misbehaving because they were getting meager fare. Abe was not only eating his own food each day, but since he was able to get to the cat bowls, I assume he got most of their food as well. His intestines were constantly full of food. Treatment was simple: Regular meals at the same time each day—and keep the cat food out of his reach.

Abrupt changes in feeding habits, exercise times, or type of dog food can also cause house soiling. A dog's digestive regularity is normally very dependable, and when it is changed there is trouble.

When a new schedule is necessary (perhaps the owner changes his job or shift), the dog has to be consistently adjusted to the new times. If the problem is a new type of food, then another type or brand will have to be found. Many elimination problems can be solved by measured feedings and rigid scheduling of feeding and exercise periods.

When a dog soils the house out of desperation, because he had the ill luck to be adopted by a family insensitive to time and nature, he has my heartfelt sympathy. Little can be done to help such a dog, outside of changing owners.

Sometimes a dog tries to communicate his need to go outside but it falls on deaf ears and unseeing eyes: The owner doesn't get the message. You must learn to interpret a dog's signs, such as a prolonged, direct stare, or a pacing gait around the door, or even a longing look toward the door. Not all dogs bark and lead their owners to the door.

The male dog who lives most of his life inside a house often needs to exert the territorial instinct of marking. Urination in a particular area (near drapes or a door) is territorial protection from passing dogs and people. Rarely will a dog defecate to mark his territory, although it occasionally happens. One Poodle I know, Cricket, became unhousebroken because her owner accidentally brought in foreign feces on his shoes. The odor of this strange dog's feces on the carpet caused Cricket to defecate in that area, asserting her territorial claims.

A neighborhood dog in heat can also cause a confined male to lift his leg around the house, and he will continue to do so long after the female is out of heat as long as the scent of his urine remains. In dealing with this problem, (and all other urination problems in the house), you should first remove the odor from carpets, drapes, and so on by using club soda or white vinegar.

If removing the odor of previous house soilings does not work, and the dog remains a habitual territory marker, castration and hormone therapy may be needed. Castration will reduce marking in 50 to 60 percent of male dogs. In uncastrated dogs, the use of hormones will reduce marking. It will also further reduce marking in castrated dogs. This combined approach of hormones and castration has been very successful in treating the problem of male wetters.

Another type of dog will wet all over the house to show that he is the boss. This behavior often also occurs in insecure pets who have overpermissive and overcoddling owners. Such dogs need leadership. And it occurs in pets who are insecure because they don't get enough attention. They must be given a proper balance of love and discipline.

Pumpkin, a Corgi, suddenly became unhousebroken on certain days. Searching for the answer, her owner and I finally realized the problem had to do with eggs. On days when the owner served eggs for breakfast, Pumpkin got her share and was in a pleasant mood the rest of the day. But on days when cereal was served, Pumpkin would emphasize her displeasure by defecating somewhere in the house. The moral of this story is not that you must do everything possible to keep you dog from getting mad at you. In fact, in Pumpkin's case, the reason for house soiling was spite for what she considered lack of attention.

Curing Pumpkin of this misdeed consisted of giving her cereal accompanied by praise and a tidbit. Eventually her attitude towards cereal changed, probably because she was getting special attention with a yummy tidbit.

Urination or defecation on clothes or personal objects (like your sofa or bed) usually indicates that the dog and the owner have difficulty relating to one another. Some dogs house soil out of jealousy, usually brought about by the arrival of a new baby, husband, wife, or friend, pet, or something else that causes attention sharing. Verbal harassment only aggravates the problem because the dog wants most to be reassured of the owner's affection. The cure is to show the dog more attention by playing games and spending more time with him. The cure for Pumpkin, was more attention. On days when cereal was served, the owner gave Pumpkin her little bowl of cereal, explained to her that everyone was having cereal, and patted her on the head. Pumpkin probably did not understand the explanation, but she did understand the attention and affection, which was enough. She quit soiling the house.

Some dogs will urinate to show submission. This is often done in front of a person, and usually when the owner is returning to or entering a room. Puppies will urinate after being punished to show submission, but most will outgrow this type of urination. Some owners, however, find themselves in a no-win situation. They punish their dogs for wetting and other bad habits, then the dogs become overly submissive and do the very thing (wetting) that caused the rebuke in the first place. Overly submissive pets have to be treated with patience. They must be helped to regain their confidence, learning not to fear their owners but to win their approval by obeying them. This means a consistent training program of play, reward, and gentleness.

If a dog is both urinating and defecating in the house, the cause is probably inadequate housebreaking or separation anxiety (fear of being alone or separated from the owner). Dogs that suffer from separation anxiety will act upset at the first sign that they are going to be left alone. The rattling of car keys, the pocketbook on the arm, the overcoat being donned, and all the other signs of departure signal to such dogs that they are going to be left alone. These dogs will pace, whine, even shake at such times. Some will act eager to go along, only to realize that they have been left behind after the door closes. Dogs with separation anxiety will mess in the house soon after the owner departs. In treating them, punishment should be avoided. These dogs should be desensitized gradually. Sometimes a radio or television set left on will allay their fear of being alone. Also, tranquilizers are helpful in calming dogs who suffer from anxiety.

Inadequate housebreaking is sometimes discovered after dogs reach maturity. Perhaps they were housebroken during the summertime when they spent most of the day outside. Then when winter forced them to be inside most of the day, they forgot their training.

There is also the occasional wetting or defecating mistake that goes unnoticed. This makes some dogs feel that house soiling is now okay, and it develops into a habit. Once this habit has developed, you must completely retrain the dog. It is similar to training the puppy but easier because the mature dog is more aware of praise and punishment and has more bladder and anal control.

If a dog is very stubborn and determined not to be retrained, you must resort to stricter and more persistent training, combined with close supervision of all the dog's habits. When you see the dog sniffing an area in the house, the dog should be taken out immediately. He is probably getting ready to lift his leg (or squat if it is a she). The dog should not be sent out alone: You should go with him so that the dog can be praised immediately when he soils outdoors. The praise (or the punishment) has to be given at the exact moment the dog performs. Ten or fifteen minutes later will not mean anything to the dog.

Urination should be restricted to a single area of the yard. This also helps decrease the incidence of household urination.

It is important to remember that all meaningful training procedures, whether praise or punishment, should come from you, the owner, the dog's leader, the one he loves and trusts. While working on the problem, you should be consoled by the fact that it takes the average dog only four days or four training sessions to learn proper habits.

The Nuisance Dog

Chewing and Other Destructive Behavior in the House

Puppies have a natural need to chew and to explore. When teething, puppies will chew on almost anything because their gums are sensitive. Whether teething or not, all puppies explore their environment by smelling, tasting, and chewing. Their curiosity sometimes seems to leave nothing unchewed, including the leg of your dining-room table. The commercial chew toys and chew sticks are ideal for puppies during this period of their development, but most dogs aren't interested in what you want them to use for chewing; they'd rather decide for themselves what to explore and tear up.

Like children, they must be taught what they may appropriately play with and chew. You should choose a toy made of rawhide, plastic, or rubber—not leather, wood, or any fabric used for household furniture and clothing. Insist that the puppy chew only his toy. It is a mistake to play tug-of-war games with a toy to get a dog interested in it. This only teaches the dog to be aggressive and encourages his interest in tearing and ripping. Instead, play fetch games, using a ball or a chew toy. Do not give a puppy an old shoe or an old sock. A shoe is a shoe to him, and your new shoes will likely be the next candidates for satisfying his chewing needs. Whenever the puppy gets something that you don't want him to destroy, take it from him, saying "No," and replace it with his own chew toy.

Prevention is always better than cure. When you have to leave your puppy alone for a period of time, put him into his crate and give him something he can amuse himself with while you are absent. If you have brought him up to consider the crate as his permanent and personal home, he'll remain there happily until you return, and your curtains will be safe.

Prevention is also crucial to the puppy's safety, for during the teething and the exploratory period, he may chew on an electric cord. A wise precaution is to unplug all accessible cords whenever the puppy has to be left unsupervised, or rub some distasteful substance on the cords, like bitter apple, ipecac, Tabasco sauce, or a chemical spray sold at pet stores for this purpose. Also, during the teething period (eight to twenty weeks after birth), give the puppy a frozen washcloth to chew on. This will help to soothe his gums.

Although puppies have natural reasons for chewing, adult dogs who continue to chew things in the house are usually suffering from boredom, loneliness, or jealousy. Chewing, relieves tension, as it does for people who chew their nails, gum, or tobacco. It can be just as habit forming for a dog. Also, for the owner, it can get terribly expensive and aggravating.

Susie, a Dachshund, would chew up personal items belonging to Vera, the maid, that were left unattended. Vera, not fond of dogs anyway, would scream and fuss at Susie, which would only further irritate the little dog. One day Susie underwent an exceptional amount of verbal harassment from the maid. Since Vera had learned to put her own things out of Susie's reach, Susie's only recourse was to chew up the rug Vera had just worked hard to vacuum. The carpet was a rare Oriental, a collector's item. The owner fired Vera and put Susie up for immediate adoption.

Susie's story is not as exceptional as it might be thought. Many dogs are put up for adoption or abandoned for a bad deed that happens once too often. But things don't need to go so far.

First, you should investigate the cause. Find out why the dog is being destructive. If you take the time to find the answer, the cure should soon follow. Sometimes the destruction stops while you are seeking the answer. Just that little bit of extra attention was what the dog wanted.

Is something physically wrong with the dog? All dogs will chew when they are hungry. Perhaps the diet is inadequate, either too small in quantity or lacking in some nutritional requirement. Or the cause may be lack of exercise, leaving unused energy that has to be spent somehow. Frequently, it will be through chewing, tearing up paper, or littering and plundering.

Does the dog have an emotional problem? Some neurotic dogs will chew and do other household mischief because of their frustration. Claustrophobic dogs will chew to get out of a confined area. Some chew through doors and walls to escape. These dogs may need tranquilizers as well as open spaces.

Is there something outside the house that causes the problem? Dogs may chew to get out for courting. A female in heat may want to get out, or a male may be trying to get to a female. If this develops into a serious habitual problem, hormone shots and castration may be needed. A dog may simply see other dogs and children playing outside, and he just wants to get out to join the fun. Being confined under these conditions is frustrating even for humans.

Is the dog jealous or angry? Jealousy and anger can provoke a wide assortment of misdeeds. These misdeeds are the dog's way of reprimanding the guilty person. Eliminate the cause, and the destruction will stop. Usually you can tell if the reason is anger or jealousy because the dog will destroy only the things belonging to one person.

Geoffrey, an Irish Setter, would get mad at his mistress whenever she had to work late. On these occasions, he would chew up the cushion in her favorite chair. Another dog, Professor, got jealous at the start of the school year because the children had to do homework instead of playing with him. After bedtime, he would chew up their school books and their homework. In both cases, extra attention brought about cures. Geoffrey's mistress started bringing home a treat and playing longer with him whenever she was late. The children started playing with Professor before doing their homework. Both dogs responded and quit being destructive.

Is the dog bored? Boredom and loneliness are the most frequent causes of destructive behavior. The destruction occurs when the owner is absent and the dog is left alone or with a person who offers no companionship. The dog will assault wastepaper baskets, chewing and strewing paper all over the house; he will spread his owner's personal belongings all around, carrying things like shoes, ties, and stockings from room to room; he will dig up house plants, chew the ferns, and, in extreme cases, seem intent on destroying the house. One Saint Bernard actually chewed the leg off a grand piano, getting a concussion when the piano fell on him. Sometimes the simplest cure is to get the dog a pet, like a kitten, a turtle or a puppy. But if the dog tends to be jealous, this sort of cure may backfire, leaving you with a dog more disturbed than before and an additional pet to look after.

An extremely good method is to leave the television set or radio on while you are away from home. This, as discussed earlier, has proved to be effective therapy for many lonesome and bored dogs. A local family discovered recently that their own two dogs, three neighborhood dogs, and two cats were congregating daily in front of the TV in the den to watch the

Mister Rogers show. The horse on the show fascinated them. Some dogs who don't seem to be able to see the pictures on the television screen respond nevertheless to the voices and sounds. For these dogs, a radio will work just as well as a TV set.

Another way to deal quickly with destructive behavior is to catch the dog in the act. At the usual time in the morning, you should go through the normal routine of departure—putting on a coat, picking up car keys, turning off lights, saying good-bye to the dog, and leaving. At first, stay away for five minutes and then return. If the house is in good order, play with the dog, praise him, fondle him, and give him a favorite treat. But if the house is damaged in any way, reprimand and scold the dog, letting him know in no uncertain terms that you are displeased.

When damage is done, shorten the period of time way from the house. As the dog improves, gradually increase the time. Most important, you should always reward the dog for his good behavior and always reprimand him for his bad behavior.

It will take patience and time before you can safely leave the dog for long periods. Some dogs learn more slowly than others do, depending on how stubborn they are and how persistent the owner is with the training program. It is a battle of wits, where occasionally the owner wins. You must be as stubborn as your pet is. Your perseverance will make your dog respect you more.

If you find no reason for the dog's destructiveness or if the conventional methods of cure do not work, don't give up. Several scare tactics work well in just such desperate times.

The best result to combat inappropriate chewing is obtained by diverting the dog's attention to articles that you would prefer him to chew. There are treated bones at pet stores which contain spaces in it that can be stuffed with all kinds of goodies—liver, beef, peanut butter or anything else that your dog enjoys. Stuff it in all the holes that you can find so that it will take him hours trying to get the food out. The longer he spends on these bones, the less time he has to chew on your furniture. Rubber bones are also available which have tiny holds that can be stuffed with food. Check out your pet store for other helpful gadgets.

For desperate owners with very stubborn dogs, severe methods have to be resorted to. One way is to set mousetraps wherever the dog is apt to chew—around chairs, hanging from drapes, inside wastepaper baskets, around house plants, and so on. Strategically placed, these traps will discourage most foraging attempts. (Mousetraps are too small to hurt dogs except the toy breeds, and toys are usually too small to cause much trouble).

Mousetraps work particularly well in keeping dogs from disturbing clothes and shoes. The mousetraps should be placed in closets or dirty clothes baskets, wherever the dog is finding items to chew. Placed in trash cans, they also discourage canine curiosity for the exotic odors emanating from those places. When the unbaited trap snaps, the dog is startled at the noise. When the dog has set off the trap a couple of times, he won't go near those places again, even when the traps are not set. After a week or so, you can be sure the dog will never disturb these areas again. For small dogs, place the mousetrap upside down so it won't hurt the pet. You can also place a newspaper over the mousetrap so it is safe for even the smallest dogs.

Another scare tactic is to spray an aerosol deodorant (the underarm-protection type) at the dog's nose whenever he starts chewing something. When he tries to sniff the can, release the spray in his face, but stop when he backs away. After he has left, spray the area that has been chewed. Continue this process every day until the misconduct stops. It doesn't work all the time, but users claim at least a 70 percent success rate.

A water pistol squirt will also work, for dogs hate to have water squirted in their faces. The drawback, however, is that you must be there to ambush the dog at the moment of mischief, and you must have a steady aim to get him in the face.

As many people have discovered, tying a piece of the chewed-up item (carpet, stuffing from chair, electric wire, whatever), in a dog's mouth for periods of time does not usually cure a dog of destructive behavior.

Furniture Sitting

Many owners will allow dogs to sit on sofas and chairs and sleep in any bed in the house. Only when the furniture starts getting soiled, the beds become a second home for fleas, and Aunt Phoebe comes to visit does the owner decide to put a stop to furniture sitting.

You should scold a dog when he jumps onto furniture. Let him know that you are mad with him. Loud noises scare him so I recommend hitting your own hand with a rolled-up newspaper. The noise will scare him and impress him that you mean business. Do not hit him directly—a loud noise will work as well. Calling him a "bad dog" will also hurt his feelings and emphasize your anger with him. The disciplinary object should be left on the furniture to add emphasis and to remind the dog to stay off. Also, when left at the scene of the crime, the newspaper or strap will be more accessible the next time the dog tries to get on the furniture. And he will try again, and again. He must be consistently scolded until he learns.

For more stubborn dogs, mousetraps will probably work. Place the mousetraps on the seats of chairs, sofas, beds, wherever the dog wants to lounge. The family may complain a bit, but the dog, after an encounter or two, will stay away from places where he has been mousetrapped. For small dogs, turn the mousetrap upside down so it won't get hurt.

A similar but more festive way to alarm the pet into a semblance of good behavior is to pin cheap balloons to the cushions of sofas and chairs. When the dog hops onto Aunt Phoebe's needlepoint chair, the loud bang of the balloon popping will startle him, thereafter he'll walk clear on the other side of the room to avoid the chair.

With the advent of ultrasonic devices, there are many products that can be used to keep animals off of furniture or other restricted areas. There are shock mats, which have a very low voltage, that will startle the misbehaving pet when he jumps on an off-limit sofa. Infrared gadgets have also been perfected to detect an unwanted guest on the sofa and set off an alarm that scares him.

Begging

To many owners, begging is not a bad habit, and they routinely slip their pets tidbits whenever they dine. To others, it is only a bad habit when company is around. For those who sincerely wish to break the habit, consistent obedience training must be carried out.

The best time to begin is with a new puppy, but the procedure is the same for the adult dog. It will just take longer for him to learn that begging will not be tolerated. When he begs, he should be told "No," and put in his crate. He should be fed before the family sits down to eat and not again until all the kitchen work has been done.

Scavenging

Few dogs are free of the urge to get into garbage containers and wastebaskets, and many dogs get a thrill out of collecting newspapers, milk cartons, shoes, and other objects from around the neighborhood. Some dogs are not fed enough at home and have to go scavenging for food. Others are enticed by the food odors and by the pleasure of tearing up papers and boxes. And some do it just to cause a commotion and get attention. Others, such as retrievers, are merely following their breed instincts when they loot around the neighborhood.

Mousetraps can be set, unbaited, just as was done for the wastepaper baskets inside the house. Another method is to sprinkle the garbage with such things as Tabasco sauce, hot Chinese mustard, and bitter apple. A few tastes of the concoctions may change the dog's mind about raiding the garbage.

A few empty tin cans, tied together and thrown at the dog when he goes near a garbage container, can prove a deterrent. Another precaution taken to prevent scavenging is to make the odor of the garbage container less tantalizing to the dog. This means emptying the container and keeping it washed with a disinfectant so that the garbage odor will not tempt the dog. Odor-neutralizing sprays are helpful both inside and outside the container.

There are probably no completely dog-proof garbage containers, but it helps to use the most difficult-to-get-into types. Some with screw-type lids are hard for a dog to open. Another kind has lids that must be depressed in the center while simultaneously lifting at the rim. Dogs have to go to a lot of trouble to get into these containers. I have brought containers like these as peace offerings for my neighbors, because my dog, Bridget McGuire, is a devoted patron of the art of garbage inspecting.

Some bad habits are difficult to correct. Sometimes an alternative solution has to be found.

The Nuisance Dog

Bridget loved milk and so early every morning she went on her rounds of raiding the neighborhood's milk cartons. She chewed off the tops and then drank the milk. The only solution to the problem was to have the milk delivered in bottles instead of cartons since Bridget could not be broken of this habit.

As for determined looters, the cooperation of your neighbors, if you are still friends, is essential in ridding dogs of this bad habit. The temptation has to be removed by situating the garbage so that the dogs cannot get to it, for example, by putting containers into dog-proof garbage racks. These are fairly easy to build, and can also be brought at most building supply stores.

If your neighbors are not committed to dog-proofing their garbage containers and if you would feel uncomfortable planting mousetraps in their trash and lurking around at night to throw tin cans in their yards, there is one last resort...obedience training. While holding a leash attached to a chain collar around your dog's neck, stand a few feet away from a garbage container full of ripe, odoriferous garbage. Any move toward the garbage should be met with a corrective jerk of the leash and a firm "No." You are trying to teach the dog that going near the garbage is a bad thing to do. Repetition for several days may teach your dog to stay away.

One ingenious owner devised his own plan. It works well if you have the time, the patience, the fortitude, and the agility to follow the rules. He gets inside a large garbage can and hides waiting for his dog to approach whereupon he springs up screaming to scare the dog. However, I would not advise this method for the average person.

Fear of Leashes

Some dogs, especially puppies, refuse to walk on a leash. Something in their earlier life may have caused them to fear a leash. In some cases, they may have been punished for some misbehavior with a leash. In others, they seem to develop the fear when the same leash used for training is also used for walking. To reassure a pet, it is best to use two separate leashes. In most instances, however, it is impossible to discover the exact cause for this fear. But there are corrective measures. The fear can be overcome by building a dog's confidence in a leash.

144

At first, a very short light leash should be attached to the collar and left dangling for several days. The hope is that the dog will get used to the presence of the leash and will eventually see that no harm will come from it. Once he is accustomed to it, his training sessions should begin. You should have these sessions before he eats, walking him around the yard while you hold the leash. End the session by walking him to his food dish. This way he will associate the walk with a food reward.

Then, using a longer but still lightweight leash, get away from him, crouch down, and call him. At the same time pull gently on the leash. If he doesn't come, pull harder on the leash. If necessary, jerk him to you—but remember, no yelling or screaming. And no physical punishment. Handle him gently but firmly.

Once the dog is used to a small leash, he should easily take to the weight of leash necessary for his size and needs.

Leash Pulling

Many large dogs take their owners for walks, literally sweeping them off their feet. Measures must be taken not only to train the dogs in obedience, but also to protect the owners. Most of these leash-pulling dogs are dominant animals who insist on being the leader. Thus, correction first requires role reversal. If you have such a dog, you must take command.

The next step is daily walks with the dog on a choke-chain collar with a strong leash. When the dog tries to get ahead, you must make a right turn, changing direction, and continue to do this until the dog realizes his place is beside you. When the dog finally conforms, he should be praised.

The dog must learn to heel at the left side, beside you. A good obedience training course will help both you and your dog, and a good trainer can show you how to handle an obstinate dog. There is a real art to handling strong-willed animals: stances, movements, voice control, and an attitude of confidence appreciated more readily (and taught more easily) when seen rather than read.

Barking

All normal dogs bark. It is how they communicate. When they see a friend passing the house, they bark, "Hello! Here I am! Come on up to the door! Wait for me! Don't leave; I'll see if I can come out to play with you." Hurrying to someone in the house, they bark, "My friend is here. I want to go out. Let me out!" Then, back to the window they run, barking "Wait! I'm coming out!" and so on.

When a stranger passes, they bark, "Don't come in my yard! We don't know you! This is my territory! I'm warning you stay away!"

But if the stranger actually approaches the house, they bark. "You're trespassing! How terrible! Get away from here! Oh, how presumptuous of you! Back up! Don't you hear me? Leave!"

And there is the barking that says the dog wants to go out to urinate, or to check on the safety of his buried bones, or to see if the family of squirrels has let its guard down and can now be caught.

So barking is normal and should not be eliminated completely. Like humans who are never allowed to speak, dogs prohibited from all barking become paranoid and withdrawn from the world. Or they become angry and belligerent. Because every dog needs to communicate and because every dog has the instinct to protect, the purpose of this section is to tell you not how to prevent your dog from barking but how to curb excessive barking under verbal control.

Excessive barking is a serious problem, especially in densely populated areas and in homes where nobody is present during the day and the dogs are left alone, locked up in the house or confined to a small pen or yard. Some cities have passed stiff antibarking ordinances designed to punish owners who cannot keep their dogs quiet. But ordinances or no ordinances, most people dislike the disturbing sounds of dogs barking, especially when it goes on all through the night. And owners begin to see the seriousness of their situations when delivery boys, postmen, garbage collectors, and even friendly visitors are put off by their barking dogs. Furthermore, some barkers tend to get more and more aggressive, turning eventually into biters.

If not properly trained, dogs do tend to get carried away with their barking. Many just love to bark; they're enchanted with the sound of their own voices. Others are highly excitable dogs who bark with little provocation. And certain breeds just normally bark more than others do. Beagles and terriers are notoriously bad about barking. Also, dogs are great imitators. If one dog barks, others are apt to join in. This happens frequently in kennels.

Owners can contribute to excessive barking themselves. Some feel more protected with a vociferous barker and encourage the barking. Others try to distract their dogs from barking by feeding them tidbits, not realizing that dogs interpret this as a reward for an outstanding barking performance. To keep their dogs quiet, some owners will let them into the house, which actually teaches the dogs to bark for entrance. Still others think barking is cute in a puppy but a nuisance in an adult dog, thereby bypassing the age when training is easiest and the result more permanent.

Most nuisance barkers, however, bark to relieve the tension of some problem. As with other misconduct, the owner must find the cause. Is the dog anxious about being isolated for punishment? Is he fenced in or tied up, with no social outlets? Is he bored? Lonely? Is he overly protective? Domineering? Is he having some personality clash with the cat down the street or a child who teases him? Look for the source of frustration. Resolve the cause, and the excessive barking often will stop.

The Nuisance Dog ─────────────────

Basic Voice-Control Training

The time to teach barking etiquette is when the dog is a puppy, when he is trying out his vocal cords for the fun of it. This is between the ages of four and six months. Although he is trying to communicate with you and eventually will use his barking to warn you of strangers approaching the house, you have to teach him that a little yap will suffice. Prolonged barking, howling, or whining must be discouraged. In training a puppy not to bark, use the words "Quiet," "Hush," "Enough," or some other simple term, said in a stern voice while you hold his jaws closed. This is often enough to get the point across. Dogs understand simple words much easier than they do multi-syllable words. Whichever word you prefer, always use the same one, and demonstrate its meaning by firmly closing the puppy's jaws. Do not yell, however, and do not use the word "No," for this may confuse the puppy and make him believe that all barking is bad. Remember, you want to control, not eliminate, the barking.

If the puppy doesn't obey your command and tries to break loose and bark, be more forceful with him. While holding his jaws shut, snap your fingers sharply across his tender nose. This will help him learn what "Quiet" means. Repeat the process every time he starts his nonsensical barking until he understands and obeys. When he does respond to your command, remove your hand from his jaws and compliment him; then give him an approving pat. Such reinforcement on your part will quickly teach him that he's done the right thing.

But if he is stubborn or still doesn't understand, then you must resort to more severe methods, such as the sound of a rolled-up newspaper or a toy water pistol, to make your point.

For the untrained adult dog, perform the same training techniques outlined above. If his barking has become a habit, a part of his personality, it will take more patience and a longer training period. Keeping him quiet may even take one of the more drastic measures described further along in this chapter. Some dogs learn quickly; others are slower or just stubborn. The severity of the technique depends on how strong-willed the dog is. Any training technique, however, must be rehearsed daily by all members of the family. When a member of the

The Nuisance Dog

family praises the dog for barking at a noise outside, he will consider this an endorsement of his barking, and it will undermine attempts to retrain him.

Bribery works as well in dogs as it does in people. Human and canine natures are similar in this respect. Bribery can help stop a dog from excessive barking as well as other misdeeds.

A dog cannot bark and smell food at the same time, so if he is barking, hold some good food in front of his nose. He'll stop barking to smell it. That's when you say, "Quiet" or "Stop." He'll soon associate the words with a food treat if he stops barking. Repeat until he learns, but always praise him as you give him the treat. He'll learn that the word "Quiet" or "Stop" means a food treat is on the way.

Loneliness and Boredom

Although leadership and training are crucial for clearing up any misunderstanding on the dog's part about what is expected of him, the primary cause of excessive, nuisance barking is loneliness and boredom. Dogs with this habit have learned that if they bark hard enough and long enough they will eventually get attention, even if it is a spanking.

If these dogs are alone in the house, try leaving on the television or radio, or even a tape recording of your voice. These sounds will mask or hide most outside noises, and they will make the dog feel less alone. Also, leave them toys, chew sticks, and a bowl of food (if the pet is still a puppy) and one of water. One dog got quite fond of a rubber doll. The extent of his fondness for it was not realized until the doll was lost. The poor dog was inconsolable, barking at all hours, until the doll was found. (This in itself sounds a little neurotic; but it made the dog happy, and he was normal in every other way).

Also, try the technique used for chewing, where you leave the house in your normal fashion and sneak back within five or ten minutes to catch the dog in his misconduct. Do not let the dog see you, but set off an alarm that sends a loud noise inside the house to scare the dog. These punishment sessions will probably teach the pet what is expected of him. Another method is to have a neighbor toss pebbles at the outside of the house, provoking the barking, while you stay with the dog to reprimand him immediately when he gets carried away with it. Smart dogs will catch on very quickly; but to reinforce the learning experience, it must be repeated several times a day for three or four days.

If the dog is outside in a pen, start giving him more time out of the pen and more of your personal attention. If this, combined with training, doesn't work, try the tin-can method.

Fill some tin cans with pebbles. Throw the cans near the barking dog, not to hit him but to startle him. He will stop barking for the moment; but when he starts up the noise again, throw some more cans. Each time, verbally admonish him. He will soon catch on, and the verbal command alone will be sufficient. (This works well with puppies too, inside or outside the house. Just use smaller cans.)

If the dog is barking to get into the house, perhaps you could install a doggie door. This pacifies many dogs. Whether you are at home or absent, most dogs feel more secure knowing they can get in the house whenever they want.

For the dog who must stay in the fenced area, another dog may provide the companionship he needs. Sometimes, however, the new dog will imitate the other barking dog, and you have two barking dogs on your hands. For this situation, use either the tin cans or a water spray from the hose directed at them. The garden hose has quieted even the most surly offenders. After a few days of being doused with water, they should stop their nuisance barking.

Night Barkers

The worst offender is the night barker. This dog usually has slept all day and is coming alive when the owner is ready for bed. Sometimes a hard run before retiring will get him too exhausted to bark. As for the night barker who is lonely and craves attention, spend as much time as possible with him before bedtime.

Again, train such a dog to respond to your voice, following the basic voice-control method for puppies. Along with this training you may need to use the tactics that startle or distract the dog. If you have neighbors nearby, don't use tin cans. Instead, distract him with a water pistol, hose, or balloons filled with water. The explosive sound of the balloon when it hits the dog, accompanied by the water, is startling enough to deter the barking. Here also, a verbal command must be given.

Another barking deterrent is the hand-held, gas-powered air horn (120+ decibels). Each bark should be followed by a verbal command and then a blast from the air horn. The barking will subside in frequency and intensity, and in about three weeks it should be controllable by verbal commands only. However, I would advise you to clear this method with your neighbors.

Ultrasonic devices are also used to distract dogs that are about to bark. The cure involves conditioning the dog to quietness rather than barking. A rape alarm is a gadget that works well in startling a dog that is barking excessively. The rape alarm is the same device that women use for protection. It can be purchased at any electronic store.

If all else fails, temporary relief can come by using a muzzle on the barker. Pet stores sell comfortable muzzles that prevent barking. Although this is not generally effective as a cure, it is an answer when it is imperative that the dog be kept quiet. And the occasional dog will associate the muzzle with punishment for barking and be cured.

Territorial and Aggression Barking

This is a difficult behavior to correct because the dog is demonstrating his dominance. This kind of barking serves as your protection from intruders, but it can get out of hand. Besides becoming a nuisance to neighbors, it may lead to more aggressive behavior and biting.

Frequently I find that dogs with this habit were praised for barking when they were puppies. As they matured, they became more vocal about their role as defender, believing themselves to be duty-bound to broadcast to everyone and everything within visual and auditory range. Also, these dogs are generally strong-willed. They want to be the leader. With these dogs, owner leadership must be clearly established. Follow the basic voice-control method used for puppies. As you verbally correct such a dog, hold the jaws closed. Further assert your dominance by making the dog lie in a prone position for several minutes. Always, with softly spoken reassurances (no yelling), maintain firm control over the dog.

The Nuisance Dog

Ways to Treat Barking

Hormones and Castration

Aggressive male barkers who will not respond to training alone are frequently helped by hormones. Experiments have proven that when a hormone, Ovaban, is given to adult male dogs, it eventually reduces or even suppresses excessive barking. This hormone has a calming effect on the dogs, making them more conducive to being handled and more obedient.

If the male is not to be bred, castration is also an effective measure in some cases. Still, both therapies are given in conjunction with training. Remember, you are striving for voice control, and no medication or surgery can substitute for the long-lasting results obtained by proper discipline and lots of attention.

Tranquilizers give poor results, because once the dog is off the medication the barking resumes.

Shock Collars

The shock collar is a device, I oppose of because it is not used to train but to punish. However, if one is used, I advise choosing a collar that is controlled by the owner and not one activated automatically by sound. The latter type can be activated by any sound, and the innocent dog is shocked needlessly. When a dog is wet, he can even be extensively burned. Also, wearing a shock collar can turn a dog into a nervous wreck, just waiting for the next shock. I do not approve of it. However, there is a collar that does not electrically shock a dog, but releases a malodorous solution similar to citronella. It is controlled by the owner and the barking is stopped in order to avoid the unpleasant smell.

There are many types of remote control training collars available for the dog owner. Most of these collars use electronically controlled sounds, not shock, as an attention getter. These sounds emphasize the verbal commands used in training.

Debarking

I am also against surgically debarking a dog. It affords only temporary relief because the vocal cords grow back. While they

152

are regrowing, the dog emits a pitiful, squeaky sound. I will not perform the operation.

One type of shepherding dog in Australia and New Zealand has to be trained not to bark because a bark could frighten the sheep and cause them to stampede from a mountain top to their deaths. This training, given daily, takes up to three years. So dog owners should not be disheartened if the barking habit cannot be controlled in short order.

Whining

A dog whines for a reason; either he wants something, or he is in pain. Before any behavioral treatment is undertaken, such a dog should be checked for any physical problem causing discomfort or pain. Perhaps it is something simple, like a splinter in his paw or a bee sting. But even if there is not physical cause, do not punish him. Verbal or physical reprimands will not usually stop a dog from whining.

If not in pain, the dog is probably whining for attention. To correct this problem, you must not pamper him. He must be taught that he cannot have your undivided attention or your visitor's lap on command. Except for daily scheduled play periods and sessions of obedience training, ignore him. When he sees that whining no longer works, he will stop doing it.

Jumping on People

It's fun and cute when little puppies climb and jump all over you, and it's hard to resist telling them how adorable they are when they are so eager and happy to see you. But this charming puppy habit is an annoying trait in an adult dog, even when he is one of the small breeds. When the dog weighs more than you do, "annoying" may not adequately express your concern.

Jumping on people has to be unlearned. Some trainers suggest stepping on the hind feet of the rearing dog. Although this may work, I do not recommend it because your weight may injure his paws.

A good training technique is to reprimand the dog, placing him in a prone position for thirty seconds. Praise and pet him while he remains calm; if he struggles, raise your voice and apply more hand pressure to the scruff of his neck. When you are outside and your dog jumps on friends or strangers, jerk his leash and firmly tell him "No." These methods are good for the puppy and the adult dog alike. With the adult, however, it may take as long as four weeks to correct a jumping habit.

For a dog too stubborn, or too excited at the pleasure of seeing you, to remember these lessons, resort to one of the following "easy" cures: (1) When he jumps up on you, grab his front paws, push him backward until he falls over, and say "No!" or (2) When he jumps up on you, bend your knee, bump him in his chest, and say "No!"

Remember, halfway measures don't work well with dogs. Their mothers would bite them sharply enough to make them howl if they were training them. One severe bump in the chest is worth twenty mild ones. Be firm, and be consistent.

However, I do not recommend using these methods with a shy dog. His withdrawn and insecure nature will worsen with any form of punishment. I advise letting this type of dog jump whenever he will. It may build his confidence and encourage him to show affection.

Another method to combat jumping on people is to completely ignore the dog. Turn your back and walk away. Instead of paying more attention by yelling at him, bumping his chest, or stepping on his toes, just turn away and ignore him. It is believed that turning your back on an excited dog will hurt his feelings and he will calm down, maybe not the first time, but after several such encounters, he will generally get the idea. It's worth a try.

Many expert trainers say that the best method to stop jumping is to teach the dog to sit on command and remain sitting until dismissed. Once he sits, give him a treat and crouch down and love the dog. Scratch his chest and neck while talking softly to him.

For more stubborn cases, it takes two people, the owner and a helper. The dog should be on a long leash and when it jumps up on the owner, the helper strongly jerks on the leash, forcing the dog to the ground while a firm command "Down" is given. When the dog doesn't jump up, he should receive enormous praise and a reward for a job well done.

Licking People

The notion that dogs lick people because of a salt deficiency is a fallacy. Licking comes from a maternal-paternal instinct that dogs exhibit when grooming their young. When a dog licks a person, it is a demonstration of his great affection for that person. With some dogs, however, it can become a nuisance. As soon as your dog starts to lick you, move him away and divert, his attention by giving him a command. Praise him when he responds correctly. Regular obedience training and play periods will usually teach him not to lick you. When the dog licks a guest or a member of the family, tell him "No" and again divert his attention with a command followed by praise. In this way, he fulfills his desire to serve and to please you without losing face. And he'll soon learn that people just don't care too much for doggie kisses.

Crotch Sniffing

Crotch sniffing is a serious fault of some male dogs, and it can be very embarrassing. Some owners privately allow this behavior but act shocked when it occurs in the presence of other people. Also, many women are worried that their male dogs will sniff them during their menstrual period. They should never allow this behavior at any time of the month. To correct this bad habit, use a choke collar and a leash, jerking the leash whenever the dog attempts to sniff someone. Accompany this with a loud verbal command, such as "No" or "Out." Make the dog aware of how displeased you are with this behavior.

For a small dog, shake a tin can filled with stones or marbles while you give the command "No."

Leg Mounting

Leg mounting can be seen in three-to-four-week-old puppies, but with them it is playful, not sexual, behavior. When leg mounting persists past puppy hood (and it is common in both males and females), it should be dealt with as quickly as possible. This habit is best corrected by diverting the dog's attention through play activity. In persistent cases, more stringent methods have to be worked out. If hormones are not helpful, castration of the males and spaying of the females may be the only solution.

Self-Mutilation

A dog who develops the habit of chewing or licking some part of his body usually has had some type of skin problem that could not heal, even with medical treatment, because of his persistent attention to the area. His obsessive attention is usually caused by loneliness, boredom, or jealousy, which in turn is caused by isolation in a house, apartment, or pen, with little socialization, or at the other extreme, by too demanding or over attentive an owner. The tension resulting from one or more of these conditions is somehow relieved when he turns his attention to the skin lesion. Many high-strung dogs develop skin ulcers as a result of excessive licking. In many cases, no underlying skin problem can be found, pointing to the likelihood that their neurotic attention to that area of their bodies actually caused the initial lesion. This is much the same as it is with people who mutilate their fingernails. And it becomes a habit.

Correction is not easy and may take up to six weeks of a careful, consistent regimen designed to eliminate the cause of the tension. To divert the dog from chewing his body, give him a chew bone or a meat-scented nylon one. Arrange to have several daily praise-and play sessions with him. If he stays outdoors in a pen most of the time, take him into the house for the play periods.

Whenever he starts to lick or chew, distract him with a loud noise using tin cans, ultrasonic devices, or even a rolling rubber ball, followed by some play and praise. He must be made to feel wanted and close to his family.

Some people have tried spraying the focal point of the chewing with foul-tasting substances like citronella or Chewstop, but the dog usually zeros in on a nearby area. In my opinion, the best of these types of substances is bitter apple. But remember, although tranquilizers, skin lotions, and bitter-tasting balms can help, they do not cure the problem. The cure depends on finding the cause and carrying out the correction program. Many dogs develop chronic sores, called lick granulomas, which are difficult to treat. Cortisone and snake venom injections are helpful; but surgery may have to be performed to rid the dogs of these unsightly growths on their legs.

Flank Sucking

Flank sucking (sucking the outer side of the thigh, hip, and buttock) is seen mainly in the Doberman and to a lesser degree in the Golden Retriever and the Brittany. There is evidence that Dobermans have a genetic predisposition to flank sucking, and some psychologists feel that they, more than other breeds, need constant reassurance and petting. They have practically no tolerance for feeling abandoned or rejected, and suck their flanks for compensatory gratification.

Flank sucking can also develop from boredom. Therefore, whether the cause is lack of attention or boredom, correction is based on increasing the dog's activity, showing him more attention, and giving him obedience training. Further, the dog should be offered a suitable substitute for his sucking needs, like a rawhide bone or a rubber toy (a pacifier, if you will).

A temporary measure is to coat the flank with Bitter Apple™ or some other foul-tasting substance. Apply it liberally and freshen it at least twice a day. This breaks the pattern and solves the problem for an indeterminate period of time. Generally, however, the dog will revert to flank sucking and the liquid must be applied indefinitely. That is why obedience training and planned attention periods are so important when aiming for a complete cure.

Tail Chewing and Chasing

When a dog starts chewing or chasing his tail, the first thing to investigate is any physical cause—skin infection of the tail or rectum or impacted anal glands. Many times, however, hyperactive dogs will chew and chase their tails when they become frustrated, bored, or lonely. Also, dogs who are seeking attention may resort to this disturbing behavior.

Scruffy was a wire-haired terrier who would attack his tail when ever his owners came home. The owners had the dog's anal glands removed, but to no avail. Then the end of the tail was removed, but Scruffy kept on chewing and mutilating himself. Several operations were performed, each time removing a piece of the tail. Finally, a muzzle was put on Scruffy's head, but he managed to rub and irritate the end of the tail with the muzzle.

When Scruffy was brought to me, I realized from his previous history that his problem was not physical but emotional. Scruffy had spent most of his time alone. Even when his owners returned home at the end of their workday, they were too tired to spend any time with him, and the tail chewing was an attempt to get attention and sympathy from them.

The Nuisance Dog

I advised nightly play periods lasting at least fifteen minutes. I also prescribed a tranquilizer to be given in the mornings before the owners left home, to sedate this overactive dog. In addition, I recommended that they leave on a television or radio to keep the dog company and that they provide rawhide bones and other toys for him to chew on. If this had not worked, I would have advised that another pet be obtained to keep Scruffy company, but it wasn't necessary. Scruffy responded well to this therapy. Eventually, the tranquilizer was omitted from the daily regimen, with Scruffy's good response being maintained by the play periods, the affection, and the television.

Running Away—the Tramp Dog

There are four main reasons why dogs run away from home: the call of the wild (the search for a mate); boredom (they are left alone with nothing to do); unhappiness (the dog does not feel wanted by his human family, in these cases, jealousy is sometimes an underlying factor); and love for children (some dogs seek out children to play with). Some dogs will break through windows and chew through doors to escape.

To cure this habit, the cause must be counteracted. If the dog wanders in search of females the whole year, hormone therapy or castration is advised. If the cause is boredom, more play time and companionship should be provided. With an unhappy dog, his orientation to the owner is not strong enough. The owner must assume a loving and masterful role with the dog.

The dog must also be taught the limits of his yard. You can usually accomplish this by walking the dog on a leash around the edge of the yard, commanding him with a "No" and a jerk backward when he gets over the limits. Also, you should get someone to hold the dog on a leash while you walk to the edge of the yard. Stop at the edge, say "No," and continue walking out of the yard while your helper jerks the dog back if he tries to follow you. This must be repeated many times over a period of days to teach him the limits of his territory. Of course, it is easier to teach this to a puppy than to a dog who is already a "tramp."

There is an invisible fence which keeps an "eye" on the dog by transmitting a harmless radio signal through a wire installed at or just below ground level. If the pet gets within 5-10 feet of the wire, an audible warning reminds the pet that they're too close to the perimeter. If the warning is ignored by stubborn dogs, the collar emits a harmless shock. The dog associates the warning sound with the perimeter, safely and effectively.

There is another type of invisible fence that does not use buried wires but sonic transmitter posts around the property. These ultrasonic devices are effective in pet training because they get the animal's attention in a harmless and humane way.

Do not punish a wandering dog when he returns home, for he will associate returning with punishment. Then his trips will be longer and longer.

Jumping Out of Car Windows

Many dogs like to ride in cars with their heads out of the windows, and some are tempted to jump out if they see another dog or a child. This, of course, is very dangerous and can prove fatal. But allowing a dog to ride with his head out a window can also be injurious to him. Besides the obvious injuries that can occur (his head being hit or his jumping out of the car), the dog's eyes are likely to become infected from the foreign particles that fly into them.

The solution is easy. Keep windows closed or closed at least to the point where the dog cannot get his head out.

I know of one family whose dog, Griffin, loved car-riding so much that he insisted on a ride at least once a day. He liked to feel the air in his face as he held his head out the window.

A clever solution was found that saved time and gasoline. The car was parked in the garage, Griffin was put in the back seat with his head out the window and a large electric fan blowing in his face. Griffin was perfectly happy with this situation.

Digging

Digging is a primitive instinct in dogs and is inspired by many different motives—seeking a gopher or other small animal, investigating the movement of insects, making a cool hole in which to lie, hiding a bone or some other treasure, or preparing a nest in which to deliver puppies. This normal behavior is considered a bad habit only when it affects the yard and garden of the owner or neighbor.

The Nuisance Dog

Habitual digging, however, can indicate some emotional or learning problems. An owner may unknowingly teach a dog to dig by allowing him to participate in gardening and planting chores. Or when a dog has been banished from the house for some misdeed and digs near the door to indicate that he wants in, the owner may respond by letting him in. This only rewards the digging. Since it is reinforced, the dog's digging episodes continue.

If your dog has the digging habit, first try to find the cause. Digging near the house usually relates to some problem confronting the dog inside the house. Digging near the fence gate may indicate that the problem has to do with the dog next door, or the digger may be bored. Monotony and frustration can create a lot of digging problems. For the lonely dog, a doggie door may save your yard, if you allow him in the house. He won't have to dig for entry, he can just go through his own door.

In curing the digging habit, it is essential to catch the dog in the act. Punishment at the time of the crime is necessary for the dog to realize he is doing something wrong. Four or five times using cans tied together and throwing them at the dog when caught in the act, will eventually get the point across.

For the dog who runs from his owner when he fears reprimand, a long rope can be tied to his collar. When he fails to come on command, he should be jerked from his digging and sternly reprimanded. For other obstinate cases, a stake can be driven into the freshly dug hole, and the dog tied to it by a short rope so that he must stand in the hole. After the dog has been tied up for about an hour, he should be released, but the stake should be left in the ground to serve as a reminder of his misdeed.

There is another method of teaching a dog not to dig in inappropriate places in the yard. Influence his thinking by teaching him to dig in one spot of your choosing.

Bury a large meaty bone in a spot in the yard that you want the dog to dig. The bone should be buried from 6 to 18 inches deep, depending on the size of the dog. It won't take him long to find the spot and dig up the bone. Keep repeating this process. It will keep the dog busy and happy, and save your yard from unsightly pot holes.

For extremely stubborn dogs, there is the water-hole method. The hole the dog has dug is filled with water and the dog's head held under the water for a few seconds. When this is done consistently, even the most hardheaded dog will get the message.

Jumping, Climbing, or Digging Under Fences

Dogs who jump, climb, or dig to escape from the fences meant to keep them confined can be costly to the owner who tries to correct the problem by building higher and more elaborately designed structures—like the ones that slant inward to prevent climbing, or the ones topped with barbed wire or medieval-looking spears. These additional fortifications are never satisfactory, because most dogs will keep on trying to escape; and those who do resign themselves to confinement will simply take up some other worrisome bad habit. The cure depends on finding out why a dog wants to get out.

Rarely will a dog climb or jump a fence for the sport of it. Some merely want to be free to chase cars, scavenge garbage cans, or beg food from the nice lady down the street. More aggressive dogs may want to get out to patrol their territory. Most often, however, they want to get out because they are lonely, because they want to mate, or because they want to escape some home conflict.

One owner came to me complaining that several days a week he would arrive home to find one of his two Great Pyrenees waiting outside the fence. Once outside, the dog would not leave. Instead, he would just sit outside the fence until the owner got home from work. The owner was perplexed about what to do and wondered why it was always the male who escaped and never the female.

At my suggestion, the owner spent the following day at home to observe his dog's behavior and soon discovered the problem. The male dog, usually very aggressive with other dogs, had become henpecked by the female dog. He was totally submissive to all her demands and was being pushed around most ungraciously. When pushed to his limit of tolerance, he would climb the fence to get a little peace of mind. In this case, the cure was obedience training for both dogs, with emphasis on curbing the female's demanding ways. It's an old story.

The Nuisance Dog

For other cases, you should follow the techniques for retraining the "tramp" dog. Always look for the underlying cause, and remember that punishment does not generally work for such dogs. They need obedience training.

For the extremely stubborn dog, an effective and relatively inexpensive deterrent is an electric fence charger, the same type used by farmers for livestock. The charge, which is not strong enough to cause injury, produces an intermittent current that merely gives a temporary shock. This, however, should be used only as an aid to "jog" the dog's memory, not as a substitute for resolving the dog's inner conflict.

A fairly new electronic innovation works well with most dogs and is called an invisible fence. A wire is buried in the soil around the perimeter of the yard. If a dog steps over the line, a mild electrical shock reminds him that he is going out of bounds. After receiving a few shocks, the dog usually remains inside the invisible fence.

Fence Fighting

In a kennel, the main form of play is fence fighting between the dogs in adjacent runs. The fence itself seems to be an integral part of the game because when the dogs are put in the same run, they will usually stop fighting and go about their business. If not, one will usually whip the other and become dominant over him.

Stool Eating

Although the exact cause of stool eating is uncertain, worms, pancreatitis, or dietary deficiencies are frequently found in dogs who have perverted appetites—eating feces (coprophagy) or dirt, stones, or other objects generally thought to be inedible (pica).

One recent theory attributes coprophagy to an enzyme deficiency, which can be corrected by the feeding of glandular organs (for example, heart muscle) and by the use of enzymes in the daily diet. Another theory is that the stool-eating dog has some vitamin or mineral deficiency, which can be corrected by daily mineral-vitamin supplements. In at least 50 percent of the cases, however, a simple adjustment in diet removes the bad habit. Some dogs, especially during puppy hood, cannot handle high-carbohydrate diets; they need more protein. For these dogs, you should increase the protein by adding meat and fat to the diet and lowering the amount of kibble or meal. You may have to experiment to get the right amounts, as each dog will react differently to the dietary change. Some experts advise giving yogurt, reasoning that the friendly digestive bacteria, lactobacillus, will pep up the stool-eating dog's digestive system.

Also, many dogs are sometimes simply overfed. They get so obsessive about eating that they will re-eat any undigested food in the stool. Sometimes, feeding dogs chicken twice a day will eliminate this habit because chicken is completely digested.

If diet and disease are not the causes, look for psychological causes like boredom, stress caused by insufficient exercise, loneliness, or at the other extreme, overindulgence by the owner. Also, some dogs overly submissive and too sensitive to the demands of housetraining, eat their own feces to hide the evidence. That is why punishment does not work well for these animals. In all cases, however, feces should be removed from the area immediately.

A German Shepherd named Sam came close to undergoing treatment for stool eating and was saved by observant children. During the weekend chore of cleaning out the pen, the worried owner confided to the children that he was certain Sam was eating his own stools because there was so little to clean. The children explained that Sam had learned to be a good housekeeper, that he would carry his feces each day to a corner of the pen, dig a hole, and bury it. Cats will bury this evidence; dogs normally do not. Sam, however, must have noticed his owner's disgust for this weekend chore and was trying to help.

Another dog, not so fastidious, would eat the stool of the Miniature Poodle next door. He would not touch any other stool but hers. Either he was in love with her, or she had something in her diet that he craved.

Still another example is the dog mentioned in an earlier chapter who was being harassed (actually ambushed) by some neighborhood cats she had tried to befriend. A neighbor, catching this dog in the act of eating the stools of one of the cats, tried to convince the owner that the dog was filthy, perverted, and should be gotten rid of. Adding to the problem, the neighbor forbade her two girls to play with the dog. This was sad because the dog dearly loved the little girls and looked forward to seeing them every day. I think the dog was trying to make himself more acceptable to the cats, like the dogs who roll in filth to change their scent so as to confuse their enemies. But who knows? The dog never did this again, or at least she was never again caught in the act.

Most dogs commit coprophagy at least once or twice. Perhaps it is only curiosity, or some primordial urge. But when it becomes a habit, you should try to understand it from the dog's point of view and remove, as far as you can, any stressful conditions that the dog is experiencing. You might also put him through obedience training and spend time playing with him.

You can further discourage coprophagy by making the stool distasteful by adding certain preparations to the dog's food. A commercial preparation available over the counter, mixed with the dog's food, gives the same result. Other substances, helpful in some cases, are monosodium glutamate, oil of anise, iron tablets, and pineapple, and papain (an enzyme used in meat tenderizers). Any of these added to the dog's food should make the stool undesirable.

For the hardy and desperate owner who has a seemingly incurable dog, there are little gadgets that you can insert in the feces which explode with a loud noise when chewed upon.

If you are present when your dog attempts to eat feces, you can let loose with a blast from a horn that will scare him. However, most dogs learn not to eat stools if you are nearby, fearing the noise from the horn, but resort to the misdeed when you are absent.

Eating Sticks, Stones, Dirt, and Such

As discussed in the section on stool eating, pica—the craving for unnatural food substitutes such as sticks, stones, dirt, and pieces of clothing—is often caused by parasites or lack of vitamins or minerals. It can also be a neurotic response to excessive tensions between dog and owner, sometimes caused by too much attention but more often by too little. A lonely or neglected dog is inclined to relieve his tensions by chewing anything available, edible or not.

Veterinarians diagnose this illness from X-rays taken of the dog's abdomen when there are reports that the dog has been vomiting, refusing food, and appearing to have abdominal pain.

I have a steady customer, a Saint Bernard named Rufus, who will eat unusual objects whenever he gets upset about something; for instance, when left alone in his outdoor pen instead of in the air conditioned house. Throughout the years I have washed out his stomach and bowels to find various indigestible objects. Once it was a molding from a car fender; another time, the car's grillwork.

Recently I had to perform surgery to remove a watch (still ticking) lodged in his small intestines. Other things that I have removed from dogs stomachs and intestines are razor blades, golf balls, rubber balls, pantyhose, and even a rubber prophylactic. You can never tell what a dog will eat.

Scolding will not effect a cure. If the cause is not a nutritional deficiency, obedience training and, if the dog has been neglected, play and more attention are the best cures.

Rolling in Filth

Rolling in excrement and other filth is an unpleasant habit, to say the least, but most domestic dogs have done this at one time or another. Their preferences range from all kinds of manure to decayed fish or the remains of carcasses, and the dogs seem to be trying to spread the scent on the sides of their neck and back. Further confounding our understanding of this dreadful habit is that most dogs have an expression of pure pleasure on their faces as they roll in this malodorous matter.

I do not know of any fully satisfactory explanation for this behavior, although I tend to agree with the theory that the dog is attempting to change his scent to confuse his enemies.

An example of this is Jekyll, a Siberian Husky, who has been rolling in horse manure with predictable regularity for years now. Jekyll's strong curiosity about male horses makes him quite a nuisance at the stables. The horses remain aloof and try to avoid him, threatening him as much as they would a worrisome fly. When he gets too persistent, however, they kick at him. So perhaps this Husky, in his frenzied state of unrequited love, is trying to make himself appealing to the horses by smelling more like them. Or maybe he's trying to confuse the stable hands (who run him off) into thinking he's just another horse.

The Nuisance Dog

In any case, such dogs are strongly motivated, and rolling in filth is a difficult habit to break. They continue to roll knowing that their behavior will be ridiculed and punished by their owners. Even the terrors of a cold bath will not daunt the enthusiasm of some dogs for this terrible sport. My only suggestion is reinforced obedience training.

People Chasers

A people-chasing dog, besides being a nuisance, may cause legal problems. The owner may be liable for any injuries suffered by the dog's victims and, in addition, may be fined or even jailed. Even if these dogs don't bite, they can cause such fear in the person being chased that he or she may be injured in flight from the dog or worse, suffer cardiac arrest. Although the severe injuries usually occur in children and elderly folks, people of any age are not immune to the fear of a strange dog in pursuit.

Some dogs seem to have a compulsion to run after small children, barking at them but not biting or even intending to bite. Often the child falls, gets hurt, and is scared half to death. The more the child screams and the faster the child runs, the more persistent the dog is in the chase. Other dogs enjoy chasing joggers and brisk walkers, anyone moving fast enough to present a challenge. Besides the fun of it, dogs chase people to assert their dominance, to protect their territory (these dogs usually quit the chase at the border of their domain), and in many cases, unfortunately, to mimic their owner's dislike of people. And some dogs, like people, take out their pent-up frustrations on strangers.

Because it is especially important to prevent the tendency to chase children, a puppy ideally should grow up with children and learn to become friends with them. If this is not possible, you should seek out children for your puppy to play with. Further, adult friends should be encouraged to pet the puppy. You might also take your puppy shopping so that he can learn that the people in the community are friendly. Strangers should be allowed to pet him.

At the slightest suggestion that the puppy, whatever his age, is about to chase a person, he must be punished with strong verbal admonition.

The Nuisance Dog

In retraining an adult dog not to run after people, you should take him out on a 30 to 50 foot-long rope. When he attempts to go after someone, you should jerk him back so strongly that he is pulled off his feet. You must reprimand him sternly and punish him severely to let him know the folly of his ways. You must also supervise him closely, especially when children are around, until he loses his desire for chasing. A muzzle is not the answer, because the dog can still knock a child down, causing injury and fright.

Vehicle Chasers

Chasing cars or bicycles is quite a sporting event for some dogs. It takes them back to primitive times when they chased game for food. Thus chasing objects on wheels may be a substitute for the food-finding instinct. Also, it is possible that some dogs are trying to protect their neighborhood from the monsters on wheels. Like Don Quixote jousting with the windmill, their intentions are good but their perceptions lead them astray. Other dogs try to herd cars. Some breeds are worse offenders than others, and without a doubt Collies are the worst. Any breed, however, is susceptible to the lure of the chase.

Kate Salley Palmer

The Nuisance Dog

Although not an easy habit to cure, car chasing should be stopped if at all possible. I have treated some dogs who have been run over by automobiles three or four times. Instead of being afraid of cars, they are off to the races again as soon as their casts are removed. If control over such dogs through obedience training does not work, more stringent measures are available.

In addition to using the rope method already discussed, you might try the following setup. Have a stranger drive by in a strange car (dogs will not chase family cars). When the dog takes up the chase, the "stranger" should spray a solution of ammonia (a weak solution, one teaspoon of ammonia to a pint of water) in a water pistol at the dog's face. This should be repeated several times. (The ammonia solution is strong enough to impress the dog with pain when he chases the car, but not strong enough to damage his eyes).

If the ammonia solution does not work, the same "stranger" can throw from the car tin cans tied together and filled with stones, or water balloons. The car can be stopped, with screeching brakes to scare the dog. Or the "stranger" can snap a whip over the dog's head. These methods can also be adapted for dogs who chase bicycles or motorcycles.

It is important to remember that if any method is to succeed, it must be carried out consistently and often—enough times for the dog to learn what is expected from him. All bad habits take time and willpower to correct.

Animal Chasing and Killing

The ancestral hunting instinct to stalk, chase, and kill will cause some domestic dogs to prey upon other animals, most often chickens, sheep, or cats. I have even seen large adult German Shepherds kill young colts and calves, and some dogs who have attempted to take on grown horses. Once a dog gets the taste of blood, chasing and killing other animals can be a difficult habit to break. The search for food is not often the motivating force, because only occasionally will dogs eat their prey. Well-trained hunting breeds—such as Coonhounds, Foxhounds, and Beagles, who are trained to hunt and kill do not eat their prey. When prey is eaten, however, it is usually chicken or sheep.

Dogs running in packs are more apt to attack and kill other animals, even other dogs. This is mob behavior, where the crowd is bolder than the lone dog would be.

Some dogs attack only when their owners are present. These dogs are evidently trying to demonstrate their prowess and ability to hunt. The owners must become more dominant and show leadership. Obedience training is important too, as well as play periods to divert the dog's attention from the hunt.

Commercial preparations, which are sprayed on and which keep a dog from scenting other animals by their obnoxious odor, are not effective in the long run because they do not teach the dog anything. They only mask the problem temporarily.

If your dog attacks other animals, you should first try obedience training. You might set up a situation, such as placing a chicken close by, and then use a leash and collar to jerk some sense into the dog while you verbally command him to stop any attempts to approach or attack the chicken. If obedience training does not work, and it should not be given up until it has been tried many times, drastic measures have to be taken.

One such drastic, but sometimes necessary, method is to use a BB gun. The dog receives a BB pellet in his hide at the slightest sign of stalking or viciousness. Although this may sound a little harsh, it will not be nearly as severe a lesson as that preferred by the irate neighbor or farmer with a shotgun.

The method that I recommend is to have the dog on a choke chain leash with a chicken walking around the room. As soon as the dog growls or makes a motion towards the chicken, you jerk hard on the leash, talking to him and letting him know the folly of his ways. When he doesn't make any mistakes, you reward him with praise and a tidbit. Eventually, when he passes several of these tests, you remove the leash and continue in the same manner—praise and reward. Some headstrong dogs need many hours of this type of training to overcome their natural instincts.

For animals who eat their prey, you can set up traps by baiting the meat with vomit-producing chemicals such as ipecac or lithium chloride. Both these drugs should be used only under the supervision of a veterinarian.

The best way to prevent a dog from preying on cats is to have it grow up with a kitten. When this has not occurred and the

The Nuisance Dog

dog has attacked cats, punishment and obedience training are needed. But investigate first. Cats have very complex personalities. Some lure a dog on, driving him almost crazy with their devious tricks. These clever cats enjoy the chase and may be teaching the dog that all cats want to be chased.

Ground Rules for Retraining Dogs with Bad Habits

Punishment

Never scold or punish a dog who misbehaves unless you are sure he knows why he is being punished. As soon as possible, within minutes, take him to the scene of the crime, talk to him, tell him he is a bad dog. Repeat the word "Bad." Use simple, single words that he can understand. Show him what you mean. Hold up the chewed-up slipper or show him the litter from the trash can. If practical, reinforce what you mean by giving him a pop across his nose with the item he has wrecked. In other words, make sure you convey to him your disapproval and your intolerance for his misdeed. But remember, punishment is most effective minutes after the deed is done. The longer you wait, the less apt the dog will know why he is being punished.

Never beat a dog in a fit of temper. And never yell or scream at a dog when you punish him physically. He will not understand, and he will lose respect for you. Count to ten if necessary, and then talk to him. Be firm, but not violent or out of control. Do as his mother would do. Hold him by the scruff of his neck, shake him, but do so in a calm, firm manner. Voice control is crucial to your success in making your dog obedient. But do not call him to you for punishment. You must go to him.

Be consistent. Repeat the training methods until the dog learns what you expect him to do and until he does it. And never let him get away with a misdeed, not even once. If you do, he will try it again and again. Don't give up, because all training takes time; retraining takes even more time.

Stand your ground. If your dog growls at you, shows his teeth, or snaps, act immediately to reprimand him or forever hold your peace. Once he knows he can frighten you, he will take advantage of you every chance he gets and make your life miserable. Don't let him trick you, either; he may try some cute, adorable little trick just to divert your attention. Don't let him deceive you when he needs to be punished.

Punishment will make some problems worse. This is why it is important to find the underlying cause. Very submissive dogs are made neurotic by punishment.

Reward

Reward is much more effective than punishment in obtaining good behavior. Dogs need attention. That is why some dogs misbehave in the first place—to get attention, even attention that is a spanking. But dogs crave approval too, and that is why reward will work best when you are trying to teach a dog something. Even when you must punish him for his wrongdoing, don't hold a grudge. Just as with a spouse, you should never let your pet's day end with any bad feelings. Let your dog know you love him.

Bribery

Bribery works well with dogs as it does with people. Human and canine nature are very similar indeed.

When working with dogs in any training procedures, their memory is enhanced by the use of some juicy morsel of food such as a piece of liver.

Obedience Training

I recommend any of the many good books on obedience training, but more important are the classes, where both the dog and owner attend and together are taught the principles of human and canine cooperation. Voice control, posture, and attitude are learned best by imitation.

Rehabilitation

THE RETRAINING PROGRAM

Sophie was a Weimaraner, about a year and a half old, and she was a "loser." That's what her owners called her when they dragged her into my hospital by the scruff of her neck.

"You can have her," said the woman bitterly. "She's no good."

"What do you mean?" I asked.

"We want her destroyed," the husband said.

"Why," I asked. "She's not sick, is she?"

The man tapped his head. "She's sick up here. She's crazy. We can't do a thing with her."

"She's not vicious-looking," I said to the couple.

"Oh, she doesn't bite or anything like that," the woman replied. "But she's unruly and obstreperous and we're sick and tired of her."

"Do you mind if I find a home for her?"

"Do anything you like with her," the husband said. "We just don't ever want to see her again. Here's her papers." And he flung an envelope on the table.

I called a friend, Tom Bradshaw, in Raleigh and asked him if he would take the dog. "Yes," he said, he'd love to have that dog. He'd always wanted to see what obedience training would do for a dog that was unmanageable.

The rest of the story is that of a canine Cinderella. Sophie turned out to have brains, and beauty. The week after Sophie went to live with Tom, he enrolled her, and himself, in an obedience class. You must remember that the discipline is just as great on the trainer of the dog as on the dog. Both go to class, but much depends on how well the human half of the temper forms between classes. The better the coaching, the better the results.

Sophie proved to be a trainer's dream dog. She went up the ladder of obedience step by step, performing brilliantly as she went along. At the same time, good food, kindness, and the security that came with necessary discipline transformed her.

172

Eventually she became a champion in the show ring and also a CDX, which in obedience trials means Companion Dog Excellent. Sophie, the dog that was "no good," became that kind of companion—and more, thanks to training. Of course, not all "unmanageable" dogs, who undergo rehabilitation programs will turn out as well as Sophie did. But most of them will be helped greatly, and many will make such progress during and after training that their owners—and their friends—will be astonished.

"This can't be the same dog," people are likely to say when they meet up with the formerly unmanageable canine. But happily it is. Training can change all but a small minority of dogs—chiefly those whose problems are organic in origin or who are hyperkinetic or psychotic—into better pets and better citizens.

Making Sure of the Cause of the Problem

Before you undertake a rehabilitation program for your problem dog, you must ascertain the cause of the problem. Most importantly, the dog should be checked by a veterinarian to be sure that the problem does not stem from disease, nutritional deficiencies, or an abundance of worms.

The next step should be honest and objective soul-searching to determine the extent, if any, of your contribution to the dog's problem. This soul-searching should run the gamut of the various problems humans have, because, as we have seen, dogs are especially sensitive to human emotions and react instinctively to them.

Once the cause of the problem is understood, a program can be shaped more effectively to deal with it.

Understanding the Dog

A good training program can correct almost any type of misbehavior, and almost any dog can be taught obedience. But in trying to train your dog out of a bad habit, be careful; he may be smarter than you think.

An intelligent dog (and dogs have different IQ's, just as humans do) can outsmart his owner in many ways. He might be the picture of good behavior when you are around. But as soon as you leave or turn your back, he is into some mischief. He knows exactly when you come home and what times of day or night he can get away with misdeeds. If he gets lonesome and wants some human companionship, all he has to do is bark or howl, and his irate master will show up trying to quiet him. And he is also curious, a sure sign of intelligence. When you are doing yard work, for example, he will sniff the ground where you're working. And to your displeasure, he may start digging up the newly planted flowers. He wants to see what you've done!

And mischievous! Have you noticed that most misdeeds are done when you're not there? Maybe he chewed up the book you were reading or dug up your house plants. After all, you did leave him home when you drove away in your car; and to some dogs riding in a car is what water-skiing is to some teenagers. Next time you take him with you, notice how interested he is in the world outside the car windows, with how keen an eye he observes it, and how he reacts to the dogs, bicycles, joggers, and other objects, animate and inanimate, that you pass. And of how most dogs hate to be left out of these trips. But maybe your dog doesn't care much for riding in cars. Perhaps he was just bored when he chewed your book. But for sure, he wants your attention and can usually figure out how to get it.

Importance of the Owner's Attitude

In many cases, a dog is a problem merely because of the lack of a consistent training program, or of any training. As there are many excellent books that deal with obedience training for dogs in general, I will limit myself to the most important points in training a problem dog.

The approach to training such a dog varies with the type of owner. Some owners cannot or will not follow the instructions designed to correct behavior problems in dogs. Some owners do not read or listen very carefully and will only partially understand what they should do. Indulgent owners need stricter instructions, whereas overly assertive people are most likely going to create more problems than they cure. It has been found that some owners need a dog's misbehavior to satisfy their own neurotic or psychotic behavior. To all these owners, rehabilitation of their problem dogs is very difficult and often ends in failure. The owner's attitude in correcting the dog's behavior is of primary importance to the success of their training.

But, whatever the case, if you are an owner trying to correct your dog's misbehavior, work with him patiently. Let him know you are trying. Play with him, exercise with him, and spend a few minutes a day concentrating all your efforts on him. Never neglect him or ignore his intelligence and sensitivity. Do not treat him like a pet rock. He is a living being who has a heart and a brain and can assimilate more than we give him credit for.

Leadership

A dog's natural instinct is to belong to a pack with one strong leader. So you, as owner, must be the leader, dominant and in control at all times. The leadership role can best be established by obtaining verbal control of the dog with simple commands, such as "No," "Sit," "Stay," "Quiet," and "Come."

Perform the necessary exercises not only in the home but in various other places outside the home. It is important for your dog to listen to you at all times and in all places. Make these exercises simple and short so he won't get bored. Ten to fifteen minutes at a time is plenty for a dog to absorb. It might take as little as one week or as long as six weeks to train him. Praise him when he does right. And give him a refresher session at least once a week.

Rehabilitation ————————————

Remember: Reinforce your show of love for your dog by spending ten or fifteen minutes a day playing with him, talking to him, and giving him plenty of attention and affection.

The prime requisite for maintaining leadership is that your commands be obeyed. Letting your dog do as he wishes will only destroy your control of him. You must be strong, and yet you must show love and tenderness toward him. Once the pack leadership role has been established, it must be consistently maintained and never given up, not even when it would be much easier to overlook a seemingly simple misdeed.

Atmosphere for Learning

Establish an emotional atmosphere conducive to learning. Although it is best that you (as leader) be the only trainer, other family members should be in on the program and be aware of the "don'ts" that could jeopardize it. Never let others hit, kick, or abuse your dog, or he will come to mistrust them. Naturally a small dog will shy away from toddlers, for he has learned that small children squeeze too hard and pull his ears and tail. When captured by the tot, he may squirm, whine, or protest in other ways, but normally he will not bite or hurt the child. If your dog shies away from older children, it may mean he has received abuse from an older child somewhere along the way. So you must be alert to what is going on and instruct children and other members of the family how to socialize properly with the dog. He will love and obey them but will look up to you as master.

Importance of Timing and Consistency

Timing and consistency are key factors in training your dog. The desirable act should be followed immediately by a reward praise or a tidbit, or both. And the undesirable act should be followed immediately by punishment. The dog has to understand why he is being punished. Hitting him with a chewed-up shoe an hour after he has committed the act will not make an impression on his brain. He will not associate the beating with the torn shoe. If he were to chew on the shoe and be hit by a snapping mousetrap or be jolted by an electric wire attached to the shoe, a more lasting impression would be made. But when you discover the misdeed some time after it has been done, don't punish him. Instead, give the dog a command such as "Sit," "Come," and so on. Reinforce the command by repetition, so as to establish control and leadership over the dog. Work with him. Talk to him, and show him the correct behavior.

Delayed Reinforcement

Delayed reinforcement can cause neuroses. Remember, when your dog misbehaves, punish him on the spot or not at all. Likewise, when you ask him to do something and he responds favorably, do not forget to praise him. He expects it. If you don't, he might become nervous and confused. A dog is a creature of habit. Treat an untrained dog like a two- or three-year-old child. Always try to do things in the same way or in the same sequence. Above all, be consistent.

A common mistake of owners is to reward or punish after the fact. Remember, the last thing the dog does is what you should reward or punish. He will associate this reward or punishment with his last action. For instance, when you are teaching him to sit and stay and he obeys your commands, sometimes he will suddenly stand up when you are giving him the reward. This is the wrong way to go about it. He should be rewarded only when he is sitting; otherwise he will think you are rewarding him for standing up.

Excessive Punishment

Excessive punishment administered long after the undesirable behavior can lead to side effects such as avoidance of the owner and the "guilty look," the sign of submission in the dog every time he is in the owner's presence. You can break a dog's spirit if the rehabilitation program is not properly administered.

In summary, behavior modification uses reward and punishment to reinforce good behavior. Immediately reward the dog's good behavior and punish the bad. If some time has passed before the misdeed is discovered, you should still punish, but try to make the reason clear to the dog by showing him why he is being punished (for example, return him to the scene of the crime).

Once the good behavior is established, keep reinforcing it by praising the dog. A dog needs a lifetime of confidence building. He needs to be rewarded constantly for his accomplishments.

Rehabilitation ─────────────────

So keep telling him how well he is doing. Keep praising him. Tell him "Good dog." This will continually reinforce his desire to please you.

But once a bad behavior pattern is set in your dog it takes time, patience, and consistency to correct it. Do not let him repeat undesirable behavior. And do not allow him to perform a bad deed just so you can scold him for it. This would be very confusing to him.

Never call a dog to you in order to be punished. He will associate you with being punished and that is not what you are striving for. He will not respond to your call the next time you beckon him. It can create a negative cycle that never gets corrected.

Training Procedures and Techniques

Important elements in a training or retraining program are, as I've said, love, understanding, determination, consistency, patience, and gentleness. These must be combined in daily command periods (which must be serious) and play periods (which must be fun). Playing with the owner can be a reward for the serious work.

Age to Begin

Training should not be started until the puppy is at least eight weeks old, when you can begin to teach him simple commands. Intensive training should not start until later.

For older dogs the same training procedures are used, but they usually take longer to be effective, especially in those dogs that have bad habits.

Procedure

Start with just one behavioral problem at a time, and do not try to eliminate everything simultaneously. Also, a command must be learned completely before a new one is undertaken. Have some treats handy. Most dogs will understand good things like food, candy, tidbits, or chew sticks as rewards. And remember, you are the leader of the pack, always in charge, and the master.

The dog must be completely relaxed before a training session and must be feeling fit. The training sessions should be carried out at the same time and in the same place each day and should never be undertaken after strenuous exercise or a meal. They should take place preferably near mealtime, with dinner becoming an extra reward. They should not be less than ten or more than fifteen minutes in length, and should be interesting because many dogs are easily bored. It takes at least four days (or sessions) for dogs to learn the average command. Simple one-word commands with accompanying gestures should be used. When a command is obeyed, a tidbit and praise should immediately follow.

Just rubbing your dog's ear or praising him are not enough reinforcement. The idea is that the two of you are working together toward a common goal—tricks and commands that he can master. So do praise and pet him when he does well, but give him that extra treat. He will be much more impressed if he gets a juicy tidbit of meat or cheese as his reward. It is not true, however, that a dog will not respond to your commands unless he is rewarded with a tidbit.

In fact, once the behavioral pattern is attained, a tidbit should not be given every time the dog responds. Verbal praise will be reward enough. But during the training sessions, that extra reward is the most effective way to make him understand how pleased you are with his progress.

Reinforcement

A trained dog has the intellect of a child between three and seven years old. And because it takes about four days for the average dog to learn a lesson, the proper response to your command after this time is considered a learned response. You must continue to reinforce each learned response by repeating the training exercises, and rewarding good and punishing bad performances.

Another important factor is consistency. Children and dogs alike want to know what to expect in any given circumstance. When they know what to expect they feel secure.

A behavior modification training session can also be called the play-and-command period. The session is important for several reasons: It gives the dog the daily attention that he wants and needs; It reinforces the image of the owner as the dominant member; and It also gives the image of the owner as the source of rewards, which makes retraining easier.

Rehabilitation

Obedience training is also used to establish leadership. It is also used in conjunction with the techniques described later in this chapter.

Anticipating a Misdeed

Often it is possible to anticipate a misdeed. At such times, a command should be given to distract the dog. Then his response should be praised or scolded accordingly. Try to anticipate when your dog is about to misbehave. You know your dog's mannerisms by your close association with him. Sometimes you almost know what he is thinking about. You know that the twinkle in his eyes means he is planning some misbehavior. So if at all possible, give him a command before he misbehaves. Try to distract him. Remember, though, that most dogs are smart. They won't misbehave when you are around but will act as soon as you turn your back.

The Guilty Look

The signs of submission in a dog are ears back, tail lowered, head down, body slightly crouched, and rolling over to expose the groin. This exposure of belly and groin is a dog's sign of conceding inferiority to another animal or human, but it is also a sign of guilt.

After a misdeed, most dogs have a guilty conscience. They know they have done something wrong and will exhibit a guilty look when immediately confronted with the misdeed.

Some owners, however, misinterpret the guilty look. They say that their dog "looked guilty" when they confronted him with the evidence of his misdeed some time after it was committed. Because of that look, the owners say, they knew the dog was aware that he had done wrong; and they punished him accordingly. They were probably in error. A dog with a guilty look might not, remember what he did wrong (if, indeed, he did anything), and might simply be reacting to the anger displayed in the owner's voice, facial expression, or body movements. Such anger naturally causes many pets to assume a fearful or guilty look—and they may further react by rolling over or crouching submissively, or by running away and hiding. A pet often picks up the emotional signals of his owner and responds accordingly. That is why it is important to make sure that your dog understands the reason he is being punished.

Overcoming Fears

Owners should learn how to help their dogs overcome fears, a process called desensitization. Some dogs fear cars; others, thunderstorms or gunshots; still others have a variety of fear-producing phobias. The aim in desensitizing a dog is to substitute a pleasant feeling in place of the fear. The feeling most often sought by trainers and therapists is relaxation. You, as owner, will know what makes your dog relax. Teach him to overcome his fear by relaxing him.

It is best to desensitize a dog's simplest fear first. Don't attempt to deal with too many varied phobias at one time. Concentrate on one fear at a time. Conquer it and then go onto another fear, if he has others. You may only see partial relief at first, but like all new learning, with repetition, conditions should improve.

Retraining the Anxious, Nervous Dog

Anxious, nervous dogs must be made to relax before they can be trained. Their fears have to be quieted. If you assume a crouching position, your nervous dog will feel more secure and that you are more approachable. Petting the throat and chest will further allay his fears. You should speak in gentle, soothing tones, and the training atmosphere should be free from outside noise and interference. The use of tin cans or water filled balloons should be avoided, for they might scare an already nervous dog too much and might create additional problems.

As mentioned before, every dog has to be handled differently in a rehabilitation program. Some dogs need gentleness, whereas others need firmness. But all need consistency and lots of patience.

Don't confuse your dog. Make your wishes known to him, but keep them as simple as possible. Teach one command at a time, or work on one problem at a time. Some dog owners unknowingly develop their own "problem dogs" by not being able to handle a nervous, growling, fear-biting, overprotective dog. In such cases professional advice should be sought from a dog trainer, a dog psychologist, or a veterinarian.

Rehabilitation ─────────────────────────

Drugs

The use of drugs or tranquilizers during training sessions is not a good idea, as they interfere with the normal learning processes of the brain. But sometimes, in obstinate cases, drugs are a necessity.

The Punishment Cage

Some dog trainers advocate the use of a punishment cage to handle stubborn, problem dogs. The principle of the cage is that a dog hates to be in solitary confinement. Whenever he does anything wrong, he is put in solitary confinement, similar to that experienced in penal institutions. He is kept confined in a small cage in a room by himself for twenty-four hours. He is fed and watered and is allowed to leave the cage only twice to heed nature's call.

A dog will associate the punishment with his misdeed. No physical abuse is necessary—verbal admonishment and being put into the cage will suffice.

This method can be used on stubborn dogs who do not respond to the ordinary retraining methods. The dog can be placed in the cage as often as necessary until he learns his lesson. But never put problem dogs who have anxiety tensions caused by boredom or loneliness in a punishment cage. It will only worsen their problems.

The Time-out Method

Time-out is an excellent method to use for social reinforcement of dogs who exhibit excessive, attention-seeking behavior. It can be used with most types of behavior problems but should never be used on a shy, withdrawn animal. It also should never be used for correction of house-soiling behavior. But it is a good method to use on the unruly dog. This method has been used extensively in the training of children.

The idea behind this method is to punish the dog by ignoring him for a period of time. He is put in a room by himself. Pick a room, a small neutral area, that he does not usually visit, such as a bathroom. Escort him by his collar into the room. Always say "No" as you do so. Do not talk to him after you have escorted him into the room, and pay more attention to him as long as he remains in the room. His behavior while in the room will tell you how long to keep him there—in any case, no less than three minutes and no longer than 20. Do not stand right outside the door because he will know you are there, and that will give him the attention he wants.

Close the door, and wait until he becomes quiet for a reasonable period of time. When you open the door, do not speak to him. Let him walk out on his own. Ignore him for 15 minutes or more, with no one talking to him during this time. After that you, may pet him, play with him, and pay attention to him. But if he misbehaves in the first 15 minutes, then he must be taken back into the room again.

Do not allow the dog to go into the room by himself. That will defeat your purpose. He must always be led into the room. Some dogs are smart—they will misbehave and run into the room by themselves. Keep the door closed to prevent your dog from doing this. The purpose of the punishment is to make your dog more aware of your dominance over him, to teach him that you, not he, are the leader, and that your wishes must be obeyed.

In using this and other training techniques, you must realize that no technique will work unless it is carried out correctly. A dog will often outsmart his owner. Indulgent people are liable to fail in training because they are too attentive to their dog and are apt to give in too easily to a mournful look or whimper. Nevertheless, if the time-out method is performed properly, it will almost always change behavior, in dogs as well as children.

Sound Devices

Researchers have found that dogs learn more quickly by sound association than by physical force and pain. For this reason, some dog trainers advocate various sound devices.

Dr. Dave Miller, a well-known dog psychologist, rattles a metal chain to get the dog's attention. Dogs immediately respond to this sound. To use this method when a dog is doing something wrong, rattle the chain, either in your hand or by tossing it near the misbehaving pet. The sound of the chain impresses on the dog that what he is doing is a no-no.

William Campbell, a famous dog trainer, uses an ultrasonic sound device to attract a dog's attention. The dog associates the sound with the correction.

Rehabilitation ——————————

There are many ultrasonic devices that can be obtained at electronic stores that will help in retraining. There is a rape alarm, the one that women use for protection, that works well to startle a dog if he is in the act of misbehavior such as excessive barking. There are shock mats, that have a very low voltage that gives a dog a big scare if he sits on your favorite sofa. Mouse traps on your furniture will also help keep the dog off a forbidden chair. Some enterprising owners have set up infra-red devices that set off alarms when the dog enters an off-limit area. All these electronic gadgets are used in controlling behavior but they do not hurt the animal.

Other trainers use things like tin cans, horns, whistles, water balloons, and so on, to impress a dog's misdeeds upon him. But remember, these devices are not recommended for the anxious, nervous dog who frightens easily.

Ultrasonic Collars

There are training collars that use high frequency sounds instead of electric shock to train a dog. It is activated by a remote button and the collar emits a harmless sonic burst that humans hear only as a click. This wireless trainer was developed at a veterinary college and is useful to help stop jumping, barking, digging, chewing, and other nuisance habits.

Many types of ultrasonic devices are effective in pet training which emphasize your verbal commands. They get the animal's attention in a harmless and humane way.

It is best to leave the collar (or a fake collar) on the dog for a long while after the animal seems cured. Some smart dogs will revert to their old ways when the collar is removed.

Head Collars and Training Halters

There are many devises, available to the trainer, both amateur and professional, that help in the training of unruly dogs who do not respond to verbal commands alone. These gadgets, head collars, and training halters, will impress your dominance upon the dog . These collars and halters do not inflict pain upon the dog but apply pressure where it does the most good; to the neck much like a mother dog soothes her puppies and over the nose and lower jaw, much like a leader dog disciplines a pack member in the wild. If properly worn and applied, these collars will help control the most stubborn of dogs.

The "Untrainable" Dog

Occasionally clients consult me regarding dogs they believe to be untrainable and uncontrollable. Although these owners have a strong affection for their pets, they often feel compelled to get rid of them. In some cases, the clients have tried obedience classes with no success. This kind of problem dog does not pay any attention to members of the family and has seemingly little or no affection for them.

In cases like this to determine why it has failed, I usually find when studying the owner-pet relationship, that the dog has taken advantage of an owner he sees as weak. He wants to be the pack leader over his owner.

To correct this problem, there has to be a dramatic change in the owner-dog relationship. The owner must demonstrate a firm, committed, unafraid, and self-confident attitude. He or she must be willing to compete for dominance, using intelligence and physical strength to overcome the dog's will. The dog must be reprimanded verbally and physically at any attempt to force his will onto his owner. The owner should use angry scolding, threatening gestures, leash corrections with choke-chain collar, and should shake the dog by the nape of the neck. Locking the dog up in a room or a punishment cage and removing his food may be required for stubborn cases. In administering the punishment, the owner must not show any fear or hesitation, or the dog will see his chance to win the battle of the wits.

The amount of force needed varies with each dog. Some respond to gentle prodding, whereas others require a strong hand. But always remember, praise as well as punishment is necessary.

There is another approach to rehabilitating an "untrainable" dog. In this approach, the owner and the dog must change drastically so that there is an image of a new owner, a new home, and a new lifestyle. The owner must provide a new shelter and a new run for the dog. If it is an indoor dog, a new crate must be provided for him. The dog should be confined in absolute isolation for a week. Other than the owner, no person or animals should be allowed near the dog. All routine work such as feeding and cleaning should be done in silence. The attention-seeking ploys of the dog should not be acknowledged in any way. On the eighth day, the dog may be taken out of the kennel on a leash for a five-minute work period. The owner must be firm and dominating. Simple obedience exercises should be performed and praise should be given if work is satisfactory. Disobedience should be dealt with in a firm manner. After five minutes, the dog may be allowed a brief play period, then returned to his kennel. Some stubborn dogs may require days and weeks of isolation; such isolation may be essential for the transitional stage of the dog's behavior modification.

If all methods fail in correcting a problem dog, transferring ownership of the dog may be the only way out. A conflict of personalities may be the cause of intractable behavior problems.

The Do's and Don'ts of Retraining

There are many good books on retraining with many different methods and special techniques devised by excellent trainers. Most of them will work if you follow instructions, spend the time required, and have lots of patience.

The list of suggestions that follows includes many ideas that have appeared earlier in this book. They are repeated here to emphasize their importance.

The Do's

- Do get to know every facet of your dog's personality intimately. Each animal has a threshold of sensitivity and must be trained according to his own temperament.
- Do teach respect by establishing leadership.
- Do get the message across—word commands have to be augmented by hand signals and body commands. I advocate using a choke collar in order to signal body commands effectively (when handled properly and gently, it can be used on the smallest and most fragile pet). When the dog has gotten the message, voice commands will suffice. The dog should be constantly talked to in quiet, soft tones—insistently. The voice tones should convey the meanings of the commands. He will learn the significance of the tones and ultimately the meanings of some words.
- Do have only one person in charge of the training program. More than one person is confusing and makes training more difficult. Once the dog has learned, other

members of the family can contribute to further training.

- Do train your dog at the same time and place each session. Continuity and familiarity aid in the learning process.
- Do hold the training sessions daily, and keep them short, ten to fifteen minutes in length.
- Do—for the best training results—confine your dog to his kennel or a separate room for an hour or two before each session. Also, do not give him food just before training. These generally make him more responsive to your directions and, also, a happier worker.
- Do reward and punish—immediately after the deed or misdeed.
- Do be consistent in requests and responses, and in aims and methods so as not to confuse or deceive. Each of the learning procedures should be followed with the same praise, reward, or disapproval responses. The dog should not be allowed to get away with a misdeed one time, and then be punished for the same misdeed the next.
- Do play with your dog after the training sessions as a reward for his serious concentration.

The Don'ts

- Don't attempt to train your dog after meals or exercise. He will be sluggish both mentally and physically.
- Don't expect miracles. It takes a minimum of four lessons to learn a command, and some dogs take longer.
- Don't lose patience. Shouting and screaming will only confuse your dog.
- Don't hit him in a fit of temper. When scolding is needed, make him understand why.
- Don't use a training lead or other training object to punish him. He will become fearful of training.
- Don't use a spiked training collar to try to impress commands on him. Cruelty does not help obedience training.
- Don't proceed with a new command until he has mastered the one being taught.
- Don't end the training session with your dog getting his own way. End it with his having obeyed a command. This way you prove your authority and leadership.

Rehabilitation

How to Help the Nervous Dog

Dogs respond to proper treatment, and it's up to each of us to find the proper way for his dog. To fight excessive nervousness in a dog here are some good rules to follow:

- Don't give him many commands at once. Go Slowly.
- Don't teach him more than he can comprehend in a 10- to 20- minute session.
- Be firm with him and make him understand that when you tell him to do something, he must do it or be punished.
- Give him plenty of companionship.
- Give him plenty of play and exercise
- Allow him to be in the company of many strangers, preferably the children in the neighborhood. Most dogs are gentle with children.

A Message for Owners Who Resist Training Programs

Many dog owners resist training programs. Some say they don't have the time. Some say, "Oh, I've tried to train him, but it didn't do much good." Usually they mean that they made half a dozen casual efforts to follow the directions in a dog-training manual and then gave up when miraculous changes did not occur overnight. Others conclude, whether after such casual efforts or without any training efforts at all, that their dog doesn't want to be trained, won't like training, and therefore can't be trained.

Few beliefs could be farther from the truth. The fact is that most dogs seem to enjoy properly conducted training sessions, especially those classes where they work with their owner, other dogs and their owners, and an experienced trainer.

Sherry Pate, who works with me at my veterinary hospital, is an experienced trainer. On Sunday afternoons she conducts obedience training sessions for dogs and their owners. One couple told her how the training sessions had changed their Beagle.

"Before she began the training," the Beagle's mistress said, "she ran away from us repeatedly, and we had a hard time persuading her to come back to us. Now all we have to do is to show her the training leash and collar, and she comes running to us."

Like most dogs, this Beagle enjoys obedience training. It gives the dogs attention; it makes them feel important. And it gives them a greater sense of security, because they learn what to do, and what not to do, to please their owners—and for many dogs that is the main goal in life.

BEHAVIOR MODIFICATION

Behavior modification is the concept that behavior can be changed by the giving or withholding of rewards. The concept originated when laboratory studies found that an animal would respond to an event in a predictable manner if his response was reinforced. That is, when put in the same situation again, he would repeat his response if he associated it with receiving a reward; or he would repeat his response if he associated it with the avoidance of pain or the avoidance of some other unpleasant event, like not receiving a reward.

From these early experiments, behavioral scientists realized that reinforcement can have a powerful effect on learning. Many of the current child-rearing practices are based on this concept.

Behavior modification as therapy works exceptionally well with animals because it provides a way to communicate that the animal will understand. A good response is followed by a reward, a bad response is followed by a punishment (which can be simply the lack of a reward). A dog will understand this and will learn to respond with good behavior.

Reinforcement is the key to success with this type of therapy. Reinforcement can be provided by both reward and punishment. Because these terms will be used in describing the retraining techniques, it is crucial that you know exactly what they mean and how they are to be used.

Reinforcement by Reward

Reward is praise, petting, or a tasty tidbit to nibble. A kind word or caress makes any dog feel that he is pleasing to his owner. Other meaningful gestures of affection that a dog can understand are taking his muzzle playfully in both hands, rubbing him behind the ears, rubbing a hand gently over his flanks and back, or handling his nose affectionately. Often just the words "Good dog" make a happy, grateful dog.

A dog has several areas on his body that when touched appropriately denote either praise or punishment. For instance, petting on the throat and chest will eliminate fear in the dog, for he associates good things with being petted in these regions.

Other pleasure areas of a dog are on top of the tail, behind the ears, and on the ribs between the front legs. The owner can use these areas as a reward, as well as to please the dog. But when you pet your dog roughly on the top of his head, you are showing your dominance over him. He will usually crouch down or turn over on his back in a submissive position when stroked in this way.

A shy dog is more apt to come to you when called if, instead of standing, you crouch down. When crouching so that you are more closely on a level with the dog, you show friendliness; and this reassures him. Bending over at the waist to pet a shy dog is not good either, for it represents signs of possible punishment. Kneel down and the dog will feel more secure. Don't rush at a shy, timid, or aggressive dog. Kneel down and let him come to you.

Reinforcement by Punishment

Punishment is a sharp look of disapproval, scolding, hitting, or, in drastic cases, isolation. Your attitude toward the dog is all-important during punishment. You should never punish with the intent of hurting or abusing your pet.

When scolding, remember that many dogs don't actually know words (although dogs who live in close relationships with their owners may know many words and respond to them). When a dog doesn't understand your words, he mainly responds to your actions in combination with your tone of voice. Do not be harsh, even though you scold. Use a firm tone of voice and an attitude of teaching.

A scolding is important in getting rid of a bad behavioral problem, but teaching the dog the right way is the objective. Don't let your dog grow up in a world of hitting, slapping, yelling, screaming, and general abuse. Attempt to develop love and respect in his attitude toward you. Proper obedience training will help immeasurably in letting him know what to expect from you.

Due to the wide variance of temperament in the different breeds, the amount of scolding in the disciplinary process must vary. For instance, for the more timid breeds, such as Beagles and toys, just a glare or a few mild words of admonition are sufficient. If you are too rough or loud with these kinds of dogs, you can permanently hurt them emotionally—you can break their spirits. Breeds such as terriers, however, usually have a more independent nature and require a more severe form of chastisement or punishment. They are strong-willed dogs and need a firmer hand.

Hitting can be effective if it is properly done. But it must be done in a way that does not harm the animal, and it must be done during or immediately after the misdeed. A gentle tap can be more effective than a fist to the abdomen. Many dog owners mistakenly resort to strong physical measures to correct a fault, a practice that usually compounds the misbehavior. Handling a dog roughly only causes him to be over stimulated, and he will resist you rather than listen to you. Don't hit him with a rolled-up newspaper unless the punishment is directly and immediately connected to the misbehavior—and then don't hit him too hard. The sound of the newspaper slapped on your own hand will get the message to him. Roughness and harshness can cause him to hate training and to develop bad habits to relieve his tensions and frustrations.

Nevertheless, you must be firm enough to make the dog understand that he has erred and must not do it again. The mother's way of punishing her puppies might teach us something about handling our dogs. She will grab a pup by the scruff of the neck and shake him, or take him by the muzzle and pin him to the ground. The pup usually shows instant signs of submission. She does not really hurt him, but she gets her message across. With small dogs, you can shake them by the scruff of the neck. Large dogs need other forms of punishment.

Be sure to treat each dog as an individual. Train, praise, or punish him as an individual. Be gentle, except when it is necessary to establish your dominance over him. And even here, use no cruelty, but be firm; your dog will know how you feel about that particular subject. You should concentrate on teaching good behavior. When you do, a lot of the bad behavior disappears.

Rehabilitation ─────────────────────

Another Technique—Praise and Reward—But No Punishment

As the name implies, behavior modification involves changing behaviors-from unacceptable behaviors to acceptable behaviors.

There are, of course, many ways to do that. But as far as I'm concerned, every way can be put into either one of two categories - the "bad dog" category or the "good dog" category. To determine which category your dog and you fall into, try this "experiment." Count up the number of times (in a day) that you say "bad dog" (or "stop that" or "get off of there" you get the picture) vs. the number of times you say, "good dog" ("atta boy," "whatta guy," etc.). By the way, I'm not talking about the times when you're purposely trying to get your dog to do something amusing like catch a Frisbee, and you say, "good dog."

Or compare the times you say "bad dog" to the times you don't say anything at all (even though your dog is doing exactly what you want him to do).

Now, compare the two totals. I'd bet that most of you fall into the "bad dog" category. That's because we all have a tendency to pay attention to negative behavior. Worse, we tend to ignore the positive behavior.

How It Works

When you respond to the negative behavior and ignore the positive behavior, you run the risk of having your dog interpret your "punishment" as a reward. It's the only way he gets attention, and attention is really what he wants, more than anything else. Well, almost anything else.

When punishment becomes the reward, the negative behavior will increase, not decrease. By definition, if we pay attention to negative behavior, we end up punishing, or "rewarding," as I've just described. But conversely, if we pay attention to positive behavior, we reward. Ignoring negative behavior then becomes the absence of reward. And just like us -adults and children alike- your dog wants to be rewarded for his good deeds. When he is, he'll do them more. Soon, all he'll be doing are the good deeds. There'll be no time left to do anything else.

This section will take you step-by-step through the process of undoing your dog's bad habits, not by punishing but by rewarding.

The types of behavior modification techniques that I recommend, by the way, work as well with children as they do with dogs. So, try it on your kids too!

Behavior Modification and Your Dog's Self-Image

Even though you may think your dog takes great pleasure in driving you crazy, especially in the beginning, he may not think he's doing anything wrong. He'll be taking all his cues from you. The more times you tell him what a bad dog he is, the more he'll start believing you. Once he really has a negative self-image, he'll start saying to himself, "What the heck? She says I'm bad, and she's bigger than I am, so she must know what she's talking about. Now, I better keep up my reputation. Otherwise I might disappoint her."

And remember this as well. If you don't reward your dog for his good behavior, how will he ever know what he's supposed to be doing?

Rewarding your dog for positive behavior has the added benefit of making your dog feel extremely good about himself. The better he feels about himself, the better behaved he'll be, so you see, there's a real "snowball" effect. It just keeps getting bigger and bigger, better and better, and faster and faster.

How Long Does It Take?

The answer to this question, of course, depends on how many negative behaviors you want to redirect and how long these negative behaviors have been going on.

Are you trying to get your dog to do something new or something different? Remember, a trained dog has the intellect of a child between three and seven years old. That's a very broad range when you really think about it. Base your very approximate determination of time on the age of your dog, both chronological and intellectual age.

Notice that I say very approximate because you will probably find that it takes longer than you want it to take. I guarantee that especially if you're using behavior modification for retraining, your dog will "test" you. His intelligence and personality (stubborn?) will determine the extent of this testing.

Essentially, he is saying to himself, "Does he really mean this? Does he really want me to change my behavior, or can I continue to get away with it if I just keep it up?"

Rehabilitation

Depending on the set of circumstances, he may be so surprised that he'll keep trying. For example, if suddenly you're just ignoring the behavior that you once threw a fit over, he'll be very confused.

"What's going on here?" he'll be wondering. "She always paid attention to me when I did this. I guess I better do it a little longer." Can you stand it? Hopefully, you can. Then as soon as he stops what he's doing, reward him. In the beginning the reward should be words and deeds (a "treat"). Gradually, you will be able to wean him off the deeds.

How to Tailor Behavior Modification To Your Dog

At least in the beginning, you'll want to start out with one behavior. While some experts say that you should start out with the most negative behavior (the "get the worst over with first" theory), I recommend just the opposite. My reasoning: Success breeds success. If you start out with the least disruptive behavior first, chances are you'll be successful faster. It'll be easier — for everyone — to adjust to the "new regime." So as you reach the more difficult levels of behavior, your dog — and you — will be used to the program. The quicker your own first success with these techniques, the more confident you'll feel.

Now for the rewards. What does your dog like? Does he love it when you pick him up and hug him or let him run around in the back yard? Will a Doggy Bone do?

Before you start up any behavior modification, sit down and make a list of things your dog likes. Now, prioritize them.

Think about his personality too — and yours. And the unique relationship the two of you have. If it's more than just you and him, you must make sure that everyone in the household is ready, willing, and able to put the program into effect. If you'll let your child watch TV an extra hour, but your spouse won't, which parent will your child seek out when the World Series is going into extra innings?

ROLE OF THE VETERINARIAN

Over the centuries a quiet revolution has occurred in the relationship between people and their dogs. Years ago, when dogs were used, to pull carts, hunt, herd, and guard, the human being was master. How the roles have reversed! The human is now the server and protector, and the dog has become the pet, the privileged and protected member of the family.

This change has brought new problems for dogs, problems of leadership, territorial rights, confinement, loneliness, and, as we have seen, boredom. Further, their greater dependence on people has caused dogs to become more susceptible to the whole array of emotional quirks that befall humans, including mental illness, stress-caused diseases, and behavioral problems.

Owing to these problems, the role of veterinarians has changed also. They no longer attend solely to the physical needs of the dogs; they also attend to the emotional health of the pets and the pet's human family. Many veterinarians specialize in treating animal behavioral problems.

Veterinarians today are better informed on the subject of normal and abnormal behavior in dogs. Besides the animal behavior courses now given in veterinary schools, the American College of Veterinary Behaviorists conducts continuing research and education. Veterinarians are not the only ones to need such information about animal behavior and customs. Human psychologists and psychiatrists can also benefit from the research, for animal behavior is a simpler, more direct expression of human behavior.

People and other animals share the same basic needs and the same motivations to fulfill their needs; thus they also share certain behavioral characteristics. Furthermore, the close companionship that exists between people and their dogs makes the study of canine behavior more germane to the issue of human psychology.

Dogs share the neuroticisms and abnormal behaviors of their human companions. Veterinarians see this in their clinics every day.

A recent survey indicates that between 8 and 10 percent of the animals brought to clinics have behavioral disorders, either inherited or caused by diet, disease, or injury, most arise from human conflict. In other words, the owner or some member of the family is often the cause of the dog's emotional problems. Without this conflict, the dog would be okay. Thus, along with keeping abreast of new medical and surgical therapies, veterinarians must keep in close tune with their human clients.

Rehabilitation

In this regard, veterinarians may play their biggest roles. To institute therapy, they must find a way to reduce the conflict. They must diagnose and treat the family's emotional problems in order to cure the dog. A renowned psychiatrist recently said much the same thing—that veterinarians are like pediatricians in that they are charged with treating the whole family. The dog is a helpless, inarticulate member of the family (just as a child is), and the doctor by necessity has to rely on family members not only for critical information in diagnosing a problem, but also for their cooperation in carrying out treatment. The dog's cure depends on both the veterinarian and the family.

In diagnosing emotional problems, veterinarians must learn more than just whatever outward signs the dog displays; they must learn what the dog means to the owner and what the owner expects from the dog. Some owners and their dogs have personality clashes—they were just not meant for each other. But fortunately, this is seldom the case; most owners and their dogs have a healthy love and respect for each other. Yet even in the best of homes, conflicts in feelings and expectations do arise. In these conflicts, veterinarians see that highly charged emotional currents exist between dogs and their owners. They witness the complex dynamics of personality and the interplay between pets and their human families. And they see that pets often mirror and localize human emotional illnesses, that peculiar and difficult pets often have peculiar and difficult owners.

In relying on human cooperation to carry out the appropriate treatments, veterinarians must teach families the proper ways to handle their pets. They share the owner's concern for their pets, which puts veterinarians in the enviable position of being able to help restore order and peace to trouble-ridden homes. Sometimes it is just a matter of instituting a little discipline or sharing more time with a pet. A veterinarian's advice is often so effective for pet problems that many owners gain valuable insight into childrearing. In such cases the advice is usually based on study, experience, and good sense.

The veterinarian's role is difficult indeed when the owners of their dog patients are themselves neurotic. It is very difficult to tell people that their own life-styles and attitudes must change before their dogs can be cured. To do so veterinarians must muster up all their diplomacy and tact, for a dog's health, and often an owner's, depends on it.

Although veterinarians often recommend an animal psychologist or a training program for an emotionally disturbed animal, many owners will not follow this course. This forces veterinarians further into the role of dog (and family) psychologist. While there are many treatment aids at their disposal, drugs and surgery among them, it is frequently found that good old-fashioned logic and lots of love and attention are the best of the veterinarian's magic cures.

Tranquilizers, steroids, hormones, and other drugs play an important role in veterinary medicine; and they can be extremely helpful in dealing with neurotic dogs. The fact remains, however, that not all animals react alike to drugs and that all drugs have potentially harmful side effects. Thus veterinarians are exceedingly cautious and selective in their use of drugs. They recognize the importance of drugs in treating mental illness, for the most part, is their ability to help occasionally, or as a temporary treatment to be used only until the proper training and rehabilitation can be initiated.

Luckily, most people respond to the genuineness of a veterinarian's concern about them and their dogs. Lucky, too, are the veterinarians, for they have unique opportunities to observe firsthand the rewards of positive reinforcement, to see that praise, affection, and attention can eradicate most emotional ailments in this stressful society of ours.

Society is just beginning to understand that veterinarians in companion-animal practice are more than luxury practitioners. They are responsible for helping maintain and improve the physical, mental, and emotional well-being of their human clients, in addition to caring for their animal patients. Many psychologists believe that in the near future veterinarians will become valuable members of mental hygiene teams. The reason for this rests on three facts:

The behavior and customs of dogs closely parallel those of people.

In mirroring the problems of people, dogs exhibit a simpler, more undisguised reaction to stress. By observing people and dogs together, we can detect more clearly the inner conflicts of people.

The love and responsibility that comes from caring for a pet has profoundly beneficial effects on human beings. One example of this is the renewed interest in life that many geriatric patients exhibit when they are given a puppy to cuddle and care for. Their memory improves, their attention to their surroundings becomes keener, and they experience a rejuvenated sense of worth, a sense of being responsible again. Even their appetites improve—all because they are able to love and be loved by that human like companion, a puppy.

ROLE OF THE TRAINER

Bruce Sessions has been a dog trainer for nearly twenty-five years. He was selected to train the Navy's first official marijuana-detector dogs, and was involved in the field of narcotic detection until his retirement. His services as a trainer have been requested from as far away as Mexico, Panama, and Bolivia. In 1971 he became training consultant to *International Dog Fancy Magazine*; he went on to become associate editor and finally senior editor. Over one hundred of his articles on dog care and training have been published in magazines and periodicals throughout the world.

Considered an expert in the field of canine behavior, his training school, Canine College, has an average annual enrollment of eight hundred dogs. His television show, *Canine College*, proved very successful.

In the essay that follows, he discusses the essential role of the trainer in rehabilitating problem dogs.

Why Training is Essential
By Bruce Sessions

It is easy for me to sit at a typewriter and tell you that you must assume the position of leader with your dog. Your first reaction will probably be, "How can I assume the position of leader when my dog won't even listen to me?" Or you might assume that you must adopt a master-slave attitude in order to become a leader, and since you're not capable of the type of behavior, the family dog is simply set free on the sea of incorrigibility.

Regardless of your present beliefs, attitudes, opinions—or anything else you may have read on the subject of dog behavior—an unruly dog is either leaderless, fancies himself to be the leader, or both! A dog will make his bid for leadership within the family (pack) between the ages of 12 and 16 weeks. Older dogs may also challenge your authority when they first come into your home. If that challenge goes unanswered, the dog will either assume the position of leader, or will be under the impression that there is no leader.

Without the feeling that a leader exists, such dogs have a tendency to revert to unsocialized, undomesticated, incorrigible beasts of the wild. In cases where the dog assumes the position of leader (with in the human family), members of the family end up being owned by the dog. The home and the occupants are the dog's possessions. In such cases, a dog will growl at a family member who comes too close while the dog is eating, will physically try to separate a husband and wife involved in an embrace, will run after and nip the children playing in the yard, and will try to control every situation within the sphere of the family circle.

A dog who assumed the position of leader will sexually mount the legs of the human family members or guests (who are encroaching on the dog's domain), whine excessively whenever attention is not being focused on him, and (if male) will hike his leg on anything and everything within the confines of the property—indoors and out!

Rehabilitation ─────────────────────────────

Once a dog has assumed the position of leader, he becomes extremely difficult to dethrone because he will oppose any effort by family members to do so. Sending that type of dog away to a training school is a waste of time and money. While a professional trainer would dethrone the dog quickly and teach him love and respect for the new leader—besides teaching him to respond to obedience commands—the situation would revert as soon as the dog was returned to his original owner.

The primary course of action for dog owners who have been kicked out as head of the household by the family dog is to institute some degree of obedience training. Just the commands "Come," "Sit," and "Stay" will be useful in helping you to reestablish your position as leader. Sure, it'll be tough at first; your dog isn't going to give up his leadership position gracefully. He likes it there, and he likes the fact that he's had his own way for so long. There will be opposition and, occasionally, a test of wills. But unless you win out in that opposition and show your dog that your will is stronger, you are destined to be nothing more than your dog's personal possession.

Dog psychologists would have to close up shop and specialize in something else if every dog were obedience trained and if everyone who owned a dog were cognizant of the big shoes he or she must fill as leader. In the wild and undomesticated state, the canine ran in packs. The leader of the pack was the strongest and the wisest. The others in the pack looked up to—and respected—the leader. Why should we expect it to be any different when a dog is placed in a family atmosphere, which becomes the dog's substitute pack? The strongest and the wisest will rule. The question is, however, shall it be human rule or canine rule? The answer, of course, is entirely up to the dog's owner. The solution to the question is obedience training. Therein lies the key!

"But my dog isn't guilty of being unruly," you say.

"Guilty of misbehavior once in a while, but not what you might call unruly." Malbehavior, as opposed to unruliness, is that type of destructive behavior that can't be considered constant. Rather it is intermittent. Malbehavior is brought on as a result of tensions stemming from boredom and monotony. Such dogs have usually been banished to the backyard after the newness or puppy stage has worn off. Thereafter the dog is ignored, except at feeding time. This feeding time becomes the highlight of the dog's day, and all other times of the day are boring, monotonous, and lonely. Consequently, holes are dug, garden hoses are chewed, fences are jumped, and the neighborhood is permeated with the sounds of excessive barking, the sight of turned-over trash cans, and much more.

Again, obedience training is the answer. Obedience training is the key that will unlock the mind of your dog and allow you to assume his control. An obedient dog is a joy to own. Obedience training is the avenue that will take you to new heights in you relationship with your dog, and both you and your dog will experience a new relationship with each other. Your dog will be happier and more secure, because he will have a leader that he can look up to—respect—and love.

Seeking Professional Dog Training

Dog trainers are generally called on after the owner has struggled along alone, asked the advise of friends and neighbors, read books and magazine on the subject, and then given up. Of course, by then the best time for training has usually passed. The cute puppy habits have developed into teenage problems.

Because dog training is not an exact science, training techniques must be adjusted to suit each individual dog. Some dogs are headstrong and require stricter methods, whereas the shy dog requires only a pointed finger with the word "No."

Even trainers themselves argue over the issue of positive and negative reinforcement versus correction and praise. Among the most competent trainers, none may approach the same behavior problem in the same manner, although they all achieve a common goal.

Dog trainers have found that 85 percent of all problems will disappear through basic obedience training sessions even when the sessions do not pertain directly to the behavior problem. They believe that the mental discipline that the dog receives helps eliminate some of the causes of misbehavior. They also believe that love itself will not cure a problem dog. It takes training combined with affection, and it takes consistency. There are training schools where a dog can be sent for several weeks or months, and there are weekly training classes where both the owner and dog are trained at the same time. I have seen well-trained dogs come back from training school only to be ruined by the owner's ignorance of obedience training or reluctance to follow the trainer's advice.

Before sending a dog to a training school or enrolling in a training class, observe the trainer's techniques. If he uses harsh methods and beats the dog into submission, look for another trainer, even if your dog is strong-willed and unruly. A bad trainer can ruin a dog. It is important to consult one whose methods seem functional yet gentle and, when needed, firm—but never cruel.

If you and your dog attend weekly obedience-training classes, you must hold daily practice sessions to reinforce the lessons. The dog trainer is actually training you to train your dog, and if the dog flunks the course, it is usually you, the owner, who is deficient.

ROLE OF THE CANINE PSYCHOLOGIST

The Importance of the Owner-Pet Interaction
By Ginger Hamilton, Ph. D., and Mollie J. Robbins, Ph. D.

There has been so much information on canine behavior made available to the lay public in the past several years that the dog owner is virtually overwhelmed with "expert" advice from a variety of sources. There are books, pamphlets, newspaper columns, and even recorded messages devoted to the subject of the care and training of dogs, especially companion dogs—the household pets whose chief function is to provide pleasure to the family. Also, of course, there is a vast store of knowledge freely imparted by next-door neighbors. Some of this information is frankly erroneous, much of it is misleading, and most of it is open to misinterpretation.

In the midst of all of this confusing contradiction, there is one common element—and almost total disregard for the effect of the owner-pet interaction process on the animal's behavior. If an owner factor is considered at all, it is generally in terms of how dog misbehaviors reflect the neurotic behaviors of, their owners. In other words, crazy dogs live with crazy people. The far more usual viewpoint, however, is that the problem resides exclusively within the animal, whether it has developed from "bad breeding," brain injury, faulty metabolism, or from some unknown physical cause. While such internal factors may be operating in certain cases, when it is medically determined that they are not, the owner is advised to use remedial methods ranging from specific conditioning techniques to a change of diet. When these procedures fail, the unacceptable behaviors are explained by the dog's stupidity or, again, craziness.

The study of canine psychology has evolved chiefly from two research areas, both of which seek deliberately to minimize the human variable. Dogs may be observed in the wild state, where no controls are imposed by the scientist, or they may be observed under the rigidly controlled conditions of the experimental laboratory. The behaviors of the family dog, on the other hand, are very much a function of the home environment in which the human variable assumes primary importance. Any attempt to understand the dog in the absence of close attention to the social circumstances in which he lives cannot succeed. Once the dog's apparently inexplicable behaviors are assessed within this framework, with all of its unique constraints, demands, and inconsistencies, the behaviors often lose their neurotic flavor and are recognized as learned ways of coping with the stresses of the animal's world.

It has been our experience that owners all too frequently are unaware of the impact of their behaviors, among themselves and toward the animal, on the animal. Generally they are nice, sensible people who know virtually nothing about the needs of this family member who is not meeting the family's expectations of a proper pet. They try to "follow the book" to no avail, the problems increase and, as their responses to the dog become progressively ambivalent, the original difficulties are compounded.

The term change agent, by which we refer to the pet owners, expresses our strong contention that owners must personally direct the social development and training of their animals. While this may be done under instruction, as in attending obedience classes, the owner must serve in the role of actual trainer. Since the dog's behavior must, to a reasonable extent, accommodate to the lifestyle of his owner, the owner is the only logical person to shape the behavior to what is desirable within that context. In this way the owner reaches a comfortable level of mutual accommodation, one that can be lived with

Rehabilitation

Kate Salley Palmer

realistically. An added advantage of the owner's personal involvement in the teaching process is that the positive bond between owner and pet is further cemented. Learning through working together is gratifying to each. By "owner" we mean the entire family, as all members must act in concert to produce the changes in question.

Our basic premise is that owner responsibility for the dog's welfare must exceed the provision of food, shelter, and medical treatment. This is not to imply that the dog should be the focus of all family concern. On the contrary, such an unhealthy emphasis is not responsible ownership. The dog does need affectionate attention to his normal requirements for exercise and play, approval for adjusting favorably to the household routine, and most significantly, well-defined limits, a structured, predictable existence.

Given a physically healthy animal, a consideration of the owner variable must be centered to any evaluation of a pet's behavior. Beginning with the premise that neither owner nor dog is crazy, knowing that behaviors do not occur in a vacuum, and recognizing that the dog is affected by his social environment, in our practice we are led to examine aspects of the owner-pet interaction in our search for factors that at least perpetuate the behaviors, if they do not foster them. In concentrating on this relationship, we strive to lay to rest some old myths and provide a clearer understanding of, and potentially more effective approach to canine behavior.

Seeking a Canine Psychologist

From a series of back-alley altercations in his youth, a dog named Butch developed an inferiority complex, which he expresses in various unsociable ways the worst of which is biting. His psychologist has given him a favorable prognosis, but the price of failure will run high for Butch. A court has ruled that if the handsome Boxer doesn't stop biting, he'll have to go to the gas chamber. Butch now is undergoing intensive therapy at the Canine Defense League's School for Problem Dogs in London.

Butch's story is not unusual. Today many dogs are suffering from the stress of modern living, and their concerned owners are seeking professional help for them. The few who receive counseling, however, represent only a small portion of the

Rehabilitation

many dogs who need such help. And even then, counseling is sought as a last resort—the last resort before euthanasia. The destructive behavior, bad toilet habits, and antisocial attitudes of these dogs are merely symptoms of their emotional suffering. And quite often, with a little counseling their fears and anxieties could be overcome and their good behavior restored.

Many dog owners, however, are reluctant to take their dogs to a psychologist for fear they will be blamed for the animal's misbehaviors. Some fear that they, too, will be analyzed. Actually, once the step is taken, owners usually enjoy the trips to a canine psychologist.

Besides the educational benefits, they offer an untraumatic means of bringing owners and their dogs closer together for harmonious living.

An owner's first step should be to seek advice on reputation and credentials, for many unlicensed persons pose as animal psychologists. A legitimate psychologist is usually one who has specialized in clinical psychology or physiological psychology and knows the relationship between human problems and dog problems.

For the initial visit, the psychologist usually will request that all members of the family be present, including all other pets, servants, and family relatives who are a part of the dog's environment. The animal is then allowed to wander freely around the conference room so that the consulting doctor can get a good picture of family-dog interactions.

Following the session, the advice might be treatment, including castration or spaying, obedience training, more love and affection, more exercise, or less confinement to one area of the house.

Dog psychologists estimate that at least 75 percent of the problems of urban dogs are caused by confinement, lack of exercise, and lack of companionship. So easy to cure! Even phobias, where dogs are turned into raving maniacs over some exaggerated fear, are fairly easy to deal with.

Most psychologists use relatively simple, easy-to-follow methods for rehabilitation, usually based on a behavior-modification technique, and their success rate is very high. Of the more than 5,000 neurotic dogs from Europe that were treated at Copenhagen's Sorensen Clinic last year, most were fit to return to their owners within one month.

Whenever possible, however, owners are used as therapists. Psychologists teach owners how to rehabilitate their pets and show owners the techniques of behavior modification. In addition, psychologists supervise the overall training programs and modify them according to the behavior of both pets and owners. Only in rare and extreme cases does a psychologist leave a dog untreated and suggest psychological help for the owner.

Preventing Problem Behavior

PROPER BREEDING

Breeding programs that have developed show dogs have also contributed to emotional abnormalities in dogs. The veterinary profession has become increasingly concerned with some of the abnormalities, both physical and mental, that dogs have been developing through generations of breeding.

Unfortunately, when a breed becomes popular, there is an influx of novices who are ignorant of the perfect specimen of the breed and haphazardly breed any two dogs so long as they have pedigree papers and possibly a few champions in their backgrounds. This is an inviting disaster for the breed. All would-be breeders should get to know the standards of perfection for a breed, attend many dog shows, and talk with knowledgeable breeders before starting a breeding program.

Good breeding kennel owners have a complete knowledge of the virtues and faults of all the ancestors of their dogs through at least three generations. They know the desired and undesired structural, temperamental, and intelligence qualities of various strains they are breeding. Studs and bitches are carefully chosen so as to avoid perpetuating weaknesses.

A bitch and stud do not, however, always give their puppies the qualities that they themselves show. They may carry recessive characteristics that will show up in later generations.

To me, there are three main things to breed for, listed in order of importance: temperament, mentality, and conformation.

Breeding for Good Temperament

Good temperament should be the first goal of breeders. Although temperament is basically controlled by genetic factors, not all temperamental failings are inherited. Environment must also be considered, since a dog's experiences after leaving the womb affect his personality. It is often difficult to decide which traits are inherited and which are acquired.

Environmental influences on temperament include such factors as a puppy's being reared in isolation, without individual care or affection, or a puppy's being the victim of bullying by larger and stronger litter mates. As we have seen, these experiences can affect the personality of the dog in later life and his reactions to humans. He may become shy, fearful, and even hostile. A nervous or shy mother can influence a puppy's behavior, even after he has become an adult. The mother's attitude toward people can affect each puppy's temperament.

Seeking to control temperament in a breeding program is a complex task. Good temperament is a dominant trait and will pass on to the puppies. Two dogs of good temperament may have a puppy who is not of good temperament; but a puppy of good temperament cannot have been bred from parents of bad temperament.

Every breeder should be on the lookout in the bitch and stud's behavior for timidity, fear of strangers, refusal to leave a familiar environment, sound shyness, fear of sudden change, sight shyness, and excessive activity. Any of these signs can be inherited in the offspring and could establish abnormal traits. Traits such as shyness or bad temper can be due to either environment or heredity. Animals showing temperamental or emotional instability should not be bred. They should be castrated or spayed.

Finding a Well Bred Puppy

It would be ideal if you, as the prospective owner of a puppy, could know not only the temperaments and physical and mental conditions of the puppy's parents, but of the grandparents as well. This is seldom possible. Most people buy a puppy with little or no knowledge of his pedigree or even of the environmental conditions under which he was born and bred. Even those who attempt to find out as much as possible about a puppy's heredity and early environment are not always successful. Some commercial dealers are too eager for a sale to have the time, or the inclination, to discuss heredity and environment. Even when they do, such dealers are not likely to disclose weakness or faults.

Under such circumstances, what can you as the purchaser of a puppy do in order to protect yourself from an unwise choice? I suggest two precautions (although neither is necessarily fool proof):

Purchase your puppy from a reputable kennel. If you are not sure which kennels are reputable, ask knowledgeable people (including a veterinarian and experienced dog owners).

When you choose a puppy from a litter, follow the suggestions in the "Puppy Selections Test."

CHOOSING THE RIGHT DOG

There is a right dog for everyone. Matching the right dog with the right people is the goal. The one advantage of purebred dogs over mongrels is that you can tell from breed characteristics what the dog's size and general temperament will be, although there are exceptions in every breed.

Choosing a Dog That Suits Your Temperament

Temperament and good health are the most important considerations in choosing a dog. Once good health is established, temperament—not appearance—should be the primary consideration. Don't choose a puppy just because he is cute.

As a prospective owner of a new puppy, you should try to match your requirements with a puppy whose breed characteristics are most likely to meet those requirements. You should choose one that you would enjoy living with for fourteen or fifteen years.

For example, if you are an emotional and rather nervous person, you should not choose a pup from among the terrier breeds, for they tend to be hyperactive dogs and might exacerbate your own nervousness.

One of my clients, a person I knew to be easily upset, chose a wire-haired terrier to be his companion. After a few months of unsuccessfully trying to live together, he brought the terrier to me.

"I had trouble sleeping before I got this dog," he said. "And now he keeps me up all night with his barking and his restlessness."

"Why did you choose a terrier?" I asked.

"Because I wanted a dog just like me, " he replied.

Obviously he had chosen a dog for the wrong reason. A person with his temperament should have chosen a calmer, more placid breed—perhaps one of the hounds, or a Dachshund or Poodle.

Never, never choose from a breed that you (or members of your family) will be afraid of. You have to be able to assume dominance over your dog.

Nor does it make sense for a small person to choose a large, exuberant dog who will be difficult to handle. Although some large or strenuous hunting breeds live apparently happy lives in small city apartments with limited exercise facilities, I suspect that many are neuroses-prone for that reason.

One-Person Dogs

For someone who wants a one-person dog, the Doberman Pinscher or the German Shepherd are reputed to be ideal. However, I feel that loyalty is not confined to any one breed.

Kate Salley Palmer

Preventing Problem Behavior ─────────────

Scottish Terrier owners often claim that the Scotties are one-man or one-woman dogs. The Dachshund has the same reputation. Certainly Chihuahua owners would contradict emphatically any attempt to impugn their pet's loyalty. I feel that the root of the matter is the love and care given to the individual dog by his owner.

Status Dogs

I go along with choosing a dog for beauty, grace, and courage that an owner may lack, so long as the dog is treated well behind closed doors. But choosing a dog simply as a status symbol, something to parade in public and treat miserably in private, is as deplorable as having a husband, wife, or lover for the same reason; and in many cases it is even more disastrous for the dog.

Choosing a Dog for Children

Although puppies and children usually get along well (they tend to relate like litter mates), it is best not to choose a toy breed for a household that has small children. Besides being fragile physically, these breeds are more often short-tempered and less tolerant of young children than larger, more placid dogs (such as Saint Bernards or Great Danes). Small, toy dogs will be much happier with mature adults.

Dachshunds, although small, are excellent with children. So are most of the hound breeds.

One Weimaraner I know, whose name is Becky, is so devoted to Sandy, the small child of her family, that she will not leave her for a moment when they are outside. One day Sandy's mother happened to look out the window. Sandy's tricycle was standing on the lawn. Sandy and Becky were nearby. At that moment one of the little girl's playmates hopped onto the seat of the tricycle. Without hesitation Becky approached the tricycle and very gently, but firmly, nudged the playmate. The little girl ignored the hint. Thereupon Becky, still in a gentle manner, pushed the interloper hard enough to unseat her. Obviously, Becky was concerned not only with protecting Sandy, but the child's property as well.

In choosing a puppy remember that he will require constant supervising. This is especially true if there are children in the family. Sometimes a strong-minded puppy tries to dominate a young child, which may create problems for both in later life. Also, rough, assertive children may be too strong for a puppy, both physically and emotionally. Be sure a child is old enough to handle a puppy before you leave them together without adult supervision.

Puppy Selection Test

Dog psychologists and trainers have scientific means of determining a puppy's future behavioral characteristics. By the age of six weeks, each puppy in a litter can be evaluated for future temperament. There are several tests that the layman can perform.

- Walk toward a puppy. If he retreats with his tail between his legs, don't consider buying him. If he approaches with his tail wagging, consider him, as he shows a liking for humans.
- Pick up the puppy and hold him above your head for about thirty seconds. Talk to him in a soft tone. If he struggles, raise your voice. If he does not respond to your command and calm down, do not choose him. The test should be repeated holding the puppy on his back and also in a prone position on the floor, and then on his side. It is important to know if the puppy will be submissive to his human family or try to dominate it.
- Clap your hands. If the puppy comes, he is normal and mentally healthy animal; if he runs away or is frightened, he will not be a good companion dog.
- Walk away. If the puppy follows in a romping and friendly fashion, he will make a good pet.
- Stroke him from the top of his head and along his back. The independent dog will try to get away; the less dependent one will accept fondling. A highly dominant one will growl and try to bite. The last kind will be an undesirable pet and difficult to train.

A puppy who will not respond to voice commands or petting will usually end up having behavior problems.

Choosing an Adult Dog

Before acquiring an adult dog, you should find out all you can about the dog and his previous owners. It might save a lot of heartaches later on.

Preventing Problem Behavior ——————

Check on the dog's temperament: Is he quiet, active, nervous, calm, protective, overaggressive?

Watch the dog closely. See how he reacts to people and to other animals.

Some adult dogs adjust well to a new home; others do not. But I believe that a dog can adjust to a new family at any age if he is basically of sound disposition and if he is treated properly. Every day people adopt dogs of all ages from animal shelters and dog pounds, and fine owner-pet relationships are achieved. In living with an adult dog, as in raising a puppy, loving care goes a long way toward establishing a rewarding association. But it must be emphasized that disposition is just as important in the choice of an adult dog as it is in the choice of a puppy.

Getting a Companion for Your Dog

To prevent loneliness and the resultant boredom and bad habits, a companion will often work wonders for your dog. Overweight and lazy dogs will also be helped by a companion. They will get more exercise and usually become more mentally alert. The most likely companion is another dog, although if you like cats, you should not rule them out. Most cats and dogs get along fine when they are brought up together.

Choosing a Second Dog

It is generally not a good idea to buy two or more litter mates at the same time. Raising two puppies at the same time inadvertently causes you to give less personal attention to each puppy; and the puppies, in turn, will relate less intimately to you. Usually they will spend more time playing with each other and be less people-oriented. They will be less responsive to your commands even though they are happy and well adjusted.

It is a better idea to get one puppy and then, after he or she has become well socialized, is responsive, and affectionate with you, choose a second puppy from another litter.

As for the gender of the two dogs living together in a family, a male and a female almost always get along well. One or both should be neutered to avoid problems during heat periods. An unaltered male usually does well with a spayed female. In a household with two male dogs, the occasional fight might

214

result until one dog dominates the other. Two females do not fight as much, but they do show signs of jealousy (perhaps more often than males), which results in occasional fretting and pouting.

An older dog usually gets along well with a frisky pup, especially when the pup is of a different gender. Indeed, as mentioned, the older dog often is rejuvenated by the playfulness of the younger companion, although he may occasionally tire of the pup's persistent attention.

REARING A PUPPY FOR GOOD BEHAVIOR

There is a great need among dog owners to learn the proper early rearing practices designed to prevent problems before they occur. In principle, these practices are similar to those advocated for raising children—early handling and fondling, proper discipline started at the right time, and consistency.

Early handling and fondling of your puppy will stimulate normal behavior. He will become accustomed to his environment at an earlier age—to noises, lights, human voices, and being held by people. This early physical contact will also help him become more responsive and adaptable to humans than dogs who are not handled until after twelve weeks of age. Trainers of guide dogs have learned from years of experience that if a puppy is not socialized before he is twelve weeks of age, the grown dog will be useless for guiding blind people.

Much of what is known about human behavior and personality was first learned by experimentation with animals. In one such experiment, designed to study what influence early contact would have on learning behavior, Scotties were reared in partial isolation. They turned out to be almost untrainable, and their social behavior was described as "aberrant in a way hard to describe." Besides responding poorly to learning tasks and abnormally to pain stimuli, they showed abnormal social development. They were dominated by normal dogs; they would permit another dog to eat simultaneously from the same food dish (something a normal Scottie will not allow); and they reacted to familiar and unfamiliar people alike with a strange approach-avoidance behavior. After they were removed from isolation, some of their abnormal behavior diminished with time; the behavior did not disappear completely, and their personalities remained grossly abnormal. From many studies, it became clear that the behavior of the adult, whether it be dog, human, or bird, depends fundamentally on the experiences of infancy.

Because dogs mature much faster than humans do, it is the first sixteen weeks that are especially important in rearing a puppy for good behavior. Each week from birth brings new perceptions that adapt the growing puppy to his environment. In the following pages, the puppy's ability for social development is divided into the critical periods of these sixteen weeks. Although the task of socialization does not end at week 16, these are the most vulnerable periods in establishing good behavior in a puppy.

Critical Periods—and Proper Handling

Birth to week 3

During his first three weeks of life, a puppy reacts only to his needs for warmth, food, and his mother. But even in this early stage of his development, gentle handling by humans is important. Daily handling is ideal; but if this is impossible, a schedule should be arranged to handle a puppy at least every other day. A properly handled puppy will benefit emotionally from this direct contact.

Weeks 3 and 4

A puppy's brain and nervous system begin to develop during the third week. In this very critical period of his social development, he will become aware of his surroundings, and daily gentle handling helps to give him an emotional stability that will help him cope with stressful conditions. He should not be exposed to any rough handling, strangers who may scare him, or loud noises. These can cause stress and have a bad influence on him, because his nervous system is developing and bad experiences will be remembered. In general, a puppy needs the security of his mother during this period. However, if the bitch is a shy, nervous one, puppies should be removed from her when they are three weeks old so that they will not take on her problem characteristics. Shyness, wetting, overaggressiviness, or overdependence can develop while a pup is still in the whelping box. The proper handling of a puppy during weeks 3 and 4, however, will prevent many of the problems that we see in older dogs. Each puppy should be handled about twice a day, and a child should also handle the puppies every day or so. It is never too early to give puppies love and care.

Weeks 5 through 7

Sociability develops a puppy's awareness of other dogs and people. In this critical period of a puppy's life, he will begin to recognize people and to respond to voices. His ability to be trained is developed during this time. The end of the seventh week is the best time to remove a puppy from his mother and litter mates. If not done then, he may become too dependent on his mother; or if left with his litter mates, he may become either too independent or too submissive. Among litter mates older than seven weeks, one may tend to become a bully (to take over at the top of the "pecking order"); and if this happens, the others will learn to submit and may develop into shy dogs. Again, handling a puppy is very important in order for them to develop normal adult behavior.

It has been shown that puppies handled after four weeks of age are highly extroverted, social toward humans, and dominant in their play with other puppies. Compared with unhandled puppies, a properly handled pup performs better in problem solving and is more aware of his surroundings.

Weeks 8 through 12

This is the most important period in developing a puppy's ability to establish a bond with humans and to be trained. His personality and traits will be formed during this time. He will learn a lot in this period of his life—things that will be permanently fixed in his brain.

Old enough now to begin being disciplined, he can learn simple commands such as "Come," "Sit," "Stay," and "No." This is also the age to start housebreaking a pup. Loud noises, noisy children, other animals that are too rough, and stressful situations should be avoided, for fear responses are learned during this period.

A puppy should not be shipped during this period. He should be shipped either before he is six weeks old or after he is twelve weeks old. Puppies also should not be shipped the same day they are weaned from their mother, because leaving the mother for the first time will be a stressful situation. Wait at least three days, until they have settled down in their new environment without the mother.

Weeks 13 through 16

This is still an impressionable age for a puppy; and what he needs most from his new owner is love, attention, discipline, socialization, and security. He will attempt to find his place in his human family, either as a dominant member, if allowed, or as an obedient, submissive one. He will see if he can push. But during this period, and until six months of age, a properly handled puppy will show few fears or phobias, will be inquisitive, and will show signs of higher intelligence.

Disciplining a Puppy

In raising a litter of puppies, we should imitate the normal mother dog. Although she is extremely affectionate toward and tolerant of her puppies, she is quick to discipline them when they do wrong.

She will give them a warning growl, a direct stare, and eventually a quick nip to keep them in line. Your dogs need the same type of discipline from you.

Strict discipline of puppies, however, should not start until after twelve weeks of age. You can injure a puppy emotionally if you spank him too hard before that age. Before then, discipline your puppies with loving care, firm but not so drastic that a permanent scar is left on their emotional stability.

There are many cases of child abuse today. For some strange reason, some parents discipline their children so forcefully that it results in physical damage and sometimes, in severe cases, in the death of the child. Humans can be more sadistic than animals, as has been shown in the past. Psychologists tell us that violence in discipline begets violence in the one being punished. Most often, child abusers were themselves victims of abuse. Likewise, cruel and harsh treatment of a puppy will make him fear and hate people—and may produce a vicious adult dog. Therefore, in disciplining a young puppy, do it gently but firmly. If punishment is carefully administered, it has a good and lasting effect on the puppy's behavior.

Preventing Problem Behavior

These are three ways to establish superiority over a puppy without hitting him: Stare directly into his eyes; shake him by the scruff of the neck; close his jaws while you push him to the ground.

A good age to start a puppy on some serious training is when he is eight weeks old. First, teach him to come. Use the basic tools of discipline: praise and punishment; repetition and consistency.

Problems of the Undisciplined Puppy

The most serious problems develop during the critical periods of a puppy's growth (during the first sixteen weeks of life). These problems can affect his behavior throughout his adult life.

When acquiring a new puppy, some people will give him free run of the house and never discipline him. The puppy then assumes that he is the "leader of the pack" and becomes the dominant member of the family. When this pup grows up, he sometimes becomes impossible to handle. By the owner's lack of knowledge or indifference to the upbringing of the puppy, he has created a monster. Such dogs may turn on their owners and become aggressively defensive of their home territory, hurting human visitors as well as other animals. It is a simple result of the human being submissive to his dog.

The Destructive Puppy

Most destructive puppies do their bad deeds out of boredom. They are not necessarily juvenile delinquents when they chew and destroy things. This is part of normal, healthy puppies' development. Before leaving a puppy alone in the home, it is a good idea to take him for a long walk—in other words, tire him—so he will nap while you are out. You might also do this before taking a puppy on a car trip.

The Nervous or Shy Puppy

Never be too lenient or too harsh with a nervous puppy. Persistence and diligent supervision are required. Puppies are great imitators, and a shy or timid dog is often reflecting those tendencies in his owner.

Also, it pays to choose a puppy's companions wisely. If there are any with bad faults, keep the puppy away from them as you would keep a child away from a juvenile delinquent. A car-chasing dog will soon teach your puppy to chase cars also.

The Hand-shy Puppy

Do not grab at a puppy who is panicky; you can scare him and he may develop hand-shyness. Talk to him first. Lean down, or better still, crouch down so that your large size doesn't scare him before you reach to pick him up. Do it gently, with no loud noises and screaming.

Talk him into coming near you, and you will be able to touch him gently. Puppies like gentleness, in touch and voice.

A shy puppy can be taught to make a good adult dog, but if he is shy and a fear biter, he may develop into a vicious dog. Be careful with him, or you might have to put him to sleep if he becomes untrainable.

The Vicious Puppy

If a puppy five or six weeks old barks and growls at people—an abnormal aggressive sign in such a young dog—watch out. He will probably grow up to be vicious. Such a pup should be put through a program of intensive socialization with strangers as well as family members.

Everyone should make an effort to play with the puppy and handle him gently, with no rough games such as tug-of-war or others where he uses his mouth. Such games would encourage his biting tendencies. Take the puppy with you when you go shopping so that he can get used to lots of people and a noisy atmosphere. Puppies who lead a sheltered life in the backyard are not prepared for the noises and excitement of modern civilization. Expose your puppy to many people at an early age.

Most biting dogs are not simply spoiled dogs. They began, as puppies, by growling and got away with it; then they tried snapping and were not punished; and so they took their first bite. Once a dog has learned he can get away with biting a human, he no longer can be trusted, for he will bite again and again. In dealing with a puppy who growls or bites, you must make him understand that you are in control, he is not. Start by taking the puppy's food dish away when he is eating. If he growls, pick him up by the scruff of the neck so that his front feet are off the ground, then slap him upward under the chin. Scold him severely. Having scolded him, make up to him immediately, and play with him again. If he starts to get rough, a warning may be enough. Repeat the play procedures later in the day, and three or four times in the followings days. In this way a puppy will form the habit of never getting too rough with anyone and of tolerating roughness from small children who do not know they are being rough.

How to Make a Puppy Neurotic

When he does something wrong, scold him using his name. This will establish a bad association with his name. In fact, the puppy should associate his name with friendliness. When you scold him using his name, he becomes confused because then his name means something bad. Don't confuse him. Do not use his name when you are scolding him.

When he does something wrong, punish him severely whenever you get around to it. This is wrong. Do not be variable, be consistent. Do not delay punishment even two to five minutes. Be quick to praise him and be quick to punish him.

When you find a mess in the house, punish him severely. This stimulates defense reflexes and only creates more problems.

When you have on good clothes, don't let the puppy jump on you, but let him jump on you when you have on old clothes. This confuses your puppy, because he doesn't know the difference between old and new clothes.

Allow your puppy to chew on your old shoes but punish him if he chews on your new shoes. The puppy can't tell old from new shoes. Don't give him any shoes to chew on.

Training Rules

The best time for training the puppy is before he is fed, so that he will be looking forward to the reward of a good meal.

- For a satisfactory training program, the puppy should have complete confidence in you. Never train a puppy while you are in a bad mood or have lost control of your emotions. Don't ever lose patience and kick a puppy in anger or throw things at him. He is still like a baby and cannot be expected to grasp everything at once.

Preventing Problem Behavior

- Allow only one member of the family to teach him commands and tricks. Once he has learned them all thoroughly, then others can help.
- Always talk to a puppy before you approach him. This goes for any dog. Let him know you are his friend.
- Don't confuse a puppy by giving him inconsistent commands.
- Don't punish the puppy with a training lead or other training object, or he will become fearful of training.
- Don't allow the training periods to get so long that the puppy becomes tired or bored. You should not train a puppy more than 10 minutes at a time, and don't expect him to remember everything you're trying to teach him. It is best to do it many times a day but in short sessions.
- A puppy should never be picked up by his ears—as one of our Presidents found out, much to his chagrin.
- Every puppy should be taught some basic commands; the most important command for a puppy to understand is "No." You have to make him know you mean it. "Quiet" should also be taught early in his life—and it should make him stop making noise immediately.

The Human-Dog Relationship

DOGS AND THEIR HUMAN COMPANIONS

A dog doesn't talk back. That's something that is very difficult to find in human relationships. A dog may not talk back, at least with words, but studies indicate that 98 percent of dog owners talk to their pets beyond giving simple commands and consider their dogs members of their families. Because the relationship between humans and dogs is relatively simple, it is easier for many people to form close relationships with dogs than with humans.

The human factor is indelibly stamped on our canine companions. It is unavoidable that our pets will try to behave as we do. After all, we are their companions, their teachers, their disciplinarians, their masters, their surrogate parents—in other words, their models. Because our dogs mimic us so adroitly, they become extensions of our own personalities, but they are usually more obvious, and less discreet. For example, if we raise Cain at the neighbor's dog for urinating on a particularly sensitive shrub, our dogs will begin to carry on with equal hostility at the intrusion. But our dogs will not discriminate between species of shrubbery, and they will not shy from voicing their disapproval when the intruder's owner is present, as we would do. Their indiscriminateness is due to their childlike intelligence (at maturity, their intelligence is only that of three- to seven-year-old children). They are perpetual children—some dogs now are even bred for infant like characteristics, such as oversized skulls, and large eyes—in constant observation of us but unable to discriminate as we do and as our human children eventually learn to do. This is why dogs mirror our behavior so well—their childlike view of the world prevents many of the subtleties and nuances of behavior that humans acquire with age. They are open and direct, and their behavior is for the most part, undisguised.

The Human-Dog Relationship ───────

Thus, here we are human models—not a single one of us completely "right" or perfect—letting our dogs show off our idiosyncrasies and neuroses to our friends, neighbors, and to the world.

What Our Dogs May Reveal About Us

Psychologists have gained insight into human personality and behavior by studying our relationships with our pets. They say that even our choice of pets may reveal much about us. Dr. F. G. Nathan, a psychologist, says that in choosing a dog, people almost always respond to a deeply hidden inner picture they have of themselves, that the dog represents an extension of what the person is or would like to be, that because of this, the dog is a person's "best mirror."

Based on this, Dr. Nathan and other psychologists have compiled a list of human characteristics fitted to particular dog breeds. For instance, Poodle owners tend to pamper and fuss over their pets and harbor the unconscious wish to be a child again (they baby their dog because they themselves wish to be babied). Owners of Doberman Pinschers wish to be thought of as ferocious, tough people. Irish Setter owners tend to show off. Bulldog owners are ultraconservative and sexually prudish. And so on.

This sort of labeling can, of course, get out of hand, and even Dr. Nathan stipulates that these appraisals are only correct about 30 percent of the time. Nevertheless, from my own experience with dog owners, I am convinced that many people do choose a dog they feel will fit into their image of who they are or who they would like to be, but that usually is not the whole story. For example, men, especially small men, do tend to choose large dogs. And shy, meek people do often choose large, aggressive dogs. They want the dog to compensate for what they themselves lack. Opposites attract even in picking out a dog. On the other hand, the choice need not be so Freudian. There are practical as well as image-enhancing reasons for choosing a small breed. And conscientious housekeepers are practical in choosing a small breed that does not shed much hair or have strong body odors. Still, many men and women will not choose the Poodle (almost odorless and not a hair shedder) because they stereotype this type of dog with prissy ladies who drive pink Cadillacs. For most people, there

are both practical as well as image-seeking considerations involved in their choices.

One type of image-seeking owner, however, invariably causes trouble. This is the status seeker. I have had to find homes for many exotic breeds because the owners belatedly decided that the unique looks of stylish dogs were not worth the time and care involved in ownership. (Status seekers are usually self-centered and not likely to devote much time to looking after a dog). Status seeking and pedigree alone do not make for a happy marriage, whether for humans or dogs.

What We Expect from Our Dog

Most important, however, for understanding people and their relationships with dogs is not the choice of breed for a pet but the expectations associated with having a pet. What does the person expect to get from the relationship? In other words, why does the person want a dog? The answer to these questions often indicates how problems arise. The expectations were inappropriate.

The Human-Dog Relationship

Certainly companionship and protection are among the basic needs of most people. And this is marvelously right. The dog that baby-sits, protects the children, and teaches them something of what nature is all about is a valuable part of the family tradition. Outside the traditional family role, the dog can offer vitality, a sense of stability, and a sense of being needed—for couples without children; for middle-aged parents whose children have left home; for working, single persons; and for widowed people.

Some expectations, however, are unhealthy. They spring from unhealthy desires, and they lead to neurotic and badly adjusted dogs. The most outrageous is the example already given, the expectation that the dog will be a status symbol. Another example is the repressed-type person who wants to dominate, to wield power over a dog. Such dogs generally end up as either spineless, submissive creatures or as vicious, fear-biting outcasts.

At other times, an owner has reasonable expectations for a dog, but somewhere along the way the relationship degenerates into one that is bad for the dog. Most owners of problem dogs fall into this category. These people are genuinely fond of their

pets, but because of their own inconsistency or overindulgence or just lack of dog sense, they let the dogs get control of them. Frequently owners buy a pet for their children without realizing that they are actually taking on another "child" to raise. Then, when the tasks of housebreaking, feeding, and midnight walks fall to them, they just can't handle the added responsibilities. There are, of course, varying degrees of this; but the worst cases end up with an owner-neglected, child-abused dog—or an abandoned one.

How We Affect Our Dog

Even though love and companionship are good reasons for wanting a dog, these two ingredients alone are not enough to engender a healthy relationship. The fact remains that owners who have personality problems (and we all do) are likely to see these same problems in their pets. Again, there are varying degrees of how severely our own quirks will affect our dogs, and there are varying degrees of how capable our dogs will be at coping. The following section lists how certain extreme personality types are likely to affect their dogs.

The Human-Dog Relationship

Overpermissive, Overindulgent Owners

Dogs, like children, do not really want to have their own way, and they grow up "deprived" when they have such owners. Dogs demand guidance and lose all sense of reason for being when this is not given.

Overloving, Overprotective Owners

They provide a great environment for pets to luck into until they achieve maturity, and then it is downhill all the way. The dogs lose all ability to cope.

Overaggressive, Egotistic Owners

The dogs are subject to nagging, underloving, overstrictness, and unrealistic demands for perfection. These dogs are usually in a family concerned with status seeking—something to master, control, show off. The dogs grow up confused, not knowing what is expected of them. More likely, they will be abandoned when they become inconvenient.

The Human-Dog Relationship

Self-Indulgent Owners

These owners consistently overfeed, fail to train or supervise adequately, and usually wait too long before bringing their dogs to a veterinarian. Such persons do not dedicate themselves to what is best for their animals, even though they claim to do so.

Mean, Vicious, Sadistic Owners

These owners tend to cow their dogs to such an extent that the animals spend their lives in fear. Or they live up to their owners" wishes and become mean and vicious. In some cases, the relationship resembles a game of Russian roulette between owners and pets.

Shy, Timid, Fearful, Self-Demeaning Owners

For such owners, dogs can be a great consolation and help develop self-confidence—they are something to love and to love back. But generally such people will use a dog as a leaning post (like the meek little man who has a German Shepherd or Great Dane to ease his fears). Such

Kate Salley Palmer

pets grow up to have the shy, timid, fearful feeling of their owners. Or, because of under socialization, the dogs become overly protective and aggressive.

Overemotional, High-strung Owners

Dogs can have a calming effect on people given to hysteria and temper tantrums—they provide the owners with something lovable to respond to. But the emotional instability of such owners can rub off on their dogs; and the dogs, too, can become subject to temper tantrums and hysteria. During such seizures, the dogs can be vicious.

Eccentric Owners

Many eccentrics are well-meaning people who often neglect themselves and their families to collect animals they believe they are rescuing from hunger or ill treatment. This can lead to coexistence in filth and squalor.

A good example of eccentricity was shown by a client of mine. Disillusioned by three failed marriages, she lived very happily with her fifteen dogs. She claimed that dogs were more loyal and trustworthy than men. All of them lived together as one big happy family.

The Human-Dog Relationship

Most dogs are dependent on people for their survival. However, there is the case of a woman dependent on her two dogs for her own life. At least that is the excuse this lady uses for not killing herself.

Whenever she drinks too much, she phones to say that she is about to kill herself and wants me to look after her two dogs when she is gone. Over and over I explain to her that nobody could take care of her dogs as well as she does, that she must stay alive to look after them. This speech of mine gives her the will to live until she hits the bottle again.

Two other types of owners are likely to run into problems if not warned of the pitfalls in their ways of handling their dogs. Although these owners do not necessarily have the extreme personality traits just mentioned, their expectations sometimes far exceed what a dog can provide. One type treats a dog as a human equal; the other, as a surrogate child.

Dogs as Human Equals

These owners relate to their dogs as they would to human beings. They usually view their dogs as companions and as unquestionable sources of affections and appreciation, and

Kate Salley Palmer

rightly so. But sometimes they seem to forget that dogs are different from people and should be treated as such. The anthropomorphic outlook can be useful and helpful to a lonely person; and yet, if excessive it may lead to problems for a dog's psyche.

The most frequent rationalization of such owners is "My dog knows better." They thereby assume that a dog is equal to a human in knowing right from wrong. Then they punish their dogs accordingly. This is a mistake. A dog who is repeatedly punished and does not know why, will eventually turn into a bewildered and emotionally disturbed animal.

Some of these people may also vent their own frustrations on a dog. One woman I knew would get a little tipsy from the wine she sipped during her gourmet cooking sessions. Unfortunately, the wine would bring out the worst of her suspicions about the ineptitude of government bureaucrats. As she would get increasingly vituperative, she would turn to her dog for moral support. "Alfred! Don't you realize what this policy means to our nation? How can you sit there with those

Kate Salley Palmer

poor dumb, trusting eyes, like our foreign policy leaders do—when you've got to know the utter jeopardy we're being placed in!" And on she'd go, while poor Alfred, thinking he'd done something bad, would start whining and howling. With this mournful support, the woman would reach new crescendos of emphasis in her bellowing condemnations of political leaders. By the time I was consulted, her gourmet sipping had become a nightly event, and Alfred had become a nervous wreck.

Dogs as Surrogate Children

Dogs often respond to their owners with a love and a loyalty rarely seen among human offspring. Thus, that dogs should be used as surrogate children is very "right" for many people. Childless couples, single men and women, widows and widowers, and the elderly, all benefit from the unconditional love bestowed on them by pets. Even gay couples say that pets can add normalcy to their childless lifestyles.

Dogs need to benefit from a relationship that puts them more in the role of a child, for they are indeed like children and need the patience and attention given to human children. But also, like children, too much pampering and babying will

233

The Human-Dog Relationship

make them lose their sense of identity and independence. Although the term "too much" is difficult to define, I must point out that excessive pampering will turn some dogs into demanding, house-soiling, jealous pets.

One childless couple actually satisfied their need for parenthood by dressing their dogs in children's clothing, seating them at the dinner table, and talking to them in baby talk. They needed desperately to be needed and to care for someone. The dogs loved the attention and chasing rabbits was the furthest thing from their minds.

Some owners, especially some elderly ones, seem to favor such demanding behavior in their pets. It gives them a purpose for prolonging the nesting instinct. They have to cook special foods for the dog, they have to clean up after the dog, they have to exercise the dog—they maintain a rigid routine to keep the dog happy. And it keeps the owners happy! I think that owners who need this type of relationship are justified in having it, for it doesn't really hurt their dog or the person.

One lady I know does indeed treat her pet as a human. The dog never is allowed outdoors and so performs her toilet

necessities on newspapers in the bathroom. As soon as the dog is finished, she jumps up on the toilet seat and whines until her Missy wipes her bottom with toilet tissue.

Another lady wants her pet to be as clean as she is, so every morning when she takes her shower, the dog accompanies her. Little does she realize that all the money she is spending on medical bills for the dog's itchy skin is due to the excessive bathing. A dog's skin can't take excessive soaping that a human's can.

For those owners, however, who want a surrogate child but do not want a demanding pet, I recommend that strict training for obedience and house etiquette be instituted during the puppy days and maintained consistently throughout the dog's life, with coddling and extra affection given as rewards for good behavior.

In summary, there are many reasons for wanting and needing a pet, some obvious, some not as obvious. The companionship between dog and human goes back as far as recorded history, and farther. Not only do the drawings of cavemen show the dog as a member of the clan, but

235

archaeologists have found Neolithic remains indicating that dogs shared human habitations in prehistoric times. The ambivalence that some present-day owners feel because they need their dogs is perhaps due to their not understanding this historic role shared between humans and dogs. In any case, whatever our needs, it is only when they lead to abuse and neglect of our dogs, or to a denial of the dogs own animal instincts, that the relationship suffers. Further complicating this are our inability to cope with our own neuroses and personality problems, especially when we see them in our pets.

DIET AND THE NEUROTIC DOG

Many dogs manipulate their owners until they get the food they want. They go on hunger strikes and will not eat anything until they get a filet mignon or New York strip steak. Once the pet gets his way, his behavior pattern is set. He will expect this tasty morsel all the time. Usually, the small toy breeds will pick out the chicken or the beef and leave all the rest. Many will eat chicken and nothing else. Then their diets have to be supplemented with vitamins and minerals or they develop a nutritional deficiency. Many dogs, and again especially the smaller breeds, will only eat the foods that their owners are eating. They think of themselves as human beings and want to be treated as such.

Although I do not believe in starving a dog into eating the food you choose for him, I believe a compromise has to be worked out. You should give such a pet a basic dog food interlaced with juicy morsels.

Be careful, though. Every time a dog stops eating, it doesn't mean he is putting on an act. Most of the time he is sick. Only occasionally does a dog stop eating to gain attention or another type of food. If his poor appetite persists more than twenty-four hours, have your veterinarian examine the dog and make the decision.

The Overeater

Statistical evidence is now available to prove what many veterinarians have long suspected: People who are overweight are more likely to have dogs who are overweight than people who are not overweight. In short, fat people tend to have fat

The Human-Dog Relationship

Kate Salley Palmer

dogs. Like their children and themselves, their dogs are overfed. The only way to get these owners interested in their dog's weight is by instilling a sense of guilt. Obese people sometimes actually try to make other members in their family, including their dogs and cats, obese because the presence of a thin person or animal makes them uncomfortable. If everyone in the family is fat, then that is the norm and nobody notices it. Also, some people feel that "plump" means healthy. You hear the expression "pleasantly plump." Mothers especially think that children and puppies should be plump. They may not know that habits and "fatness" carry over into the adult's way of life.

Some people believe that when they hear a dog's stomach grumbling the animal is hungry. They immediately feed the dog. Although these intestinal sounds are quite normal in dogs, the uninformed owner thinks they are signs of distress of an empty stomach. The result can be an obese dog.

Some dogs seem to always be hungry and will eat anything. A friend of mine has a dog like that. Every night near the end of dinner, the dog tries to steal someone's napkin. When she succeeds, she eats the entire paper napkin. It is hardly necessary to say that the dog is obese.

Kate Salley Palmer

Dogs on Their Owner's Diet

Dogs are at the mercy of their owners. Their dietary habits—either overeating to the point of obesity or dieting to the point of emaciation—often mimic those of their owners, not necessarily from preference but from necessity. They simply eat what they're given.

I have known several owners who have inflicted the same dietary restrictions on their dogs that they do on themselves. One woman gave her dog a daily dose of her own thyroid tablets because she believed her dog suffered from an underactive thyroid as she herself did. When I examined this nervous, emaciated dog, I soon became aware of the woman's diagnosis and treatment of her pet.

Periodically I see owners who give their own diet pills, which contain benzedrine and other appetite suppressants, to their dogs. I'm always surprised by this; but again, like the lady who gave her dog thyroid pills, I suppose they think that what's good for them is good for their dogs.

Another example is the client who took part in the rice diet program started at Duke University and who conscientiously maintained her dog on a similar sodium-free diet of rice and diuretics. The owner seemed quite pleased with her dog's thin, lithe body and didn't understand why he was sick. The dog's "lithe" look was due to his emaciated condition, and his sickness must have been likewise provoked. Nutritious food soon restored the dog's health.

There is another dog who is the victim of his owner's dieting and has become obese because he is given all the food that the owner doesn't eat.

Vegetarians, likewise, can't accept the fact that dogs need protein—especially meat. Many of their dogs resemble half-starved refugees, or they are overactive, nervous wrecks.

High-sugar or high-carbohydrate diets tend to make dogs more active and, in some cases, nervous. Just a little bit of sugar or candy will make a hyperkinetic dog go crazy with wild and bizarre antics. Also other nutritional deficiencies will cause dogs to exhibit abnormal behavior or to crave unnatural food substitutes.

Don'ts About Diet

- Don't overfeed a dog. Dogs are resourceful little beggars, so don't be taken in by their tricks. If several daily feedings are necessary, as they are in puppies, limit the amount of food to small servings. Remember, it is quality, not quantity that you are striving for.

- Don't underfeed your dog either. To be healthy and active, dogs need sufficient calories and nutritional substances.

- Don't completely ignore your dog if he becomes a finicky eater. It probably is a passing fancy, but he may be sick. Have him examined by a veterinarian.

- Don't give your dog foods that are high in sugar. Dogs like treats, and like children, they are fond of candy. A better treat for your dog, however, is a beef stick or a dog biscuit, or even an occasional nibble of cheese or saltines. But please, no sugar.

- Don't prescribe pills or drugs for your dog. Many drugs are given according to body weight, so you may overdose your dog. Besides, most drugs are just as harmful to dogs as they are to people. Just because you need a drug does not mean that your dog needs it too. That kind of thinking may end up killing the dog.

LOSING A PET

Owners grieve over the death of a pet. Some cry; some men as often as women, get hysterical. This is normal. It is normal and healthy to let your inner feelings out. Unfortunately, some owners prolong their anguish for weeks and months, getting into a depressed state, even to the point of mentioning suicide. Veterinarians are often called upon to give psychological counseling to pet owners who cannot get over their grief. Often such an owner is associating the death of his pet with the recent loss of a close family member. The pet's death comes as a double shock. Others prolong their grief because the pet was a surrogate child for them.

Some owners prolong their grief or they experience intense physiological reactions (nausea, vomiting, loss of weight, or depression so severe as to require sedatives or hospitalization)

The Human-Dog Relationship

because they feel guilty. Often people blame themselves for not taking the pet to the veterinarian sooner.

Replacing the Pet

Replacement of the lost pet with another animal is the answer to the problem, but most people need some time to think it over. They have to wait until the inner hurt heals. Usually grieving owners say that they will not replace their dog. I know that it hurts to bring a new puppy into the house while still mourning for the other, but I try to reason with the owner that the loss of a dog should not prevent getting another.

MacKinlay Kantor, Pulitzer-Prize-winning author, worded his sentiments beautifully in a letter to a friend after the death of his dog: "Some silly folks cry and beat their breasts and yell, I will never have another dog. Can you imagine anything more absurd? It is like saying, I owned a supreme friend. He gave me laughter, courage, tenderness, power. He gave me all those things and more—yet now he is gone. Therefore, I want never to have another friend. You do not get another dog to replace the old one. No dog can ever replace another. But one dog can take over the responsibilities and duties of another. Dogs have a keen sense of fitness and propriety."

I agree with Kantor. You can soon learn to love another dog, although maybe not in exactly the same way as you loved your dead pet. But all dogs are individuals, and they all have their own particular and wonderful ways of becoming part of your family. And it is unreasonable to say that you will not have another dog because some day he will die. Just look forward to the ten to fifteen years that he will give you happiness, love, and loyalty. Depriving yourself of love is not the answer. Love another dog, and you will have years of happiness with him. The joy that the dog will give you will more than compensate for the grief you suffer when he dies.

Putting a Dog to Sleep

Euthanasia—the providing of a quiet and easy death to end the suffering of a loved one, human or otherwise—has long been debated. I am constantly asked, "What would you do if he were your dog, Dr. Vine?" The question haunts me, as do the faces of the doomed dogs and the tragedy in the eyes of those who love their pets and must make the decision. To those who have decreed a quiet and easy death rather than a life of suffering when such suffering is inevitable, let me say that if he were my dog I would do the same. I can say no more than that.

I firmly believe that any animal who is diseased beyond all hope, and to whom there is no adequate relief from suffering, should be allowed out of his misery. The two questions I ask myself are: Is the dog undergoing undue suffering that cannot be relieved? and Is the dog enjoying life? If the answers is obviously unfavorable, then I wholeheartedly advise euthanasia.

But if the dog is healthy, enjoys life, and is not vicious, I will not perform euthanasia. I still all to vividly recall the incident I told about at the beginning of this book—when I was too inexperienced to protect a healthy young dog from that distraught couple who were divorcing and who demanded their pet's death.

Even a vicious dog should not be put to sleep until all other possible solutions have been tried. One man confided in me that when his terminally ill wife died he thought he would have to put Smutt, her Cairn Terrier, to sleep because she had so pampered the dog that he was jealous and vicious with other people. But surprisingly, after the wife died, Smutt's disposition changed. He became meek as a lamb. The dog obviously knew that he could be overly protective and dominant with the wife but behavior of that sort would not be tolerated by the husband.

Finding a New Home for a Dog

If a dog simply has to be gotten rid of, euthanasia is not the answer. If, for any reason, owners must get rid of a pet, I advise them to tell their veterinarian about their decision. Many times the veterinarian will know of someone looking for such a dog. Also local chapters of the Animal Protection Society are always willing to place pets in new homes. Never abandon your dog. In many cases, this is a worse fate for the animal than euthanasia would be.

Unfortunately, people sometimes have their dog put to sleep because they believe that the dog would be heartbroken in a new home. Such a belief is almost always mistaken. Much as

it might hurt an owner's ego to realize it, a dog will rarely die of a broken heart if placed in a new home.

The extreme adaptability of the canine species makes it possible for a dog to become a valued companion to different kinds of people. A dog will usually adjust to another owner if he is treated kindly, petted, played with, and assured by words and deeds that this new human being wants to be a friend. You can teach an old dog new tricks. It only takes time, patience, kindness and love.

PETS AS THERAPY

Pets alleviate some of the stress and loneliness and add good humor to our lives. Because of this, studies have been carried out to determine just how therapeutic pets may be for people who are incapacitated, lonely, and unable to deal with stress. The results of these studies have surpassed all expectations.

Helping Heart Patients

The human heart rate and blood pressure are lowered significantly during the petting of an animal. Therefore, physiologically it is very relaxing to a person to pamper and stroke a pet. There's nothing as relaxing as a good moist lick in the face. Also, speaking baby talk to a dog has a calming effect on the speaker, perhaps because the speaker knows that the dog will listen without ridicule, without prejudice, and without demanding anything in return. Because of these factors, investigators wanted to discover if dogs could have a therapeutically calming effect on heart patients.

The dogs were an added impetus for daily walks and gave the patients companionship during these exercise periods, which made exercising a less dreaded task.

Contributing to Mental Health

Dr. Bruce Max Feldman, a veterinarian, believes that, "Pets help people cope with the complexities of contemporary life and they make an enormous contribution to the mental health and emotional well-being of the people they live with, simply by giving them the opportunity to love and feel love in return." And psychologists agree.

Workers in the mental health field are just beginning to realize how helpful a pet can be in getting through to patients who have withdrawn from human help. Many now believe that a pet dog may help fulfill two urgent needs of mental patients: the need to love and be loved, and the need to feel worthwhile to themselves and to others. Dogs have the ability to love without criticism; thus the patient feels no threat from the dog, only acceptance. Sometimes pets can help the emotionally ill where drugs, electroshock, or analysis fail.

Recent research at the Ohio State Psychiatric Hospital shows that dogs often facilitate psychotherapy with mental patients who are nonresponsive to traditional forms of therapy. The experimental work, started at the hospital and continued for nine months, involved fifty patients and twenty dogs. The patients were permitted to groom, exercise, and play with the dogs. The psychiatrists noted that the patients' behavior changed almost from the start. They livened up. They established a bond of love with the dogs by means of which they were eventually able to begin communicating better with the doctors and nurses.

Pets have even been used successfully to treat certain forms of schizophrenia where human therapists had failed. "Feeling

Heart" dogs, chosen for their warmth and friendliness, serve as constant companions to some schizophrenic patients and offer the kind of love a psychiatrically sick person needs.

Helping Disturbed Children

With mentally disturbed and retarded children, pets work extremely well. These children have a particular need for cuddling. Having physical contact with a living creature soothes their fears and anxieties. A dog gives them a point of orientation and makes them feel less confused. The dog will usually become attached to the child, thereby providing constant reassurance for the unstable and unsure child that the dog does love him.

Dr. Boris M. Levinson, author of *Pet-Oriented Child Psychotherapy* and a famous psychologist who has treated mentally disturbed children for many years, says, "Pets are important to the mental health of all children and of the elderly. The very young and the very old need dogs and cats to relate to when it is difficult to relate to humans." He points out that 10 million children in the United States exhibit disturbed behavior, and that pets could prevent many of the conditions leading to their emotional disorders. "Pets are crucially important in mental hygiene," he says, "helping the disturbed child get rid of his pent-up emotions. They provide someone who still loves you when you get home.

"A pet enlarges the scope of a child's experience," he adds in one of his articles. "The child can develop empathy for living things and compassion for pets in distress, which in turn, may transmit itself into sympathy and understanding of the emotional suffering of the people he lives with."

Helping Older People

People of all ages, but especially the elderly, benefit from the companionship of animals. Older people who are depressed over the loss of relatives or friends can learn to love again by caring for a pet, and they feel less lonely. As people get older, they sometimes feel less needed by family and friends and, therefore, abandoned. This feeling of uselessness results in depression and, as some researchers think, in illness. Scientific evidence shows that the companionship of pets both reduces the frequency of serious illnesses and prolongs life, and has led to pet programs in nursing homes. In several states nursing homes are seeking to enact laws that permit live-in pets for their patients. Such a law has already been passed in some states.

In a Visiting Pet Program in Santa Barbara, California, on certain days dogs are allowed to visit the city's various nursing, convalescent, and rest homes. These visits seem to rejuvenate the older people, both physically and mentally. They smile and talk about their own pets of years gone by. They hug, fondle, kiss, and talk to the pets and are more communicative and happy after the pets leave. They all look forward to the pets next visiting day.

Phyllis Daley of Cleveland, Ohio, has started a similar program in her community. Her dogs, Paucho, Muffy, and Pachuco, visit nursing homes regularly and act as "therapists" to residents who have sunk deep into themselves and have no interest in life. She says that the dogs, "Bring God's unquestioning love to these demoralized men and women. They do what no human being can do—get through to people who for one reason or another have soured on humans."

Others Who are Helped

Prisoners and institutionalized inmates may benefit from pet companionship. One study has shown that there is a strengthening of moral fiber among criminally insane inmates who are allowed to keep pets. Other studies have also shown that most prisoners respond well to pets. Prisoners who are allowed pets are less demanding, they cause fewer problems, and—most importantly—they show more determination to return to society and be good citizens. Moreover, they are less likely to develop the institutional syndrome of giving up on life.

Alcoholics

Dogs help alcoholics. The director of a halfway house in Bridgeport, Connecticut reports that his dogs, Brandy, Ginger, Blackberry, and Cognac have helped the residents to "beat the bottle." A reformed alcoholic himself, he believes that many people turn to alcohol because they are not able to satisfy their emotional needs. Seeing how the residents responded to his dogs, he felt that obtaining dogs to live in the halfway house would be just the medicine many residents needed. The dogs would give love and affection, ask no questions, and make no demands. Most residents became so attached to "their" pets that after the "cure" they took them home to continue the companionship discovered during their rehabilitation.

Disabled People

Dogs have long been friends of disabled people. Seeing Eye Dogs are priceless assets to the blind, and now dogs are also being used for the deaf. Audio Canis, a nonprofit organization for the deaf or hard of hearing, uses all breeds and crossbreeds who pass the evaluation test for alertness, hearing, and sight. The deaf people work with the dogs for fifteen weeks until they and the dogs are alert to routine sounds such as telephones, doorbells, and knocking—as well as out-of-the-ordinary sounds like smoke detectors, or, in the case of a mother, a crying baby.

But one need not be disabled, elderly, mentally disturbed, or suffering from stress-related disease, like heart problems or alcoholism, to benefit from the good therapy of a dog. Many psychologists think of companion dogs as preventive medicine, like an apple a day.

Certainly we've seen how dogs teach our children about life: about loving, mating, dying, feeding, and grooming—in short, about the joys and responsibilities of nurturing a living being, and about the peace of mind that comes from a dog's loyalty and uncritical devotion. History, too, has told us about the strong bonds between great men and their dogs. Kings, Prime Ministers, and Presidents have found solace in their dogs.

Lonely People

But it is not people, whether powerful, prosperous, or poor, who share their lives with other humans who have benefited most from the unique companionship that dogs have to offer. It is, I think, the lonely people of this world.

The lonely need companionship and affection so very much. For one reason or another they cannot find it among their own kind. Often a dog gives it to them in overflowing measure. The dog, whether purebred or just plain dog, seems to know the needs of the human. Given any encouragement he dedicates the rest of his life to one end, the pleasing of his one-person-in-the-world. You know how wonderful you feel at the end of

The Human-Dog Relationship ────────────

a hard day when your dog greets you with a madly wagging tail, jumps up, and tries his best to show you how splendid you are. To lonely people, this kind of response means the difference between emptiness and meaning in their lives.

The Power of Love

I end this book—as I began it—with a true story about troubled people and a dog. This story, unlike the first, is not about the consequences of human hatred. Instead it is about the triumph of love.

One day George Plummer and his wife brought in a small mongrel named Josephine who was suffering from bronchial pneumonia. They were middle-aged and plain country people who had endured hard times and suffering.

"Will she be all right, Doctor?" the woman asked.

"She'll need special nursing care, Mrs. Plummer, " I replied. "I wonder if you wouldn't like to leave her in the hospital for a few days."

"The wife and I'll nurse her," the man said. "She'll get good care."

Ordinarily I would prefer to have such a case under my personal supervision, but I knew this was a case involving more than the dog. To the Plummers, Josephine had brought not only a return to a good life, but a return of the self-respect they had supposed gone forever.

They had been alcoholics for years. I'd known them because George had done odd jobs for me around the hospital. They were childless. They were poor. Life was drab and getting more so as the years went on. They began drinking. They drifted apart. The farther they drifted, the harder they drank.

Then one day they found a small, nondescript dog. The starved creature followed them home. The man threw it some food. Soon it came on the porch. Then into the house. Once again those two human derelicts knew what it meant to have a living being look upon them with admiration. Once again they felt the urge to take on responsibility. Within six months they found that other urge, to drink until everything became nothing, was fast disappearing. They were needed! To Josephine went all the affection they had held back for so many years. She was more than a mongrel dog to this man and woman. She was a way of life.

The Human-Dog Relationship

And now she was desperately sick. No, they wouldn't leave her to be nursed by others. Josephine's two bright eyes saw nothing but her beloved human companions. She know they would not fail her. And they did not.

Index

Suggested Reading

Dog Behavior and Training
by Dr. Lowell Ackerman

TS-252

292 pages, over 200 color photographs.

Joined by editors Gary Landsberg, DVM and Wayne Hunthausen, DVM, Dr. Ackerman and about 20 experts in behavioral studies and training set forth a practical guide to the common problems owners experience with their dogs. Since behavioral disorders are the number one reason for owners to abandon a dog, it is essential for owners to understand how the dog thinks and how to correct him if he misbehaves. This book covers socialization, selection, rewards and punishment, puppy-problem prevention, excitable and disobedient behaviors, sexual behaviors, aggression, children, stress and more.

Training Your Dog for Sports and Other Activities
by Charlotte Schwartz

TS-258

160 pages, over 200 full-color photographs

In this colorful and vividly illustrated book, author Charlotte Schwartz, a professional dog trainer for 40 years, demonstrates how your pet dog can assume a useful and meaningful role in everyday life. No matter what lifestyle you lead or what kind of dog you share your life with, there is a suitable and eye-opening activity in this book that both you and your dog will enjoy.

The Atlas of Dog Breeds of the World
by Bonnie Wilcox, DVM and Chris Walkowicz

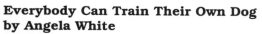

H-1091

896 pages, over 1,100 full-color photographs

If you love dogs you'll love this book. It's the most comprehensive guide to all types of dogs around the world— 409 different breeds receive full-color attention and individual study. Traces the history and highlights the characteristics, appearance and function of every recognized dog breed in the world.

Everybody Can Train Their Own Dog
by Angela White

TW-113

256 pages, full-color photographs throughout.

This book is a fabulous reference guide for all dog owners. This well written, easy-to-understand book covers all training topics in alphabetical order for instant location. In addition to teaching, this book provides problem solving and problem prevention techniques that are fundamental to training. All teaching methods are based on motivation and kindness, which bring out the best of a dog's natural ability and instinct.

The Most Complete Dog Book Ever Published: Canine Lexicon
by Andrew De Prisco and James B. Johnson

TS-175

896 pages, over 1300 full-color photographs.

This encyclopedic dictionary contains up-to-date information for the dog person. It is the most complete single volume about the dog ever published, covering more breeds than any other book, as well as other relevant topics, including health, showing, training, breeding, anatomy, veterinary terms, and much more. No dog book has ever offered this many stunning photographs of all breeds, dog sports and topics.

Suggested Reading

Choosing a Dog for Life
by Andrew De Prisco and James B. Johnson
TS-257

384 pages, full-color photographs throughout.

Choosing a Dog for Life offers the first-hand experience and advice of hundreds of dedicated breeders and owners that will save you time, money, and possibly the life of your next dog. It answers all your questions about over 160 different individual breeds, including what to look for in a puppy, the genetic, medical and behavioral aspects of each dog and the positive and negative traits of the breed. It is the best possible gift you can give yourself and your new "dog for life."

Owner's Guide to Dog Health
by Dr. Lowell Ackerman
TS-214

432 pages, over 300 color photographs.

Winner of the 1995 Dog Writers Association of America's Best Health Book, this comprehensive title gives accurate up-to-date information on all the major disorders and conditions found in dogs. Completely illustrated to help owners visualize signs of illness, different states of infection, procedures and treatment, it covers nutrition, skin disorders, disorders of the major body systems (reproductive, digestive, respiratory), eye problems, vaccines and vaccinations, dental health and more.

Skin & Coat Care For Your Dog
by Dr. Lowell Ackerman
TS-249

224 pages, over 200 color photographs.

Dr. Ackerman, a specialist in the field of dermatology and a Diplomate of the American College of Veterinary Dermatology, joins 14 of the world's most respected dermatologists and other experts to produce an extremely helpful manual on the dog's skin. Coat and skin problems are extremely common in the dog, and owners need to better understand the conditions that affect their dogs' coats. The book details everything from the basics of parasites and mange to grooming techniques, medications, hair loss and more.